How Language Works

How Language Works

Madelon E. Heatherington

Department of English
University of California, Los Angeles

Winthrop Publishers, Inc.
Cambridge, Massachusetts

Library of Congress Cataloging in Publication Data

Heatherington, Madelon E
    How language works.

    Includes bibliographies and index.
        1. Linguistics. 2. Language and languages.
3. English language. I. Title.
P121.H45   410   79-21603
ISBN 0-87626-333-3

Design by Dianne Smith Schaefer/Designworks

© 1980 by Winthrop Publishers, Inc.
17 Dunster Street, Cambridge, Massachusetts 02138

Printed in the United States of America

10   9   8   7   6   5   4   3   2   1

Contents

Preface

All native speakers of a language know how to use that language to talk, whisper, command, plead, inquire, joke, murmur, tell stories, or any of the other tasks language can perform. But not all native speakers know how to analyze their language practices. Most speakers do not know how they use language, or why they use it in certain ways, or what other choices of use they might have. Indeed, few speakers really think about language at all; or, if they do think about it, their responses are likely to be charged with emotion rather than productively analytical.

For example, many speakers seem to regard language as a sacred or magical totem, fragile and needing protection from the indignities they feel are committed by a scientific inquiry. Other speakers often associate language analysis with the feelings of helplessness they acquired in high school as they struggled to distinguish fine points of usage. Still other speakers have been trained to believe that language needs no analysis, only drill, for in their eyes, language use is either right or wrong and that is all that needs to be said.

These responses to language analysis are very common. But none of them does much to advance our understanding of how language actually works (as opposed to how we wish, fear, or hope it works). This book is addressed to anyone interested in what is now known about the realities of language function, language production, and language use. Students of psychology, anthropology, sociology, and education, as well as students of English or other languages, can find useful material here. The book can serve as a review for people already acquainted with various ways of analyzing language, but it is specifically directed at those who have never taken any courses in linguistics. It is a general, introductory book intended for a non-specialized audience.

How Language Works has three interrelated aims: (1) to provide as accurate and current a survey as possible of various areas of theory and practice concerning language; (2) to present this survey in an intelligible, coherent, and interesting manner; and (3) to demonstrate that the necessity of approaching language objectively does not make the subject less interesting, but more so. These aims will be realized if the reader who finishes the book is convinced of the value of looking at language carefully and can apply to her or his own language behavior the observations described in the text.

The book begins with three chapters on language in general, any language: its possible origins (chapter 1), the stages by which it is acquired (chapter 2), and some universal principles which apply to it (chapter 3). The next three chapters analyze aspects of the English language in particular: its system of sounds (chapter 4), its system of forms (chapter 5), and its system of syntax (chapter 6). Chapter 7 deals with the history of English, and chapter 8 with the dialects of English. In chapter 9, the subject is meaning: meaning as the speaker intends it, as the audience understands it, and as the language conveys it. Chapter 10 deals with the manipulation of meaning for purposes of gaining power.

The first ten chapters investigate the most common form of language behavior, the spoken form. Chapter 11, however, is concerned with the less common form, writing, and chapter 12 deals, not with language behavior, but with the teaching of language. Like the rest of the book, this final chapter is directed to anyone who uses language, not merely to those who formally teach it. Therefore, this final chapter serves as an overview of the entire book.

Each of the twelve chapters is accompanied by a bibliography of selected additional reading. There is also a general bibliography of works covering much of the same materials as does this book, but from different (usually more technical) perspectives. In addition, each chapter is followed by a list of ten questions reviewing the salient points in the chapter. A separate teacher's resource guide provides suggested additional material for study in each chapter.

Any writer who attempts to provide a survey of the several disciplines within a broad field owes so much to the specialists in those disciplines that the debt is virtually incalculable. I acknowledge with profound respect my debt to all the scholars and investigators whose works appear in the bibliographies, but any errors and misinterpretations are of course my own.

In addition, I should like to direct particular thanks to the individuals who assisted in the gestation and preparation of *How Language Works:* to Waller B. Wigginton of Idaho State University, for helping get it started; to Louise Greene, for expert and patient typing; to my colleagues and students, whose advice and comment I solicited at invariably busy times; to Paul O'Connell, Janet Schreiber, and Clive Martin, of Winthrop Publishers, for editorial insight and care-taking; and above all, to James W. Goshorn, my colleague and husband, for everything.

How Language Works

1
The Origins of Language

Language use—speaking, reading, writing—is perhaps the most visible and distinctive of all human activities. It accompanies virtually every other form of conscious behavior; we talk all the time, while we are doing the infinite number of other things that we do. Indeed, many people believe that it may be our special use of language that sets us apart as a species from the other anthropoids who share part of our evolutionary background. And yet, although we have learned more in the last century than we ever knew about how language works, many aspects of its functioning still remain unclear. One of the more obscure features is the origin of language.

There has been speculation about language origin since at least as long ago as the ancient Greeks, who speculated about everything. Such a flurry of theories was proposed in the mid-nineteenth century that in 1866, the Linguistic Society of Paris banned any further formal speculation. Although the likeliest answer to the question of how language came into existence is that nobody really knows or is likely to find out, theories about language origin can be roughly categorized into two types: monogenetic and polygenetic.

Monogenetic and Polygenetic Theories

The monogeneticists hold that language originated from a single source, from which the many languages of the world then diverged. Divine inspiration or gift is the usual source suggested. The Hebrew God, it is often supposed, spoke in Hebrew, as did Adam and Eve; the divinely descended Egyptian pharaohs brought the Egyptian language to their peoples; the Chinese emperor, also descended from the gods, gave the gift of the Chinese language to his peoples, and so on. As in the biblical Tower of Babel, when humans grow away from the gods, or "first speakers," they also lose their ability to converse directly with the gods: the multiplicity of languages is connected with a fall from grace. Nearly all cultures have language-origin myths of this sort, and in nearly all of these myths, the god (or descendant of the god) who gives language to humankind is also a god of light. Origin myths imply so strong a connection in the human mind between language and light (insight or revelation) that we might be tempted to suggest something almost miraculous about language.

3

But one need not believe in a divine source of language to be a monogeneticist. To believe in any single origin, such as "the nature of things," is to take a monogenetic position. Plato, for example, asserted in the fifth century B.C. that things have names by nature, that the first speakers gave names to things according to how the sounds fit the concepts named. By this reasoning, there is a single "nature" inherent in every creature, idea, rock, tree, or person, and it remains the task of the name giver merely to discover what that "nature" is. One need only wait until the "proper" name somehow reveals itself. We know that this cannot be so, however, else why should English speakers use "egg," French speakers *oeuf*, Spanish speakers *huevo*, German speakers *Ei*, and Russian speakers *yaitsó* for the same object?

Even if we reject the notion that everything in the universe has a "natural" name, we may still wonder whether there were not some single stimulus for the origin of language, such as in the imitation of nature's sounds, in play, in tool making, in art, or in hunting. Many theorists have speculated along these lines, too, and perfectly serious explanations have come about thereby, with names likely to make us smile. The "bow-wow" theory, for instance, suggests that language is onomatopoetic, echoing the sounds of nature, such as a dog's bark. The "yo-he-ho" theory proposes that speech developed from the rhythmic grunts people make as they work at a shared and difficult task, such as rowing a ship. The "pooh-pooh" theory (the name sarcastically given to Darwin's monogenetic proposal by a contemporary who disagreed with him) suggests that human beings developed language as an outgrowth of emotional cries, "pooh!" representing the puff of air expelled when one makes a noise of disgust. These versions of the monogenetic position assert that we were stimulated by a single cause to develop language through imitating the world around us, but none of them accounts for the fact that the complexities of language transcend the original sounds or stimuli. Language use goes far beyond mere imitation.

On the other hand, polygenetic origin theories suggest that the sources of language are multiple rather than single, that no one cause produced language, but rather a combination of causes. Language began to develop possibly as long ago as half a million years, based on archaeological sources, although our evidence for the existence of writing only goes back some ten thousand years. Most polygeneticists believe that such development began in several different places, among several different groups of human beings, perhaps at more or less the same time. Polygeneticists, then, do not believe that only one group was given the gift of language, or that there was necessarily a single original language developed from a single cause.

Most commonly proposed as the multiple causes for language origin are several physiological developments in the structure of human bodies. It is commonly recognized that our human forms have evolved from hominid (humanlike) ancestral bodies to the human shapes we know today. Chief among these developments is that of the brain, with the hand, the upright posture, and the vocalizing apparatus also playing significant roles.

The Brain

So much has been learned in just the past fifty years about the workings of the human brain that although there is much yet to be discovered, we can confidently assert that without the present organization of the brain, there would be no language. Indeed, "language" can be regarded as separate from "speech" precisely because of the brain. *Language* is a body of knowledge, stored in the brain, about sounds, forms, structures, and ways to use them, whereas *speech* is the vocalizing (or gesturing) performance of that stored knowledge. But if language lies in the brain, how did it get there, and what makes the brain specially suited for language?

We cannot answer these questions in precise detail, for we do not yet have enough exact information about how the brain evolved or how it works now. But we do have more sources of objective information than Plato or Darwin had, so we can be more educated in our speculation. Among those sources are anthropological data about the evolution of the human body, work with people who have language disorders (disorders collectively called aphasia), neurophysical examinations of the brain itself, and use of a technique called dichotic listening, in which earphones direct different sounds into each of a listener's ears so that interpretation of sounds by the brain can be evaluated.

All of these sources have indicated that among its many other functions, the brain has become specialized for using language. We know that the human brain is large in proportion to body mass, that it is subdivided into several parts, the "thinking" or "higher" part of which is called the cerebral cortex, and that this cortex, which developed quite late in human evolution, is further divided into two halves, left and right, connected by a mass of nerve fibers called the *corpus callosum*. We also know that the areas controlling perception of sounds and muscular control of speech are located in the left side of the cortex. Incidentally, purely primitive vocalizing in animals other than man, such as howls of pain or shouts of rage, is not controlled by the cortex, but below it in the cerebellum. Since language production is located in the left side of the brain (is lateralized to the left), if the left side of the brain is damaged, language performance may be disrupted, as often happens to people who have suffered a blow to the head or a stroke. They "lose" certain capacities of speech: sometimes pronunciation or articulation, sometimes groups of words (like verbs or tense endings), sometimes connections between words (like which kinds of noun to use in connection with which kinds of verb). Injury to the right side of the brain, however, does not seem to provoke language disruption, although other capacities, such as spatial perception, may be disrupted.

All human infants apparently develop lateralization as they grow, the process being completed at about five years. Specialization for speech, then, probably developed in the species as a whole, but since a few birds also have lateralized brains, this asymmetrical specialization is not enough by itself to account for the development of language. There is a specific location for language in the brain, but why did we develop language in the first place? For even a tentative answer, we must move to the connections between the brain and the human hand, upright posture, and vocalizing apparatus.

Hand, Stance, Voice

The brain, of course, is the control center for everything: speech, thought, feeling, action, survival. Because the human species, like all creatures, is survival oriented, those evolutionary changes that contributed to the survival of the species are the changes that have lasted. Although anthropologists disagree about when the various survival-supporting alterations took place, it is fairly clear that, in addition to the development of the brain, the specialization of the hand and the adaptation to an upright posture have much to do with our becoming human. Furthermore, these three changes—in the hand, in the stance, and in the brain—are all closely connected with one another and indirectly with the evolution of language. The hand is important because it leads to tool making; upright posture is important because it leads to the development of hunting as a subsistence base; and as the hand and the posture changed, so did the demands made on the brain, specifically the demand for increasingly sophisticated communication.

Without the opposable thumb—which distinguishes a hominid hand from that of other primates in that it can touch, or be opposed to, the other four fingers—the kind of dexterity to which we are accustomed would be impossible. Tuck your thumb into your palm and try to thread a needle or button a button and you will see why. This opposable thumb made it possible to create and use more specialized tools, which in turn made it possible for the protohumans to extend their control over the environment, thus also extending their chances for survival. They could make weapons for long-range killing, pots for storing food, scrapers for shaping branches for shelter and scouring furs for warmth, and eventually plows for tilling the land.

More or less at the same time as the opposable thumb was developing, the hominids were moving from an arboreal existence to a terrestrial one. As a result of that move from trees to the ground, they were adapting to an upright posture and bipedal locomotion. When our ancestors stood up and walked on two legs rather than four, they acquired a number of survival advantages: the ability to run farther (because the legs had lengthened), to see for greater distances with greater acuity (because the eyes had shifted from the side to the front of the skull), and an increased dexterity with the fingers (a result of the realignment of shoulders and chest). Increased visual acuity and manual dexterity, of course, meant more skill at making tools.

Upright posture also brought about changes in the physiology of the neck and head. When the head is held upright instead of parallel to the ground, the trachea and pharynx—the "windpipe"—are pushed away from a horizontal axis toward a perpendicular one. The windpipe becomes less like a curving tube and more like a right-angled tube with a long, straight stretch above the larynx, or vocal folds (figure1.1). This realignment of the "pipe" increases the space available for resonance in the throat and accompanies the restructuring (of jaws, palate, and tongue) that now permits *Homo sapiens* to produce and shape language sounds. Half-a-million-year-old Neanderthal man, in whom all of these physiological alterations were but partially complete, could produce only a limited range of sounds. A few ancient skulls promote some expert speculation that Neanderthalers probably could not have spoken many vowel sounds at all and only a few consonant sounds, for they lacked the capacity for differentiating between closely related sounds. This differentiation is required by all spoken languages, as we shall discuss in chapter 4.

In addition to development of the thumb and the posture, changes in the culture helped in the development of speech. As our ancestors gradually became omnivorous instead of herbivorous—that is, began to eat everything, including meat, not just vegetation—they changed their food-getting tactics. Instead of one individual gathering what plants he or she could eat at a single setting, communal hunts became the subsistence base. Hunting requires a good eye, a steady hand, a fleet foot—and increasingly sophisticated communication between the members of the hunting party, especially if they are out of each other's sight. The better the communication, the better the hunters' chance of catching their prey, and therefore the better their chance of survival.

Hunting would have required more sophisticated tools than plant gathering did, because one can use one's bare hands for plucking leaves, but it is difficult to kill and dress a large mammal without a weapon of some sort. Now, in order to make tools, use tools, and transmit information about tools, one must necessarily use gestures, and it may not be at all coincidental that language-use and tool-use capacities are both left-lateralized, in the same general area of the cerebral cortex. Many researchers therefore theorize that speech had its beginnings in gesture, for with the hands occupied by tools, gesture could no longer suffice for accurate communication, especially if one meant to communicate something about the very tools one held. By the time

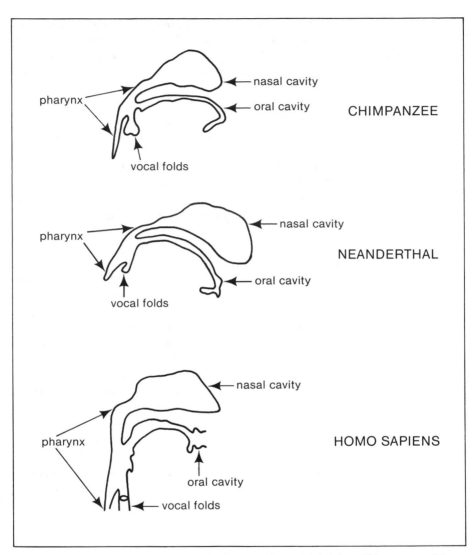

Figure 1.1   Speech-Production Chambers in Hominid Adults: Chimpanzee, Neanderthal, and Homo Sapiens. *Adapted from Philip Lieberman,* The Speech of Primates. *The Hague: Mouton/Humanities Press, 1972, p. 109.*

tool making became a clear advantage for survival, it is possible that gestures had become stylized enough to serve as a kind of "language"—modern-day sign language, of course, shows that gestures serve as a perfectly adequate language—and that vocalizing was already taking place.

Sound and gesture may already have been related, before sound took over from gesture as the dominant mode of communication.

But why should sound have taken over at all? Up to this point, what we have said about the physiology of speech and language is based on evidence we can verify. From here on, however, we can only rely on a careful reconstruction of what might have happened to make sound the dominant medium. We must first keep in mind the point that language, like everything else human, almost certainly evolved. Language did not appear overnight in the species, any more than fully formed sentences emerge from an infant before he or she has gone through the stages of language acquisition discussed in the next chapter. As with any evolutionary process, the changes in the human brain and body that lasted were the ones that led to survival of the species. We should therefore ask what benefits of sound over gesture might have prompted speech as a survival mechanism. And we discover many advantages: sound reaches around corners, unlike the vision required to see gestures; sound can function as well in darkness as in daylight; sound can accompany gesture; sound is faster than even the quickest gesture language; and—most important of all—sound can be so manipulated as to signal many more narrowly distinctive meanings, and many more abstract meanings, than a simple gesture "language" can.

Thus, it seems likely that the hominids who had learned to use rudimentary speech to supplement their gestures simply lived longer than those who remained mute or used sound only for expressing emotion. When speech itself became a survival factor, then speech also became evolutionary: from simple grunts and emotive cries, vocalic utterances became more and more refined and systematic, capable of more and more specialized discriminations and a faster speed of transmission. As speaking became the dominant mode of communication, the physiology of speech began to take over from the physiology of eating and even of breathing. The human pharynx is now extraordinarily vulnerable to blockage by hastily swallowed food. We have evolved into beings for whom speech is at least as important as the ingestion of food and the respiration of air, strong evidence that to be human is to speak.

Clearly, the evidence favors a polygenetic theory of language origin, not a monogenetic one. A number of factors, and not a unilateral cause, must have contributed to the development of language in human beings. But one aspect of the polygenetic theory approaches a kind of monogeneticism, almost drawing polygeneticists and monogeneticists together. That point lies in what we know of the development, not of the species' aptitude for language in the abstract, but of the development of the multiple languages that human beings now speak. We will be dealing with this point in more detail in chapter 7, but it will suffice here to say that all of the languages for which we have records do seem to have developed from a very few ancestors. This is not the contradiction it might seem, for true monogeneticists believe that all languages originated from a single language caused by a single stimulus—which is not at all the same as hypothesizing that many factors may have prompted the emergence of a small number of languages. Nevertheless, the central point must be repeated: all theories about language origin are just that—theories. Nobody really knows for certain, and nobody is ever likely to know.

Review Questions

1. What are the differences between a monogenetic and a polygenetic theory of language origin?

2. Which kind of origin theory, monogenetic or polygenetic, most often appears in myth and religion?

3. Identify and define these three examples of origin theories: (a) bow-wow, (b) yo-he-ho, (c) pooh-pooh.

4. What are the differences between language and speech?

5. What is the cerebral cortex? What is its connection with language?

6. In what part of the brain is language lateralized? What does "lateralized" mean?

7. What do aphasia victims and dichotic listeners have to tell us about language?

8. What are opposable thumbs and bipedal locomotion? What do they have to do with language?

9. How are the pharynxes of a chimpanzee and Neanderthal man different from the pharynx of *Homo sapiens?*

10. What benefits are there in sound over gesture as a medium of human communication?

Selected Reading

Darwin, Charles. *The Expression of the Emotions in Man and Animals*. New York: Appleton-Century-Crofts, Inc., 1913.

Gazzaniga, Michael S. *The Bisected Brain*. New York: Appleton-Century-Crofts, 1970.

Hewes, Gordon W., ed. *Language Origins: A Bibliography*. 2 vols. The Hague: Mouton Publishing Co., 1976.

LaBarre, Weston. *The Human Animal*. Chicago: University of Chicago Press, 1954.

Langer, Suzanne K. *Philosophical Sketches*. Baltimore: The Johns Hopkins Press, 1962.

Lenneberg, Eric H. *Biological Foundations of Language*. New York: John Wiley & Sons, 1967.

Lieberman, Philip. *On the Origins of Language*. New York: The Macmillan Co., 1975.

Robins, R. H. *A Short History of Linguistics*. Bloomington: Indiana University Press, 1967.

Stam, James H. *Inquiries in the Origin of Language*. New York: Harper & Row, 1976.

Stross, Brian. *The Origin and Evolution of Language*. Dubuque, Iowa: William C. Brown Co., 1976.

Swadesh, Morris. *The Origin and Diversification of Language*. Chicago: Aldine Atherton Press, 1971.

Wescott, Roger W. *Language Origins*. Silver Spring, Md.: Linstock Press, 1974.

Journals   *Brain and Language; Cognition; Studies in Linguistics; Visible Linguistics*

2
The Learning of Language

Until not too long ago, the babbling of babies was usually dismissed as nothing but baby talk—cute, perhaps, but not significantly related to adult speech. Similarly, animal communication systems were for a long time held to be either completely esoteric and removed from man's comprehension or so rudimentary as to be unworthy of human attention. Many of us have yearned to be like Dr. Doolittle and talk to the animals, but we assumed that we could not do so, or we romanticized our fantasies—and the animals—by turning animal communications into parables of human speech. Only in the last few decades have researchers begun to focus on what both babies and animals are really doing, instead of on what we wished they would do, and so only recently have we begun to learn how complicated "baby talk" is and how intricate, but nevertheless limited, animal "languages" are. As we learn more about both fields, we also learn more about the nearly miraculous functions of speech in human beings.

Animal Languages

The flood of ethological, or animal-behavior, studies in the past few years has advanced our knowledge of animal "languages" considerably. We can no longer hold, for example, to the kind of earnest fantasy that led the founder of the DuPont family to compile a dictionary of birds' "words." That animals use signals and codes, we can be sure; that animals communicate with each other is undeniable; but that they use words and languages is highly doubtful. To explain why *Homo sapiens* is the only creature who uses language, we must investigate the nature of the animals' communication systems.

An important point about all of the systems by which animals communicate with one another, rather than with man, is that for the most part, the systems are stimulus-bound. That is, their signals—bees' dances, wolves' howls, whales' songs, dolphins' whistles, and so on—appear in response to a particular stimulus from the environment, and only in response to such a stimulus. There is virtually no spontaneity in a bird's song. Equally important, minimal learning and creativity are involved: elements of an animal's signaling code are genetic. Once a bee learns the patterns it can dance to demonstrate where the pollen is, it cannot signal anything else. The signaling code may be very intricate and may contain elements that can be shifted around to express variations of a message, as wolves change their cries to indicate alterations in the progress of the hunt; but the code will not accommodate any situation outside its range of information. No animal "language" can deal with the past or the future, or with the details of appearance of a strange creature newly met, or with the specifics of a problem with which the animals have never dealt before. Dolphins, for example, were thought to "talk" to each other in humanlike ways, but a famous experiment showed otherwise. A male and a female dolphin were placed on opposite sides of a barrier. They could only get food if the female signaled to the male to "direct" him to press certain levers. But it turned out that her signaling had nothing to do with his understanding of the levers. She whistled only because she had learned, through a conditioned response, that whistling would get food for her—never mind what happened to him! Her whistles were hunger stimulated and had nothing to do with "communicating" with her mate.

But what about animals who have been taught forms of human language, especially the marvelous chimpanzees like Washoe, Sarah, and Lana? Beginning in the 1960s, Washoe was raised from infancy by Allen and Beatrice Gardner, Sarah by David and Ann Premack. Washoe and Sarah have shown much more intelligence, specifically a linguistic intelligence, than has ever before been conclusively demonstrated by a nonhuman species. Most interesting of all, the chimps have shown an astonishing capacity for language use.

Using colored plastic tokens (Sarah), American Sign Language (Washoe), or computers (Lana), the chimpanzees have learned to use and to create quite complicated sentences. Washoe and others like her are not merely responding on command, like parrots or trained lions, nor are they limited to the expressions that their own communication system can provide for emotive responses, as to danger or motherhood or food. They can respond to and signal entirely new constructions, like "Open (the) refrigerator"; "Sarah (want) water"; "Play (with) me"; and "Insert apple dish banana pail" (Put the apple into the dish and put the banana into the pail). Furthermore, some chimpanzees can actually "talk" to each other in these new languages, not just to their human companions and trainers.

In the first years of experimentation with the chimpanzees, linguists and ethologists were very excited by the results, but later results proved a bit of a disappointment for those who wanted to talk to animals. Washoe and her companions learned much faster than human infants in their earlier years, but they seemed to stop at about the human equivalent of four years, perhaps because of limited cognitive capacity. They had a smaller number of words in their vocabularies and a much smaller number of ways to combine those words than the average human child had after four years. Additional experiments may give different results, of course, but as of now, it appears that one difference between the chimpanzees' use of human language and humans' use of language is that the humans keep on acquiring words and constructions, but the chimpanzees do not.

Another difference, many researchers suggest, is that chimpanzees must be formally taught to use human language. They cannot learn it, as humans do, simply by existing among human beings who are talking. Human children are not formally instructed in their language until they are already using it, whereas nonhuman infants either must undergo instruction (as Washoe, Sarah, and Lana did) or, as we have seen with bees, are born with the entire "language" already genetically coded. And a third difference—which cannot be tested until this generation of chimpanzees has children of its own—may be that the chimpanzees will not teach the human language they have acquired to their own offspring.

Washoe and the other chimpanzees have shown that some of the cognitive capacity (if not the vocalizing skills) for human-language acquisition is undeniably present in chimpanzees. They have also shown, however, that capacity alone, even supplemented by the remarkable adaptability the chimpanzees have shown in learning, is probably not enough to promote language use beyond a fairly rudimentary level. So far, the best we can say is that human beings may take longer than any other species to acquire language, but they learn it better, and they keep on learning it all their lives.

Language Acquisition in Humans

The study of language as a human trait is called psycholinguistics. Psycholinguists who focus on children's acquisition of language have drawn their information from many sources, among them archaeology, comparative linguistics and grammars, neurophysiology of the brain, and child development. All sources are piling up more and more evidence that human beings are genetically predisposed to learn language. That does not mean, of course, that infants are programmed to learn a particular language, but rather that something in our genes probably leads us to learn language of some kind. Indeed, some researchers suggest that this predisposition is so strong as to constitute a kind of knowledge all its own. It is like a genetic acquaintance, acquired before birth, with very basic and fundamental rules of language use. Some researchers further argue that this predisposition is so strong and so distinct that it not only defines us as human, but also marks us off from other animals, who do not have the same kind of inherent drive toward language that we do.

No one proposes that children know everything about language from infancy onward or that children are not trained to some extent in their use of language by the people around them. Rather, the argument is that children's language acquisition is so universal and so consistent in its stages—regardless of the particular language in question and regardless of whether the children are given much or little reinforcement from parents or other children—that each child must have been born with an innate drive to learn some language.

Support for this innateness theory comes from several sources. One source is provided by the so-called "wild" children, technically referred to as feral, who managed to survive without human contact until they were well past infancy. All of these children, the most recent being a girl in Los Angeles named Genie, lacked language. Feral children could provide themselves with the basic necessities of survival, food and shelter, and most of them could communicate basic emotional responses, but they could not speak. More important, they found it very difficult to learn language once they had been brought into contact with other human beings. Their difficulty suggests that there may be a "critical age" for initial language acquisition, and supports the common observation that learning a second language when one is in junior high, high school, or college is much more difficult and painful than learning one's native language was.

Unlike feral children, all other infants learn to speak, even those born to nonspeaking parents. Furthermore, as long as they are in contact with signed or spoken language, young children learn to speak without being formally taught to do so. Most of us have to be trained to read and to write, but none of us is trained to talk. It is true that once we have begun to speak, our language behavior may be modified by parents or teachers or other children, as when a mother says to her daughter, "That's not pronounced 'fol-edge,' but 'fo-lee-adj' " (the word was "foliage"). But these kinds of correction come after the fact, after the child has already begun the extraordinary act of sorting out his language for himself. Language use begins with the child, not with the parents, and it progresses in a remarkably regular way, virtually regardless of what the parents do to support or shape the child's speech.

Let us pause here to take account of two theories about children's speech that have held sway for a long time, the imitative theory and the reinforcement theory. The first theory goes back at least as far as John Locke in the seventeenth century, who held that a child's mind is a *tabula rasa*, a "blank tablet," without any innate or genetic predispositions at all. The child acquires his habits and character solely from his surroundings, by imitating what he hears in his environment. The "imitative" theory, then, is a version of the "bow-wow" theory of language origin referred to in chapter 1. Although the imitative hypothesis has merit when applied to a child beyond infancy, after his initial acquisition of language, it has a serious flaw if applied to infants: infants do not hear from adult speakers the sounds that the infants make. Even the so-called baby talk that some adults use to children is not really the same as the speech of the children themselves. The speech that adults customarily use in talking with one another (and, more often than not, to the baby) is quite different from the speech that children first develop.

Like imitation, reinforcement comes later in the child's life, after he has already begun to speak on his own, and in the context of the child's innate predisposition to acquire language. The reinforcement theory holds that infants begin to speak because parents or other teachers reward the children for speaking correctly and withhold reward from, or actually punish, utterance of incorrect sounds. This theory has some merit, but in a very limited way, for most parents spend far more time accommodating to the child's speech than monitoring it as closely as the reinforcement theory suggests. Many parents, in fact, reward any sound the infant makes, whether that sound bears the slightest resemblance to adult speech. Furthermore, if there is more than one child in the family or the neighborhood, each of the children is talking with others who are speaking as he does, not as adults do, and therefore he is reinforced for children's speech.

Stages of Language Acquisition

As a result of the many psycholinguistic studies of children's language done in the past fifty years or so, we have to conclude that children learn language because human beings are simply born to speak, not because they are taught to speak. But children certainly do not speak as fluently as adult native speakers do; children acquire language in a fairly regular and systematic fashion. The critical age for acquisition of language—allowing for the perfectly normal variation in children's individual development—seems to lie between approximately four months and five years. During this critical period, the child moves through four overlapping stages: babbling, holophrastic, telegraphic, and recursive. It is important to remember, in the following discussion of these stages, that not all children begin to babble when they are four months old, that children move through the stages at different rates, that some children may move so quickly that they seem to skip a stage, and that all children appear to move backward sometimes, from telegraphy to holophrasis or from recursion to telegraphy.

The babbling stage. Lasting from about four to about twelve months, this stage might more properly be called the "prelinguistic" phase, for the infant is not yet using language. He or she is merely making sounds, often stimulus-bound ones (hunger, messy diapers, fright) but just as often random. Some investigators have suggested, in fact, that during this stage, the infant—the word "infant" comes from a Latin word meaning "without speech"—is running through all the sounds that the human vocal apparatus can produce, and that some language learning is already taking place. Contact with adult speakers during this period may begin to shape the baby's sounds as he imitates the sounds he hears, or through reinforcement by the parents of babbling that most closely approximates adult sounds. By the age of about twelve months, the baby can repeat whatever language sounds are clearly spoken to him. He has begun to select out and practice those sounds that belong in his language and to drop those that do not.

The holophrastic stage. Around twelve months of age—sometimes as early as eight months or as late as eighteen months—the child moves into the holophrastic stage, when he or she can convey the meaning of an entire sentence with a single word. ("Holophrasis" means "whole phrase" or "whole concept.") This "one-word" phase marks the point at which most parents exult that the baby is learning to talk, that is, is becoming able to refine sounds so that they are intelligible to the parents and are identifiable as referring to something the parents recognize. In other words, the infant begins to demonstrate his skills at associating sounds with concepts.

The most common words during this period are nursery words, names for things with which the baby is most familiar: "mama," "potty," "papa." (Nearly all infants, regardless of the language they are learning, begin their holophrastic speech with words in which the "a"-sound of "mama" and "papa" is prominent, surrounded by "p," "b," or "m" sounds. These are among the easiest sounds, physically, to produce.) In the holophrastic stage, the single word stands for a complete concept, such as "Mama's here"; "I need a potty"; "Where's Papa?" Tone and pitch, rising and falling notes, together with loudness of voice, will serve to differentiate the "sentences" implied: "mama" said one way means, "I want my mama," but said another way means, "I hate you, Mama!"

Many children first express overgeneralization during the holophrastic stage. A word like "papa" is applied not just to the child's father, but to all adult males, "mama" to all adult females, "ball" to anything round, from the moon to a carousel, "dog" to any animal from a chipmunk to an elephant. Overgeneralizing may seem regressive, but it probably is not a sign that the child is slipping backward linguistically. Rather, it suggests, even at this stage, that the child is practicing some important rules about language. In the case of "ball," for example, the child may first correctly name the object in question and then incorrectly—to an adult ear—misname the moon by calling it "ball" too. But he may actually be acquiring and testing a complex principle about language that might awkwardly be translated like this. There is a category of objects in the visible universe; all members of that category may be classified as round; the name of the objects in this category is "ball." Later, he will learn that some particular objects in the "round" category have different names, but meanwhile, he has internalized a theorem about the relationship of language to things in the universe around him.

As he learns to differentiate specific people, objects, and feelings during this stage, he is also learning to differentiate sounds, both in others' speech and in his own. He can usually distinguish sounds before he can pronounce them. A year-old child can usually tell the difference between "sky" and "kite" or between "tall" and "ball" or between "bath" and "back" when an adult pronounces these words, but the baby may not be able to say "ball" until after several months of pronouncing it like "bah." Furthermore, it appears that even at this stage, the child can do something that few other animals can (and unlike the child, the animals have usually been coached). The holophrastic child can use displacement speech: he can talk about people or things that are not present, as in "Papa!" or "Dada!" when the child hears his father's car in the driveway.

The telegraphic stage. In this stage, two or more words are spoken together. The words are differentiated (not like the common holophrastic utterance "allgone") but are clearly connected. Recognizable sentences appear here, but with most of the pronouns and tense markers and all of the conjunctions left out: hence the name "telegraphic." This stage lasts from about eighteen months to about thirty-six months and might more accurately be subdivided into two phases, the joining, or two-word, phase and the connective, or three- (or more) word, phase.

In some ways, the joining phase, in which two words are linked together, is the most miraculous linguistic performance a child makes. He moves here from the simple association of one word with one thing or idea to the extremely complex level of association within language itself. Now words can be joined with each other and not just to an object. He also learns that an infinite number of word combinations is possible. Hence, the joining phase is a period of much playing with words, endless repetition of syllables (especially rhyming sounds), and testing of combinations. Children will often put themselves to sleep at night by murmuring a string of connections like "Block, clock, dock, rock, tock. Yellow block, yellow clock, yellow dock, yellow rock," and so on. Commonly, too, a single word will be tested against a variable number of others: "Hi, book; hi, TV; hi, postman; hi, kitty; hi, cereal." This testing suggests that during this joining stage, the child may be learning that language works in combinations of words: one base word ("Hi"), a base word plus a variable word ("Hi, kitty"), or a variable word by itself ("kitty!").

In the connective phase, the child uses more words in a string (at least three) than he did in the joining phase. He also begins to use organizing, or "traffic-directing," words like pronouns, prepositions, and some tense markers. Consequently, this phase marks another crucial leap in the child's acquisition of language, for in addition to combining words—usually nouns—he begins to signal what function the words serve. Until now, the function of the words has to be guessed at by the listener. Does "Allgone cookie" mean: "They ate the cookies yesterday"? "There will be no more cookies after this one"? "The cookie is out of my reach"? "The dog ate my cookie"? Or what? Many parents become quite skilled at extrapolating meaning during the joining phase, relying on the child's posture, gesture, expression, and tone of voice to tell them what he is saying. With the connective phase, however, the child can begin to make himself clear through words alone, for he begins to signal what belongs where and when: *"Those* cookies all gone *soon"; "In* California *last year"; "My* yellow block lost."

In the connective phase, too, the child begins skillfully using some of the more complex patterns in sentence structure. Now he can correctly state negatives, questions, replies, guesses, and commands. Instead of simply signaling a negative construction by beginning with "No," as in "No water!" if he doesn't want a glass of water, he can say, "I don't want water." He can say, "What do you want?" instead of "What want?" To the question "Where are you going?" he can say, "I'm going home," instead of "Go home." This stage, involving a great deal of language manipulation, may also involve a great deal of overgeneralizing as well, especially with the deviant forms, such as irregular verbs, which often continue to give adults trouble. It is very common in the connective phase to hear "He goed," "We bringed," "They sleeped," as the child incorporates a rule of tenses that might be phrased like this: For something that took place in the past, add a "t"- or a "d"-sound to the verb. Later, he will learn that many verbs have irregular past-tense forms.

The recursive stage. This phase begins somewhere around three years of age and continues, in varying ways, until the child is well into school. Indeed, refinement in various recursive techniques may go on forever as the speaker acquires stylistic fluency. The basic elements of recursiveness, however, are probably acquired by the time the child is five.

Recursiveness refers to the ability to fold language in on itself, that is, to combine one or more structural elements of language with or within another structural element. In the babbling stage, the child begins separating sounds into those that belong to his native language and those that do not. In the holophrastic stage, he combines sounds and begins separating words. In the telegraphic stage, he combines words into structures involving two or more words together. In the recursive stage, he combines structures and can recognize the underlying similarity of apparently different structures.

For example, a five-year-old might not say, "The dog was given its dinner by Marilyn," but he can understand it. He also can explain that the sentence conveys essentially the same information as "Marilyn gave the dog its dinner," and he can recognize and use such complicated constructions as "Tell Marilyn to give Friskies to the dog" or "I want you to feed the dog," both of which contain several ideas and structures, not just one. The first sentence, for example, contains three underlying structures: "You tell Marilyn something"; "Somebody will give the dog Friskies"; and a switching of the indirect object to a prepositional phrase.

The child who is mastering such recursiveness is also acquiring skill in making stylistic and contextual selections among various structures, according to what is appropriate for the circumstances. He will say, "Give the book to me" when he wants to emphasize the recipient (himself, not his sister), but "Give me the book" when he wants to emphasize the object (the book, not the fire tongs). These two sentences are basically the same, except for a surface difference in phrasing, a difference that shows a sophisticated grasp of the demands of different situations. Although the child will spend the rest of his life refining his skill in recursiveness and selection, he has acquired the basic tools for recursiveness and selectivity by the time he is five or six. Everything speakers learn about language after this is simply modification of the remarkable, even incredible, achievements they made in their earliest years.

Other Kinds of Language Acquisition

We have talked so far about the "normal" (whatever that means) progress a child makes in acquiring language. Our discussion has been generalized and based on three assumptions: the child can hear and is around adults who speak out loud; the child is learning his language from competent native speakers; and the child is learning only one language as he grows. These assumptions suffice for most children, but they do not account for deaf children or children born to parents who do not speak, nor for twins, nor for bilingual children. Many studies are continuing even now with such children, so fresh information may change our conclusions, but this is what we can summarize today about other children.

Deaf children, or children born to nonspeaking parents, go through the same stages as children who can hear, except that after the babbling stage, a child who hears no spoken language but is taught sign language will use sign language for the remaining three stages. But deaf children have trouble learning to speak, because they do not hear the sounds. They also appear to have difficulty learning to read, perhaps because reading depends so much on an internalized awareness of how words and syllables sound.

Many twins develop language systems of their own, along with the language used by others in their home. The twins can understand their private language, but no one else can. Most twins abandon their private language, or use it only seldom, when they are brought into contact with other people besides the family. Some especially isolated twins, however, such as the Kennedy children in California recently, seem to learn their twin language so well and find it so useful that they do not bother learning the language used by other speakers around them. In this case, the twins will face some of the same difficulties with other speakers that bilingual children must often cope with.

Truly bilingual children, raised to speak two or more languages from infancy, appear not to have much trouble with language acquisition, moving through the four stages in both languages and switching back and forth with ease from French to German or English to Spanish, as required. It has been suggested that a truly bilingual child will be able to acquire still other languages more easily than children raised with only one language. Often, however, a child is raised with one language in the home and another, later, in the rest of his environment, so that a linguistic tug-of-war develops over the child's language skills. These are the children for whom the confusion of languages causes the most difficulty. Many Native American and Spanish-American children are put in this awkard position, as are many speakers of "nonstandard" English dialects. Some theorists favor teaching such a child in his or her native language, while others believe that the child should be taught the language used by the majority of speakers in his or her environment. Still others feel that using both languages is the best way. At present there is no consensus about how best to handle bilingualism or bidialectalism. We shall discuss this subject further in chapter 12.

Review Questions

1. What does it mean to say that nonhuman communication systems are stimulus-bound?

2. The communication systems of which nonhuman species have been most extensively studied?

3. What factors seem at present to differentiate the speech of human beings from the "speech" of other primates?

4. Define "psycholinguistics."

5. Describe the innateness theory and distinguish it from the imitative and the reinforcement theories.

6. What can feral children tell us about normal language acquisition?

7. What is the critical period for normal language acquisition?

8. Describe each of the four stages in language acquisition.

9. What is overgeneralization? How is it different from regression?

10. What is displacement speech?

Selected Reading

Bar-Adon, Aaron, and Werner F. Leopold, eds. *Child Language: A Book of Readings*. Englewood Cliffs, N.J.: Prentice-Hall, Inc., 1971.

Bloom, Lois M. *Language Development*. Cambridge, Mass.: M.I.T. Press, 1970.

————, and Margaret Lakey. *Language Development and Language Disorders*. New York: John Wiley & Sons, 1978.

Brown, Roger. *A First Language: The Early Stages*. Cambridge, Mass.: Harvard University Press, 1973.

————, ed. *Psycholinguistics*. New York: The Free Press/Macmillan, 1970.

Chomsky, Noam. *Aspects of the Theory of Syntax*. Cambridge, Mass.: M.I.T. Press, 1965.

Curtiss, Susan R. *Genie: A Linguistic Study of a Modern-Day "Wild Child."* New York: Academic Press, 1970 (reptd. 1977).

Dale, Phillip S. *Language Development,* 2nd ed. New York: Holt, Rinehart and Winston, 1976.

Deese, James. *Psycholinguistics*. Boston: Allyn and Bacon, 1970.

Ferguson, Charles A., and Dan I. Slobin, eds. *Studies of Child Language Development*. New York: Holt, Rinehart and Winston, 1973.

Greene, Judith. *Psycholinguistics*. Baltimore: Penguin Books, 1972.

Hopper, Robert, and Rita C. Naremore. *Children's Speech*. New York: Harper & Row, 1973.

Jakobovits, Leon A., and Murray S. Miron, eds. *Readings in the Psychology of Language*. Englewood Cliffs, N.J.: Prentice-Hall, Inc., 1967.

Jakobson, Roman. *Child Language, Aphasia, and Phonological Universals*. Trans. Allan R. Keller. The Hague: Mouton Publishing Co., 1941 (reptd. 1968).

Liberman, Philip. *The Speech of Primates*. The Hague: Mouton Publishing Co., 1972.

Lilly, John C. *The Mind of the Dolphin*. New York: Avon Books, 1969.

Linden, Eugene. *Apes, Men, and Language*. Baltimore: Penguin Books, 1974.

Lorenz, Konrad Z. *King Solomon's Ring*. New York: Crowell, Collier, and Macmillan, 1952.

Maruszewski, Maruisz. *Language Communication and the Brain: A Neuropsychological Study*. Trans. Grace W. Shugar. The Hague: Mouton Publishing Co., 1976.

McNeill, David. *The Acquisition of Language*. New York: Harper & Row, 1970.

Olmsted, D. L. *Out of the Mouths of Babes: Earliest Stages in Language Learning*. The Hague: Mouton Publishing Co., 1971.

Piaget, Jean. *The Language and Thought of the Child.* New York: Harcourt, Brace, and World, 1926.

Schrier, Allan M., and Fred Stollnitz, eds. *Behavior of Nonhuman Primates,* vol. 4. New York: Academic Press, 1971.

Sebeok, Thomas A., and Alexandra Ramsay, eds. *Approaches to Animal Communication.* The Hague: Mouton Publishing Co., 1969.

Slobin, Dan I. *Psycholinguistics.* Glenview, Ill.: Scott, Foresman and Co., 1971.

Smith, Frank, and George Miller, eds. *Genesis of Language: A Psycholinguistic Approach.* Cambridge, Mass.: M.I.T. Press, 1966.

Von Frisch, Karl. *The Dance Language and Orientation of Bees.* Trans. L. E. Chadwick. Cambridge, Mass.: Harvard University Press, 1967.

Journals *Child Development; Cognitive Psychology; Journal of Verbal Learning and Verbal Behavior; Language and Speech; Language Learning; Perceptual and Motor Skills; Psychiatry; Science; Scientific American*

3
The Universals of Language

It is clear that certain innate or genetic predispositions lead human beings, as a species, to use language. Some of us may take a little longer than others to acquire language, and we may move at different paces through the four stages of acquisition, but nearly all of us pick up a language eventually and use it all our lives. Obviously, we do not acquire the same language initially; equally obviously, the native languages we acquire are quite different from one another. Since linguists do not always agree on how to classify what a particular group of people speaks—is it a dialect or a separate language?—there is no exact count of the numbers of active languages in use today, but around five thousand is an informed approximation.

These five thousand or so languages are mutually unintelligible; that is, without training, speakers of one language cannot understand speakers of any of the others. Nevertheless, all the languages of which we know have several characteristics in common. Characteristics that apply to all known languages, everywhere, at any time, are called universal traits. The exact number of such traits will vary according to the classifying system used, but here we shall discuss five major ones:

1. Language is human.
2. Language is spoken.
3. Language changes in various ways.
4. Language is systematic.
5. Language is symbolic in various ways.

Language is Human

As we saw in chapter 2, all animals appear to have signaling systems among themselves, and some animals, notably the chimpanzees, can be taught to use versions of human language. Nevertheless, no other species besides *Homo sapiens* appears to use the communication system of language in the same way that human beings do. Belonging only to human beings, language is therefore species specific.

We also saw in chapter 2 that all children (with the exceptions of the isolated feral children and of the physically impaired) do acquire language.

Some children may use language more competently than others; for instance, children who are severely mentally retarded often have severe speech impediments as well. But with the exceptions noted, there is no known instance of a human being not using language. Belonging to all human beings, language is therefore species universal.

Only *Homo sapiens* uses the mouth and windpipe as much for talking as for breathing and eating. Indeed, most human beings spend far more time talking than they do munching or swallowing, and their talk consists of much more than the rudimentary cries of warning or anger or other basic emotive responses that animals utter. Genetically and in practice, then, we are chatterboxes: to be human is, above all, to speak.

Language is Spoken

We shall have more to say in chapter 11 about differences between spoken and written language. Here, it is important to make the point that all languages, whether they are now or were ever written, were and are first spoken. Children learn to speak long before they can write; and children do not need to be formally taught to speak, as they usually do to write. Furthermore, all adult language users speak more often, and speak many more utterances, than they ever write.

After several hundred years of indoctrination, we are well trained in our faith in the written word, so it may be difficult to accept the notion that from a linguistic point of view (although not from a cultural-historical one), writing is of less significance than speech. To get an accurate impression of what a contemporary language is really like—not how it should be according to some users, but how it actually is—a linguistic researcher must take samples of spoken usage.

Because speech is primary, both in time (we learn it first) and in degree of use (we speak more often), speech behavior changes more quickly than the written form of language does. Although print preserves words, it does so belatedly; there is always a gap between what people say and what they write. This is not just a stylistic gap—we all tend to write in a slightly more self-conscious manner than when we speak—but a chronological lag as well. A slang phrase, for instance, can travel by word of mouth from Los Angeles to New York with intermediate stops in Houston, Chicago, and Washington, D.C., well before it has ever made its way into print. Often such a phrase will be out of date by the time it finally gets translated into writing, as happened a few years ago with Chevrolet's appropriation of the phrase "Whatever's right": the young and modish consumers at whom the advertisement was directed had dropped the phrase several months before the ad agency picked it up.

Language Changes

All languages change in various ways, and any language is in a constant, slow, not always steady process of alteration. Constructions are dropped or added, old patterns combined in new ways, new words coined from old parts. This form of change is chronological or historical: change over time. In chapter 5, we shall look at some common patterns of historical change in languages, and in chapter 7, we shall address some large-scale historical alterations in the English language.

In addition to changing over time, all languages show variation over space. At any particular time, many different versions of the same language will be being spoken in different regions by different types of people. These variations are collectively known as *dialects,* and we shall discuss the major types of dialects in chapter 8. It is important to note here, however, that a dialect is not a debased or less worthy form of a language; it is just a variant form. Every speaker of every language uses several dialects, depending on what he or she is doing at any particular moment; we do not ordinarily, for example, speak the same way in church as we do in a bar.

Furthermore, no matter how widely divergent the dialects within a particular speech community might be—a speech community is simply any group of speakers held together by a common purpose and a common dialect—these speakers will have more in common with each other than with the speakers of a different language. To the ears of an Arkansan, for example, a Bostonian-dialect speaker may sound peculiar indeed, just as the jargon of, say, economists seems strange to one not familiar with their specialized terms. But all of these people still speak English and can usually understand one another with more ease than they could comprehend a speaker of Spanish or Flemish or Quechua.

Changes in time and space. Besides the changes that are primarily spatial, other types of change in language go on more or less constantly. Time and space are involved in two in particular: conversion and openendedness.

Conversion. All languages have the capacity of converting one kind of structure into another kind of structure. As an ongoing process, conversion takes place as a matter of course and may be represented here by three examples.

Part-of-speech conversions. All languages, as a first instance, have some way of indicating those parts of speech that, in English, we call nouns and verbs; and all languages have ways of converting a noun-type word into a verb-type word: ''choice'' (noun)–''choose'' (verb); ''example'' (noun)–''exemplify'' (verb); and so on. The process works in reverse, too, from verb-type words to noun: ''teach''–''teacher''; ''cancel''–''cancellation.''

Modifier conversions. Second, all languages have modification systems, ways of limiting, restricting, or clarifying the basic units or features. In English, the basic units are nouns and verbs, so the modification system consists of adjectives (noun-modifiers) and adverbs (verb-modifiers). For instance, the noun "apple" can be modified by any number of adjectives to become something like "the large, round, shiny, tasty, red apple," and the verb "grow," with adverbs modifying it, can be turned into "slowly grow warmer in the sunshine." (This additive capacity is also a function of another kind of change, open-endedness.) Note that in English the placement of adjectives is much more restricted than the location of adverbs: adjectives usually come before the noun, and in a certain order, whereas adverbs can regularly appear either before or after the verb. That is, the positional conversions possible for English adjectives are fairly limited. In addition, a whole group of words, called a phrase, can act as a single modifier, as does the prepositional phrase "in the sunshine." Phrasal modification is true of most other languages as well.

Furthermore, all languages can convert adjective-type modifiers (of nouns) into adverb-type modifiers (of verbs), as when the adjective "conversational" (itself derived from the noun "conversation") becomes the adverb "conversationally." This process, too, works in reverse, adverbs converting into adjectives, as in "speedily" to "speedy" (and back to the noun or the verb, "speed"). These kinds of conversions—nouns to verbs, verbs to nouns, nouns to adjectives, adjectives to verbs, adjectives to adverbs, and adverbs to adjectives—involve a change in the form of the word, adding or dropping a syllable. Much less common in English than in other Indo-European languages, these changes in form are called *morphemic* and *morphophonemic* alterations, which will be discussed in greater detail in chapter 5.

Sentence conversions. The third and most important kind of conversion common to all languages is the reshaping of entire clauses or sentences. For instance, every native speaker of English recognizes that all the sentences listed are essentially variations of the same basic idea:

1. Did the members read the new procedures? (A question)
2. The members did not read the new procedures. (A negative)
3. The new procedures were read by the members. (A passive)
4. Will the members please read the new procedures? (An indirect command)
5. Read the new procedures! (A direct command)

On the surface, these may seem to be five different sentences, but it is clear that all have the same underlying construction: "The members read the new procedures." It is possible to take almost any sentence in English and apply the same types of structural conversion to it: question, negative, passive, and imperative. It is possible to do this sort of exercise in every other language of the world as well, although the particular methods of conversion and the resulting patterns will not be the same as in English. In Spanish, for instance, the affirmative sentence *Yo puedo hablar* becomes negative by the insertion of the negation signal *no* in front of the helping verb, *puedo,* and not after it, as English would do: compare *Yo no puedo hablar* with its English translation, "I cannot speak."

Open-endedness. All languages show a built-in flexibility and receptivity to new words or constructions. Languages are not closed sets, frozen forever in a particular state; they are open-ended and adaptable to changing social circumstances, changing needs of their speakers, changing conditions in the general human situation. Particularly are languages open-ended with respect to the lexicon, or word stock: new words come into a language more easily than new structures. Relatively speaking, English is remarkably flexible about its lexicon, more so, perhaps, than other languages in its "family."[1]

A few languages allow comparatively little alteration in the word stock. Some speakers of French, for instance, periodically express alarm at the French-English mixtures in their lexicon, such as *le drugstore* and *le sport,* and chase them all out in a ritual of purification. German speakers make up most of their new words from forms already in stock, so fewer words need to be imported in German than in English. To an ear trained in English, the result produces such accurate but jaw-breaking compounds as *Bombenziel-vorrichtung,* literally translatable as "bombing-an-object device," that is, a bombsight. English, on the other hand, readily absorbs words from other languages without very much change in their native form or much disruption in English structure. We have in English such words as *patio* from Spanish, *blitz*[*krieg*] from German, *algebra* from Arabic, *rendezvous* from French, and *smorgasbord* from Swedish. All languages, however, have an open-ended capacity for adopting new constructions, dropping old ones, and adapting to change, for change is a constant in language, as in living.

Language is Systematic

Every language in the world regulates itself, fits its units and unit groups together in predictable ways, and produces systematically intelligible sounds and sentences. No language's systems are more "primitive" or more "advanced" than any other's—which is to say, there is no correlation between the technological complexity of a culture and the complexity of its language. So-called primitive societies (those with a relatively low level of technology) frequently have language systems far more complicated than the languages

---

1. We shall discuss the classification of language families in chapter 6.

of more technologically advanced societies. All languages are complex but regular at all levels, from sound to form to sentence.

Usually the means or patterns of regulation—the systematic structures—are fairly limited in number. For example, depending on the expert you talk to, English has about forty-five sound patterns and about fifteen to thirty basic sentence-structuring (syntactic) patterns. A general principle about English syntax is that over the centuries it has been in use, it has tended to become syntactically more complex because it also has become inflectionally simpler. That is, with the decline of word endings (inflections) as a structuring device, English had to develop more ways of putting individual words together to form sentences. The earliest forms of English, for example, required only one word plus some inflections to convey a shift in the tense of a verb, whereas Modern English may require four or five separate words to indicate the same change: consider a Modern English construction like "will have been being baked," which Old English would have rendered with two words: *wille bacan*.

Arbitrary and conventional. That languages are systematic comes about in part because any language is arbitrary and because any language functions by means of convention. To say that all languages are arbitrary is to note that there is rarely any logic in the structure or meaning of language *except* an internal, self-consistent one. There is no reason traceable to connections between language and the outside world why any particular word means what it does: it just does. Nor is there any externally logical reason why one language should produce a subject-predicate-object syntax and another language should not: they just do. None of the systematic patterns in any language can accurately be called right or wrong, good or bad, better or worse—although we may be tempted to do just that when we do not understand the system—because judgments like "good"/"bad" are social or moral evaluations, not objective linguistic conclusions.

To say that languages function by means of convention is to point out that when a system (of sounds, of word meanings, or of syntax) does operate in a language, such a system works simply because a majority of speakers of that language actually use the system. In other words, the systems of language function by a sort of majority rule of usage. Any word, for instance, will continue to have a certain meaning only so long as most people continue to use that word to indicate that meaning. If the majority of English speakers decided tomorrow to make the word "table" mean "a drawing compass or divider," and then used "table" consistently to refer to the object that we now call a "compass," "table" would conventionally come to mean "compass."

If most of the systematic functioning of languages were not based on conventional (majority-rule, commonly accepted) usages like basic word meanings, then no two people would be able to talk with each other without eventually having to make up a shared language. If they did that, they would merely be agreeing on a new set of conventions. And if most of the systems of language were not arbitrary, then it would not be possible for languages to change over space or time. Change happens in language because words are *not* bound to single, unshakable meanings, nor are syntactic patterns immovably and eternally limited in kind or number.

Language is Symbolic

To repeat a key point: words have no inherent, innate, or divinely decreed meanings. Words merely stand for, represent, or symbolize meaning. The creature we call a "whale" is not so named because "whale" has some innate connection with large, aquatic mammals, but because a majority of English-speakers use that name. Other language-speakers use other names: *la baleine* (French), *der Walfisch* (German), *la ballena* (Spanish). All of these different terms are symbols for the creature itself, for the referent— that is, the figure (or idea or action) to which a word refers.

Sound and letter symbolism. This sort of symbolism (word to referent) in language is but one type. There are other kinds of symbolism as well. For example, most users of English are aware that the Roman alphabet—A, B, C, D . . . Z—does not mean anything all by itself, but is merely a collection of twenty-six distinguishable squiggles inherited from the Egyptians by way of the Akkadians, the Phoenicians, the Hebrews, and the Greeks.[2] A few of the squiggles, which we ordinarily call letters and linguists call graphemes, may seem to mean something when written alone (A, I, and possibly O), but there is actually only a very loose connection between the letters of the alphabet and the meanings signaled by the sound-sequences that those letters try to represent.

　For instance, the combination of letters we read as the printed word "chair" uses five squiggles but really represents only three sounds: CH, AI, and R. Those three sounds are symbolic, as are the letters representing the sounds (rather poorly), since the written word "chair" or the spoken CH-AI-R direct our attention toward the agreed-upon name for a particular example of furniture upon which people and cats sit. When we utter the sounds, or read the letters that symbolize the sounds, we will be classifying the article, describing it, introducing it into our linguistic code. But the name we give the article is not the thing itself, just as the letters "chair" are not really the sounds we utter. As the philospher Ludwig Wittgenstein pointed out, echoing many earlier observers, "The word is not the thing"; the word or name merely symbolizes the thing.

---

2. See chapter 11 for more on alphabets and other writing systems.

Thus, we have at least two levels of symbol making inherent in language. First, the written word "chair" symbolizes a combination of sounds in a certain sequence, roughly indicated here by CH-AI-R: the spoken word, symbolized by the written word. A second level is the reference of the sounds-in-sequence to something presumed to be "out there," beyond the language, in the "real world" universe of objects, activities, ideas, feelings. That something out there we have already identified as the referent. In the case of our example, the referent is a particular article of furniture over which the cat is draped.

Now, we know what the written or spoken word "chair" means, in the sense that we can go find an example of one if someone asks us to. But suppose we rearrange the letters in "chair" to make a new combination of letters (representing sounds): "hirca." If we ask someone to pronounce it, he will probably make low noises in his throat that sound something like HUR-KA. But when he says the word "hirca," he cannot mean anything by it because there is no referent in English for such a thing, nothing we can point to or pick up and carry back to him. We could make "hirca" mean something if we wanted to, because the letters and sounds are arbitrary. We need only declare that it does, in fact, have a referent; we will say that "hirca" is the name of a golfball with a blue stripe around it. But "hirca" would only become a word in English if large numbers of speakers accepted and used the word conventionally.

This method of discovering meaning by discovering a referent works fairly well so long as we are dealing with furniture and golfballs, tangible things. A word like "chair" covers a whole class of varied referents, representative examples of which we can point to. But when we get away from the referents of "chair" into intangibles like concepts or ideas, we often find ourselves in dangerous semantic waters. With intangible referents, we cannot, you and I, both point to the same thing any longer to clarify what our spoken or written symbol stands for. The meanings of abstract words, words that have intangible referents, are therefore often difficult to define. The referents for abstractions like "loyalty," "run," or "graceful" are completely internal, in each of our brains, although we might be able to point out instances of what each of us thinks is loyal behavior or the activity of running or graceful gestures.

Cultural symbolism. All of us are sending messages about ourselves to other people all the time. Some of the messages are sent consciously; some are not. Some of the messages are linguistic; some are not. The way we speak—not just what we say, but also how we say it—is one such message. In addition, the cultural environment as a whole constantly sends us messages, through the media, the buildings, the schools, the highways and national parks and Gross National Product Index—indeed, through all our contacts with the world "out there," beyond our own heads. As members of that wider environment, we pick up some of the messages and overlook, ignore, or reject the rest. Since speech is a part of the environment, all speakers of any particular language will share a common stock of words, meanings, and ways of connecting the words—lexicon and syntax—even though each one of us will vary slightly in our language behavior from everyone else. Linguists say that each person has his or her own idiolect, or special way of using the linguistic patterns drawn from the common stocks.

Because language is a form of human behavior, it is a cultural artifact. As potsherds, arrowpoints, and trash middens tell anthropologists something about the people who made and used those artifacts, so do words, structures, and intonations tell linguists something about the people who uttered them. Indeed, some reconstruction of defunct cultures is possible through a careful study of language, even if nothing else remains of the culture. For example, the earliest ancestors of most European languages—people who spoke the long-dead Indo-European language—probably lived in north-central and northeastern Europe and southwestern Russia, were stockmen rather than farmers, and set up families under the patriarchal system. How do we know this? Because what we know of their language contains no words for southern trees, but does contain northern terms; it has no words for grains or vegetables, but does have several words for domestic-animal food sources; and it contains a word for daughter-in-law but none for son-in-law, suggesting that a bride moved in with her husband's parents, not with her own.

Similarly, hundreds of years from now, researchers may wade through whatever survives of old TV videotapes and movies in order to get some sense of what the United States was like linguistically in the fourth quarter of the twentieth century, but it is not necessary to go into the future for such research. Just listen to the different people you know and correlate their speech behaviors with other things they do: how they dress, stand, walk, take notes, comb their hair. Generally, you will find that their several behaviors form a more or less coherent pattern of signals that tells an observer who they are or who they think or wish they were.

Coherence of pattern is characteristic of speech behavior, too—the words each of us uses and the ways in which we use them. The relationships are fluid among the three key components of a speech community: the individual speaker's idiolect, the dialect groups he or she participates in, and the stocks of words and structures common to the language as a whole. Each of us shares common, conventional patterns, but also departs from them. Each of us projects something of ourselves onto the society at large, but also receives signals from it. Each shapes society in various ways and is shaped by it. To the degree that our idiolectic use of language is molded by society in general, we are said to be linguistically enculturated, a concept that brings us to an important and sometimes disputed theory about language.

The Whorfian Principle. Called the Whorfian Principle of linguistics, after Benjamin L. Whorf, who proposed it, the theory (simplified here) contends that the language each of us speaks is a product of the society we live in. Our language, like our culture, to some extent predetermines what we can perceive. The principle suggests that without a word for, say, "hirca," we could neither think of nor understand nor learn from a hirca if we should ever encounter one. There is no meaning for a concept, and thus no comprehension of the concept, if there is no word. This does not, of course, include responses that are purely pictorial or emotional, nonlinguistic, as to a painting or a ballet or a brawl.

Thus, Whorf indicates, all cultures are linguistically—therefore perceptually—limited, because no one culture or language encompasses *all* the possible attitudes in the universe. English, for instance, predisposes its speakers to think and react in linear ways, to assume causality, logic, connectedness, and ordinal sequences, because there is such a preponderance of words in our language having to do with lines, points, edges, sequences, causes, and consequences: "line of sight," "point of view," "on the verge of," "chain of command," "sequence of events," and so forth. English-speakers therefore are limited in their capacity to understand nonlinear ideas, such as those in Oriental philosophies.

If Whorf is right (and many do not agree with him), if we are in fact perceptually limited by what our linguistic stock has prepared us to perceive, then the reverse may also be true: the greater the stock, the greater the possibility of perception; the more words and structures available for reference, the better our chance of understanding and (we hope) the less likely we are to be trapped in a limited or jangled construction of reality. Vocabulary may extend the capacity to understand.

Each Language is Unique

Ultimately, of course, each language is unique, as is the particular culture of which each language is a part. It is possible, we know, to group languages into related clusters or families according to their lexical and/or syntactic similarities, but to analyze any given language in detail, we must approach it on its own terms. To treat one language as if it were another language (that is, to deny uniqueness) is a grave error. For instance, it simply does not work to try to analyze English by using Latin grammar (except in a few instances where Latin and English do share structural patterns), on the mistaken assumption that English is little more than a corrupt and debased form of Latin. But for the past three hundred years, that is exactly how English has been taught.

Again, therefore, we are confronted with the same kind of two-way pull we have experienced with nearly all the universals: languages have many features in common (they are spoken, systematic, symbolic, etc.); at the same time, each language renders its version of the universal in its own particular way. But this two-way pull, toward universality and also toward individuality, is a paradox we are familiar with in many areas of living. All of us eat (but different foods), all of us have hair (but arrange it different ways), all of us walk (but at a different pace), all of us vacillate between the need for order and the need for variety. Paradox appears in language because it appears in human life.

Every time we use language, we are making a choice among sounds, forms, words, and structures. In selecting one pattern to utter, we cut out all others for a moment; we briefly narrow our perceptual universe down to one fleeting "shape," whatever shape our needs or experiences might dictate for that microsecond. With every utterance, spoken or written, we build more and more such shapes, all of which (if we could ever see all of them) combine into an exploration, explanation, expression, and creation of the connections between us and our universe.

Review Questions

1. What is a universal of language?
2. What does it mean to say that language is human?
3. Why is it important for the linguist to deal with the spoken language rather than with writing?
4. Besides changes over space and time, in what other ways do languages show alteration?
5. What does it mean to say that languages are arbitrary and conventional?
6. Define these terms: inflection, lexicon, syntax, idiolect, dialect.
7. What is a referent? What is an abstract word?
8. Discuss the meaning and implication of the Whorfian Principle.
9. Why is it important that each language is unique?
10. Why is it *not* true that some languages are more primitive than others?

Selected Reading

Bach, Emmon, and Robert T. Harms, eds. *Universals in Linguistic Theory.* New York: Holt, Rinehart and Winston, 1968.

Fodor, Jerry A., and Jerrold J. Katz, eds. *The Structure of Language: Readings in the Philosophy of Language.* Englewood Cliffs, N.J.: Prentice-Hall, Inc., 1964.

Greenberg, Joseph H., ed. *Language Universals with Special Reference to Feature Hierarchies.* The Hague: Mouton Publishing Co., 1966.

——, ed. *Universals of Language,* 2nd ed. Cambridge, Mass.: M.I.T. Press, 1966.

Herskovits, M. J. *Man and His Works.* New York: Alfred A. Knopf, 1947.

Kluckhohn, Clyde. *Mirror For Man.* New York: McGraw-Hill, 1949.

Sapir, Edward. *Language: An Introduction to the Study of Speech.* New York: Harcourt, Brace and World/Harvest, 1921 (reptd. 1949).

Whorf, Benjamin L. *Language, Thought, and Reality: Selected Writings of Benjamin L. Whorf,* ed. John B. Carroll. New York: John Wiley & Sons, 1956.

Journals   *Language Sciences; Working Papers on Linguistic Universals*

4
The Sounds of Language

Regulated sounds are the building blocks of language. Not all sounds that human beings can utter are linguistic sounds, of course, and not all languages use the same sounds, but every language is built from a pattern of specific sounds. The regulation or patterning of sound is the crucial point, for random grouping of language sounds produces only babbling. As a baby learns to select the sounds that regularly occur in his language, he is beginning to learn to talk. Nobody ever learns his native language by beginning with complete sentences or even with words: we begin—and therefore language itself begins—with the sounds that form the words. In particular, once we are into the holophrastic stage, we begin language acquisition with speech sounds, as contrasted with emotive cries or random noises from our anatomy.

Phonology is the study or science of speech sounds. Its two principal subdivisions are phonetics and phonemics. In the rest of this chapter, we shall investigate these two subdivisions, complementary and interlocking ways of scientifically investigating the sounds of language.

Phonetics

Phonetics is the analysis of actual speech sounds: how the sounds are produced or articulated, how the sounds are physically expressed by means of the acoustic properties of sound waves, and how the speech sounds are perceived and, in particular, notated or transcribed in symbols. These three aspects of phonetics result in three branches of the discipline: articulatory phonetics, acoustic phonetics, and transcription. We shall not be concerned here with the highly technical field of acoustics, with its attention to periodicity, overtones, and so on, but we shall deal with articulatory phonetics and phonetic transcription.

Articulatory phonetics. Speech sounds are produced by those parts of the human anatomy collectively called the speech organs (figure 4.1). The speech organs include the nasal cavity, the oral cavity (teeth, lips, tongue, hard palate, soft palate), the jaws, and the throat (the pharynx, the larynx, the vocal cords, the trachea).

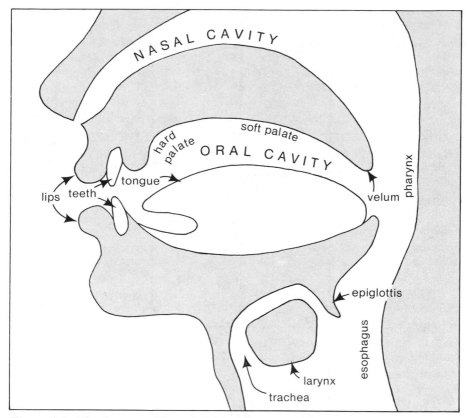

Figure 4.1 The Organs of Speech (Not drawn to scale)

Speech production begins when the bellows action of the lungs pushes air up the trachea, the part of the "windpipe" below the folds of the vocal cords. Still rising, the air goes past the larynx (vocal cords), which can be activated, that is, made to vibrate at various speeds or pitches, like a tuning fork. The combination of air and vibration is what produces sound. Then the air goes into the pharynx, the windpipe above the larynx and behind the tongue and palate; the pharynx branches out into the oral and the nasal cavities. Resonating in these cavities, the air is then shaped—or articulated—in various ways by the lips, teeth, and tongue. Finally, the articulated sounds pass through the lips and nose into the surrounding atmosphere, where the waves are picked up by the ears of a listener.

The study of the different ways in which that flow of air can be manipulated is called *articulatory phonetics*. It is the aim of articulatory phonetics to describe the physical activities that will produce particular speech sounds.

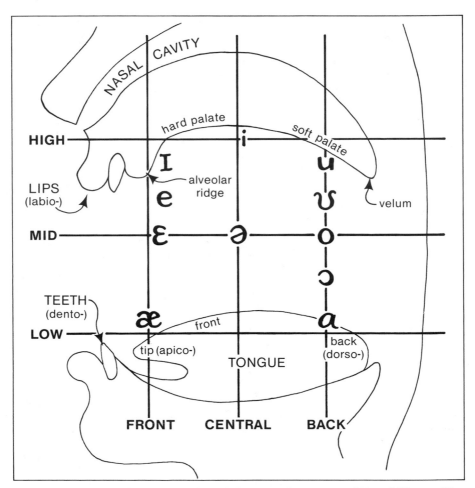

Figure 4.2   Points of Consonantal Articulation and Positions of Vowel Phones (Not drawn to scale)

To make an accurate description, the linguist must refer to three aspects or dimensions of articulation: the physiology of the oral and nasal cavities, the activation of the vocal cords, and the control of the flow of air.

Physiology of oral and nasal cavities. Figure 4.2 shows eight key places in the oral cavity: (1) the lips (the adjective form of the word "lips" is "labio-"); (2) the teeth ("dento-"); three parts of the palatal area, at the top of the mouth: (3) the alveolar ridge, just behind the teeth; (4) the hard palate,

	Stop	Fricative	Affricate	Nasal	Lateral	Glide
Bilabial	p, b			m		w
Labiodental		f, v				
Dental		θ, ð				
Alveolar	t, d	s, z		n	l	r
Palatal		š, ž	č, ǰ			y
Velar	k, g			ŋ		
Glottal						h

Table 4.1   Description of American English Consonantal Sounds. The first sound in the paired groups (/p/, /t/, etc.) is voiceless; the second is voiced. Unpaired sounds (/m/, /w/, etc.) are voiced, except /h/.

behind the alveolar ridge; (5) the soft palate and velar area, at the very top and back of the mouth; and three parts of the tongue, on the bottom of the mouth; (6) the tip of the tongue (adjective form: ''apico-''); (7) the middle or blade of the tongue, called the front; and (8) the back (''dorso-'') of the tongue. The lips, teeth, and tongue are the articulators, or shapers, of the flow of air pouring into the oral and nasal cavities from the pharynx.

To give a physiological description of a speech sound, a linguist will begin by noting which articulator is placed on which point of articulation to produce that sound. Table 4.1 lists examples of such descriptions for the consonantal sounds. These are produced in English by placing lips and tongue in various positions relative to the teeth and the parts of the palate. The technical names for each consonantal sound are also noted in table 4.1. A bilabial sound like /p/, /b/, /m/, or /w/[1] involves the upper and lower lips but not the teeth, whereas a labiodental sound like /f/ or /v/ is made by using the lower lip and the upper teeth. To make a dental, one places the tongue between the teeth. Moving to the palatal areas, we find that alveolar sounds are made with the tongue on or near the alveolar ridge, just behind the teeth, and the palatal, velar, and glottal sounds involve arching different parts of the tongue—tip, front, back—toward articulation points located farther and farther toward the back of the mouth.

Activation of the vocal cords. Whether or not the vocal cords are activated is the second factor an articulatory phonetician considers in describing speech production. If the cords are activated, the resulting sound is said to be voiced, or to have the feature [+ voice]. If the cords are not activated, the sound will be produced by the rush of shaped air only; such a sound is called

1. The reason for using the slash marks around the letters ''p,'' ''b,'' etc., will be explained in the next section. You might also want to look ahead to table 4.2.

unvoiced, or voiceless, that is, having the feature [− voice]. In English, the distinction between [+ voice] and [− voice] is often crucial. In many cases, that will be the only difference between one speech sound and another. For example, /v/ and /f/ are articulated the same way, with the lower lip touching the upper teeth, but /v/ is voiced and /f/ is not. Check the other pairs in table 4.1 for that [± voice] distinction among the consonantal sounds.

The feature [± voice] cannot be distinguished for vowel sounds, however, because vowel sounds are all produced with the vocal cords activated. Thus, a distinctive feature of vowels is that all are [+ voice], none [− voice]. Consequently, in describing vowel sounds, a linguist will refer to the relative positions of tongue and palate, which combine to produce each vowel sound. (The positions of the lips are not used as reference points, for, as ventriloquists know, it is not really necessary to move one's lips much to produce vowel sounds.) Figure 4.2 indicates the "positions" of vowel sounds in the mouth, that is, where and to what degree the tongue arches against various locations on the palate. As three examples, consider /u/, /ə/, and /æ/. The high back vowel /u/ is produced by activating the vocal cords and curling the back of the tongue up, with the sound wave bouncing far enough back on the soft palate that the resulting sound may almost be nasalized as /ũ/. The mid-central vowel /ə/ resonates almost exactly in the middle of the mouth, with the center part of the tongue arching slightly and the tip of the tongue placed near the back of the bottom teeth. The low front vowel /æ/ is produced by keeping the front and tip of the tongue low, with very little arch at all.

Constriction of air flow. The third factor involved in a phonetic description of speech sound is an indication of how much the flow of air from the pharynx is constricted and how much is let pass unobstructed through the mouth or nose. Five terms, indicating five degrees or points of constriction, are commonly used here: stop, fricative, affricate, nasal, and lateral (table 4.1). In a stop, the air flow is completely cut off, as in the bilabials /b/ and /p/, the alveolars /t/ and /d/, and the velars /k/ and /g/: "bag," "tip," "cud." A fricative narrows the flow so that the air comes through with a rasping sound, as in the labiodentals /f/ and /v/, the dentals /θ/ and /ð/, the alveolars /s/ and /z/, and the palatals /š/ and /ž/: "voice," "thief," "zebra," "sugar." An affricate is a momentary stop followed by a fricative release; we hear it in the sounds /č/ and /ǰ/, as in "church" and "judge." If the air goes through the nose as well as the mouth, we hear a nasal like /m/, /n/, or /ŋ/, as in "monster" or "mango." And if the air goes around the sides of the tongue, the sound is lateral /l/: "lullaby." Sometimes /r/ is a lateral, too: "murmur."

The sounds in /y/, /w/, /h/ (and sometimes in /r/) are produced as much like vowels as like consonants. That is, they are [+ voice], as vowels are, but the

	IPA Symbol	Sound Represented	Trager-Smith Symbol
Consonants	[p]	*p*arson, u*p*	/p/
	[b]	*b*ill, sla*b*	/b/
	[t]	*t*ry, po*t*	/t/
	[d]	*d*ark, en*d*ure	/d/
	[k]	*c*at, qui*ck*	/k/
	[g]	*g*aze, pi*g*	/g/
	[f]	*f*law, enou*gh*	/f/
	[v]	*v*ain, re*v*eal	/v/
	[θ]	*th*in, *th*rough	/θ/
	[ð]	*th*is, *th*erefore	/ð/
	[s]	*s*eal, re*c*eive	/s/
	[z]	*z*ebra, ea*s*ed	/z/
	[ʃ]	*sh*ip, *s*ure	/š/
	[ʒ]	mea*s*ure, sei*z*ure	/ž/
	[tʃ]	*ch*urch, *ch*atter	/č/
	[dʒ]	*j*ud*g*e, *j*angle	/ǰ/
	[m]	*m*ain, sta*mm*er	/m/
	[n]	*n*eo*n*, differe*n*t	/n/
	[ŋ]	si*ng*, a*n*xious	/ŋ/
Liquids	[l]	*l*eap, rumb*l*e	/l/
	[r]	*r*anch, sc*r*atchy	/r/
Glides	[j]	*y*et, *u*niversity	/y/
	[w]	*w*ander, q*u*ick	/w/
	[h]	*h*elp, thresh*h*old	/h/
Vowels	[ɪ]	*i*ndex, p*i*t	/i/
	[ɛ]	*e*ver, tr*e*mble	/e/
	[æ]	*a*fter, c*a*n	/æ/
	[ə]	*a*bout, ros*e*s	/ə/
	[ʌ]	j*u*st, th*u*nder	/ə/
	[ɑ]	f*a*ther, b*o*ther	/a/
	[ʊ]	b*oo*k, p*u*t	/u/
	[o]	(no example in English)	/o/
	[ɔ]	l*a*w, bl*o*nde	/ɔ/
	[a]	*au*nt (some dialects)	—
Diphthongs	[i]	s*ee*, cl*ea*n	/iy/
	[ɛɪ]	w*ay*, bl*a*me	/ey/
	[aɪ]	fl*y*, b*i*nd	/ay/
	[ɔɪ]	n*oi*se, b*o*y	/ɔy/
	[u]	m*oo*n, bl*ue*	/uw/
	[oʊ]	t*oe*, m*o*tor	/ow/
	[aʊ]	h*ow*, r*ou*nd	/aw/
	[ɛh]	*yeah*, *e*ver	/eh/
Post-Diphthong [r] *or* /r/	[ɚ]	fe*ar*, fai*r*, fa*r*, tou*r*	/hr/

Table 4.2   The International Phonetic Alphabet and the Trager-Smith Phonemic Alphabet for Standard American English.

airflow is interfered with or obstructed in the oral cavity, as with consonants. Their sounds are such that /y/, /w/, /h/, and often /r/ frequently alter whatever sound is in their immediate environment, as the articulators glide from one sound to the next. These four, then, are often called glides or semivowels.

There is one final category, noted in table 4.2 but not in 4.1, of diphthongs. Sounds in this category are not consonantal but vocalic. They are produced by a very rapid motion of the tongue from one vowel sound to another, so that the two sounds almost seem to blend together, as in the [a] + [ɪ]—or [a] + [i]—sounds that combine to make up what we informally call the "long-*i*" of words like "tie," "bind," or "shine." Say the diphthongs very slowly and you can hear the blending of two sounds, even though the spelling may indicate only a single letter.

Phonetic transcription. Most speakers of American English use around forty-five different significant speech sounds. Since there are only twenty-six letters in the Roman alphabet, it is clear that the conventional alphabet does not permit a one-to-one correlation between letter and sound. Because such a one-to-one correlation is important in phonetics, linguists have developed more accurate symbols to indicate specific speech sounds.

One such system is the International Phonetic Alphabet, or IPA, listed in table 4.2. In an alphabet such as the IPA, each distinctive speech sound is symbolized by a different graph. *Phone* is the term for an actual speech sound produced by a speaker on a particular occasion. Phones are what a phonetic linguist will transcribe, using IPA symbols. In addition to the basic phonetic symbols, linguists often use other notations as well to show slight variations in articulation. For example, a very small *h* following one of the phonetic symbols would indicate that the speaker had uttered the basic sound with a slight puff of air, aspirating the sound, like this : [tʰ], as in a word like "type" (as contrasted with the unaspirated "t"- sound in a word like "aspirate"). Note that phonetic symbols are enclosed within square brackets.

Another kind of alphabet used by linguists is properly termed a phonemic rather than a phonetic one. The system developed by George L. Trager and Henry L. Smith, Jr., is such an alphabet. Although some of the graphs in this system differ from those used by the IPA, and although the symbols here are enclosed in slash marks, the Trager-Smith, or T-S, system is most fundamentally different from the IPA in intention rather than in form. The T-S alphabet is not intended to represent actual phones as they are produced by a speaker (which is what a phonetic alphabet is designed for). Rather, each graph in a phonemic alphabet symbolizes a range of sounds. The next section discusses the differences between phonetics and phonemics.

Phonemics

Phonemics is the analysis of the relationships among phonetic sounds. Phonemics proposes to describe the rules by which combinations of sounds influence one another to produce words or parts of words. Phonemics builds on careful phonetics, for a study of the patterns of sound cannot be accurate unless the sounds themselves, on which a phonemic study is based, have first been accurately transcribed. Thus, phonetics must first describe the actual sounds of phones as speakers ordinarily produce them in customary discourse.

Although no two people ever say the same phone exactly the same way, native speakers of a language nevertheless can still understand one another. For example, the word "the" is sometimes pronounced with an [i]-phone, sometimes with an [ə]-phone—that is, there are two different phonetic representations of "the"—but both pronunciations are recognized by native speakers as the same word. Linguists have discovered that meaning-signaling sounds in language are distinctive from other meaningful sounds or combinations of sounds (as "the" is distinct from "a," or "cat" from "hat" from "pat"), but that each meaningful sound is tolerant of slight "internal" variations. Thus, each meaning-signaling sound actually represents a range of variations in pronunciation—that is, phonetic differences—within which the same meaning is still conveyed.

Phoneme and allophone. The term for this range of meaningful sound is *phoneme*. Every phoneme is an abstraction, a sort of summary of the similar but phonetically not identical sounds that still signal the same meaning. The Trager-Smith alphabet is phonemic rather than phonetic, because each T-S symbol represents the bundle of variant sounds that collectively make up a phoneme. The tolerable variants, phonetically different but phonemically the same, would be distinguished from one another by the specifically phonetic symbols on the IPA chart.

It is important to recognize that the same phoneme or series of phonemes, as in the word /pɪktyur/, "picture," may actually be pronounced in different ways by different people and thus may have several phonetic representations: for example, [pɪkčɛr], [pɪtčɛr], [pɪčɛr], [pɪkšər], or [pɪktyur]. These variant pronunciations—all indicating the same series of phonemes, /pɪktyur/—are called the *allophones* of the phonemes involved. Each individual phoneme ordinarily has at least two allophones.

Context will usually tell us whether a phonetically distinct sound is also phonemically distinct, that is, whether a phone we have just heard is an allophone or a phoneme. Many English speakers, for example, pronounce the /t/-phoneme almost as if it were [d], so that a word like "bitter" frequently sounds like "bidder." In one kind of utterance, that phonetic shift between [t] and [d] makes no difference in meaning, as when a speaker says [ðɪs waɪn ɪz bɪdər]. The rest of the sentence tells us that the [d]-phone here is clearly allophonic, not phonemic. But in another utterance, the phonetic representation may also have phonemic significance. For example, in the sentence [wi eid it], is the [d] an allophone of /d/, or is it really an allophone of /t/? We will need to know something else from the surrounding context of the sentence, such as the reference of the pronoun "it," before we can tell whether the speaker is saying "We aid it" or "We ate it"—a difference in meaning that might matter a great deal to the "it" in question.

Minimal pairs. A useful technique for discovering what is a phonemic rather than a phonetic difference is the use of controlled sets of sounds. These minimal pairs are two words that a native speaker knows have different meanings, but that sound alike—except for a single (i.e., minimal) distinction in sound which signals the difference in meaning. It is not the spelling but the sound that is important, and we must change only one sound at a time to discover which sound is phonemic. "Pair" [pɛr] and "bare" [bɛr] in English are minimal pairs, because they sound alike except for one sound. That one sound distinction, [p]–[b], signals difference in meaning. That is, /p/ and /b/ in English are different phonemes, not different allophones. We could not use "bare" [bɛr] and "cared" [kɛrd] as minimal pairs, though, because two sounds, not one, mark the difference between these words—[b]–[k] and [r]–[d]—so we could not tell which of the two sound-changes was the phonemic one.

Suprasegmental phonemes. Articulated phones, such as those listed in table 4.2, form a continuous, linear stream of sound, one phone after another in sequence. Riding along with this stream, accompanying each segment of articulated sound, is another kind of phone that may alter the phonemic significance of the flow. This "accompanying" type of phoneme is called a suprasegmental—literally, a phoneme on top of the segmental ones listed in the IPA and Trager-Smith charts. There are three types of suprasegmentals overlaid on the segmentals, and each can make a difference in the meaning of an utterance: stress, pitch, and juncture.

Stress. Stress, or emphasis, in the voice can be phonemic when it distinguishes between a pair of words that are otherwise phonetically identical. For example, only the stresses indicate the difference between /ɪnklaɪn/ (a slope or slant) and /ɪnklaɪn/ (to lean toward or be favorably disposed toward). Spelling will not show the difference between the two words— "incline"–"incline"—nor will the IPA or T-S notations, although linguists sometimes use diacritical marks just in front of the most strongly stressed syllable, like this: /ˈɪnklaɪn/ (noun) and /ɪnˈklaɪn/ (verb). Note that the segmental phonemes are identical; thus, it is the suprasegmental stress which is phonemic.

Pitch. Relative height or depth of tone (high-voiced or low-voiced quality), called pitch, can also be phonemic. The pitch of a speaker's voice can tell an auditor the difference among such utterances as a statement, a question, or a command, even if all three utterances are otherwise phonetically the same. Two significant changes in pitch occur in English: falling and rising. A falling note at the end of an utterance usually signals commands, completed statements, and generalized questions of the sort that cannot be answered by "Yes" or "No": "Close that do~ !" "I went to town this morn~ ." "Whatever was she do~ ?" The other change in pitch is a rising note, indicating polite requests or commands, incomplete or hesitant statements, and questions: "Would you bring me the pap~er?" "What on~earth . . . !" "Has everyone finished the~test?" Graphically indicating pitch is difficult except for general up-and-down trends, although linguists have tried every system from musical notes to curving lines. But there is no doubt that pitch can make a phonemic difference: "Sit~down" with a falling note (command) has a different meaning, is phonemically distinct, from "Sit~down" with a rising note (invitation).

Juncture. Junctures between sounds (sometimes called transitions) are no easier than pitch to notate consistently. Sometimes it is very difficult to tell at what point one syllable ends and another begins, and it is even more difficult to get any two linguists to agree on the same point. Furthermore, the written language can confuse someone trying to listen carefully to the way people actually speak. "What did he say?" in print is four syllables and four words, but vocally, especially if the speaker is excited or lazy, it may come out as something closer to three syllables: /hwa di sei/. Nor do speakers always pause where the written words would indicate that pauses should occur. When a speaker says /kohrsɛks/, is the written version "course X" or "core sex"? How about /aiskrim/: is that "I scream" or "ice cream"? Since the segmental phones in the two phrases /kohrsɛks/ and /aiskrim/ are identical, it is not possible to tell what meanings are being signaled without some indication of juncture or transition. Only the juncture will distinguish between one meaning and another; therefore, the juncture is phonemic here.

Distinctive and redundant features. Individual phonemes (whether segmental or suprasegmental) do not exist in a vacuum, pure and uncontaminated by the surrounding sounds. On the contrary, one sound often intrudes into another's phonetic territory, modifying the articulation, as when the nasal consonants /m/, /n/, and /ŋ/ nasalize the vowels in their phonetic environment: [sĩŋ], [donẽĩt]. A question of much concern in phonemics is, when does that phonetic modification by one phone (like the nasal consonant) of another phone (like the nearby vowel) turn into a change in meaning? In other words, what features of phonetic sounds are *distinctive,* or phonemic, and what features are nondistinctive, allophonic, or *redundant?* The nasalized vowel in the environment of /m/, /n/, or /ŋ/ is nondistinctive—redundant—because there is no difference in meaning between [sɪŋ] and [sĩŋ]. The nasalized form [sĩŋ] is only allophonically different from the non-nasalized form. But it often happens that over many hundreds of years, a feature that was originally redundant does turn into a distinctive feature.

For example, the [f] and the [v] sounds in English about a thousand years ago were phonetically but not phonemically distinct. Their variation was allophonic (nondistinctive, redundant) in the speech of the time, as are nasalized and non-nasalized vowels now. The fricative phoneme would be voiced, as [v], when it occurred in the environment of two voiced phonemes, as in [he′ovənəm], *heofonum* ("heaven"). But it was not voiced—as [f]—in all other environments, such as in *hlāf* ("loaf"), pronounced [hla:f], the [a] here being held for an extra beat. This phonetic change, from voiced to voiceless fricative in the presence or absence of certain other sounds, did not involve a phonemic change; it was a nondistinctive feature. But when many French words began entering the English language in the twelfth century, the new words often did make a phonemic distinction between [f] and [v]. Influenced by this imported phonological rule of distinction, the English language gradually changed its redundancy rule, and now [f] and [v] are different phonemes in English, too, as witness /fil/ and /vil/: "feel" and "veal."

Morphophonology

If we can identify the distinctive features of a phoneme, and if we can also identify the redundant features for each phoneme—those features that are phonetic rather than phonemic—then we may start to make sense out of the complex relationships between patterns of sound and patterns of form. When sounds begin to cluster together in regular ways, the resulting cross-influencing of one sound upon another begins to build up into forms: parts of words and then whole words. Sound clusters that begin to produce forms are known as *morphophonemes,* sometimes shortened to *morphonemes,* from the Greek *morph-* ("form") plus *phon-* ("sound"). *Morphophonology* is the general study of this in-between area where sound and form come together.

In morphophonology, where we are dealing not with just a single sound and its variants but with sound clusters and their variants, the task of accurate description becomes more complicated. It becomes, therefore, even more important to identify distinctive and nondistinctive features, so that morphophonetic representations can be differentiated from morphophonemic ones.

Consider, for example, the morphophonological question of plurality in English. The concept "plurality" is phonemic and is distinguished, by opposition, from the concept "singularity": the word "books" has a different meaning from the word "book." But the concept of plurality is expressed in several different ways: most commonly, with a [s] phone, with an [əz] phone, and with a [z] phone, as in the words "books," "houses," and "pens." Most native speakers of English know without thinking when to use which sound cluster; we don't use [z] with a word like "book." At the same time, most native speakers also know without thinking that the [s] of "books," the [əz] of "houses," and the [z] of "pens" all signal "plurality." We know that the phonetic and formal differences among those three variations are not really meaningful; they are redundant, nondistinctive, not phonemic.

What we know more or less unconsciously about the sound-and-form patterns in our language, a linguist wishes to identify and describe clearly and consciously. Concerning plurality, then, linguists must specify a set of phonetic features by which the three variants or versions of the morphophoneme "plurality" can be represented. A simplified phonological rule for the three most common representations of "plurality" might be written like this:

$$\{Z\} \longrightarrow \begin{cases} \text{[əz] after [s, z, š, ž, č, ǰ]} \\ \text{[s] after other [− voice] consonants} \\ \text{[z] after other [+ voice] sounds} \end{cases}$$

The letter {Z}, with the surrounding braces to indicate its morphophonemic status, is an arbitrary symbol denoting "plurality." The arrow translates into this signal: "will take the form of" or "will be expressed as." The long brace in front of the three choices means: "choose one and only one of the possibilities listed here." Then the three choices and their phonological environments are described. From such a rule as this, you should be able to predict what particular phonetic form indicating plurality will be attached to each of the following words: "bath," "bush," "church," "clog," "curtain," "garage," "gap," "judge," "pack," "slab."

Morphophonological changes, such as those observed in the representations of plurality, occur in regular and predictable ways. Such changes in the form of a word or word part are themselves the result of changes in classes or bundles of sound. At the morphophonological level, it is not merely one sound which alters, but groups of sounds together, as from [s] to [əz] in the plural. There are many other examples of morphophonological changes, of course, such as possessives, verb endings, or the conversion of nouns into verbs ("beauty"-"beautify"), nouns into adjectives ("beauty"-"beautiful"), verbs into nouns ("grow"-"growth"), and so on. When sound influences form in such manners as these, then we are already into the next significant level of language, the analysis of forms and form combinations, words and parts of words, syllables and pieces of syllables—that is, morphology.

Review Questions

1. Define these terms: speech sounds, organs of speech, phonology, phonetics, phonemics, morphophonology.
2. What are the two major subdivisions of phonetics studied in this chapter? How are they different from one another?
3. What are the four major speech organs?
4. What is the principal difference between a consonantal and a vocalic sound?
5. What three factors are involved in a phonetic description of a speech sound?
6. Define these terms: phone, phoneme, allophone, phonemic, phonetic.
7. How is the ordinary (Latin or Roman) alphabet different from the Trager-Smith and the International Phonetic Alphabet? How do the last two differ from each other?
8. What are distinctive features, redundant features, and minimal pairs?
9. Name the three kinds of suprasegmental phonemes. How are they different from segmental phonemes?
10. What is morphophonology? Give an example of a morphophoneme *besides* the plural.

Selected Reading

Abercrombie, David. *Elements of General Phonetics*. Chicago: Aldine Press, 1967.

Anderson, Stephen R. *The Organization of Phonology*. New York: Academic Press, 1974.

Bowen, J. Donald. *Patterns of English Pronunciation*. Rowley, Mass.: Newbury House, 1977.

Bronstein, Arthur J. *The Pronunciation of American English*. New York: Appleton-Century-Crofts, 1960.

Chomsky, Noam, and Morris Halle. *The Sound Pattern of English.* New York: Harper & Row, 1968.

Gleason, Henry A., Jr. *An Introduction to Descriptive Linguistics,* rev. ed. New York: Holt, Rinehart and Winston, 1961.

Harms, Robert T. *Introduction to Phonological Theory.* Englewood Cliffs, N.J.: Prentice-Hall, Inc., 1968.

Hyman, Larry M. *Phonology: Theory and Analysis.* New York: Holt, Rinehart and Winston, 1975.

Jones, Daniel. *An Outline of English Phonetics,* rev. ed. West Orange, N.J.: Albert Saifer, 1976.

Kenyon, John Samuel. *American Pronunciation,* 10th ed. Ann Arbor, Mich.: George Wahr, 1961.

Ladefoged, Peter. *A Course in Phonetics.* New York: Harcourt Brace Jovanovich, 1975.

————. *Elements of Acoustic Phonetics.* Chicago: University of Chicago Press, 1962.

Langacker, Ronald W. *Fundamentals of Linguistic Analysis.* New York: Harcourt Brace Jovanovich, 1972.

Schane, Sanford A. *Generative Phonology.* Englewood Cliffs, N.J.: Prentice-Hall, Inc., 1973.

Sloat, Clarence, Sharon Henderson Taylor, and James Hoard. *Introduction to Phonology.* Englewood Cliffs, N.J.: Prentice-Hall, Inc., 1978.

Thomas, Charles K. *An Introduction to the Phonetics of American English,* 2nd ed. New York: The Ronald Press Co., 1958.

Journals   *General Linguistics; Journal of the Acoustical Society of America; Language Sciences*

5

The Forms of Language

There are many parallels between phonology, the study of the sounds of a language, and morphology, the study of the forms of a language. The specialized terminology belonging to each discipline is an example of such paralleling, as table 5.1 indicates. There is no equivalent in morphology of phonetics, for when we wish to represent the sounds of a morpheme, we simply use a phonetic transcription. But what is a morpheme?

	Sound (phon-)	*Form* (morph-)
Study of	phonology	morphology
Smallest Unit	phoneme	morpheme
Variant	allophone	allomorph
Actual Speech	phone	morph
Transcription	phonemic symbols / /	morphemic symbols { }
	phonetic symbols [ ]	—

Table 5.1   *Comparison of Terms in Phonology and Morphology*

The Morpheme

Let us first state what a morpheme is not: it is not a word, nor is it a syllable. Like the phoneme, the morpheme is frequently an abstraction, covering a range of possible variant forms (or allomorphs). But here, the abstraction is a unit of meaning, not a unit of sound: a *morpheme* is the smallest unit of meaning in language.

Lexical and syntactic meaning.   Immediately, however, we encounter trouble with the word "meaning," which itself has many meanings. We shall examine the question of meaning in much more detail in chapter 9, but here, let us stipulate that there are two basic kinds of morphological meaning: lexical, or semantic, and syntactic, or structural.

Lexical meaning.   Lexical, or semantic, meaning is the type we ordinarily intend when we use the word "meaning." Lexical meaning has a sense of content or reference about it; morphemes having lexical meaning are listed in dictionaries or thesaureses. Lexical meaning is then further divided into denotative meaning (ordinary usage, common, widespread) and connotative meaning (private or localized, not widespread). Thus, the usual lexical denotation of "apple" is: a red, yellow, or green fruit from the tree *Pyrus malus*. But the connotations may range all the way from pleasant (tastes good, supposedly keeps the doctor away) to unpleasant (symbol of strife, temptation, destruction). A morpheme that has more lexical than syntactic meaning is called a lexical morpheme.

Syntactic meaning. The other principal kind of meaning, syntactic, has less to do with content or reference and more to do with what we might call internal traffic directing. A morpheme that has syntactic meaning—a syntactic, or structural, morpheme—tends to direct other, more lexical morphemes, to signal relationships within a syntactic unit, to indicate what is subject and what is predicate, for instance.

Frequently, a syntactic morpheme is attached to a lexical one, in which case the attachment is called an *inflection*. The plural allomorphs are inflections, as are the tense markers, possession markers, and comparison markers. Such inflections as these do not have much lexical meaning themselves; the {ed} that signals the past tense in English does not have the content-meaning of a lexical morpheme like the word "apple." But the inflections are necessary to show how one lexical morpheme is related to another, as in the phrase "John's book," where the possessive inflection {'s}[1] indicates that the book belongs to John. Similarly, tense signals a relationship: the word "pour," which lacks an inflection, indicates action going on right now, in the present, whereas the word "poured," composed of the lexical morpheme {pour} plus the inflection {ed}, signals a condition that has already occurred in the past. The relationship here is of time rather than of possession.

Just as frequently, however, a syntactic morpheme is not attached to a lexical one, but occurs alone. Separate forms that primarily serve a syntactic rather than a lexical function are called function words, or sometimes operators. Examples of such words include "and," "there," "because," "or," "but," "so," "than." Like inflections, these words are low in lexical meaning but high in traffic-directing or relationship-signaling function. The operator {and}, for example, primarily serves to connect two or more lexical words in a way that shows the two to have equivalent weight: "cats and dogs," "red, white, and blue." (Note that the connection is not "cats and dog" or "red, white, and cow.") Like other function words, "and" does not

---

1. Strictly speaking, the apostrophe (') is not morphemic, but appears here because the word "John's" is written rather than spoken. The possessive morpheme actually is {s}, pronounced [z].

mean much, as we ordinarily use the word "mean," but it *does* much in those phrases. If we changed "and" to "or" in each phrase, the relationship signaled among the words would be quite different.

Often it seems nearly impossible to distinguish lexical from syntactic meaning; there is much overlap between the two. Thus, almost any given morpheme may be classed as lexical or as syntactic, depending on how it is functioning in an utterance.

Morphology

Morphology, or the study of morphemes, can be most usefully subdivided into two types of analysis. One type, called synchronic morphology, investigates morphemes in a single dimension of time—any particular time, past or present. Essentially, synchronic morphology is a linear analysis, asking what are the lexical and syntactic components of words, and how do the components add, subtract, or rearrange themselves in various contexts. Synchronic morphology is not concerned with the word's history in our language. If we bring in a historical dimension, however, and ask how a word's contemporary usage might be different from its first recorded usage, then we are moving into a field of historical linguistics called etymology, or diachronic (two-dimensional time) morphology.

Anyone concerned with a full examination of a word's or a morpheme's meanings will, of course, pursue both a synchronic and a diachronic inquiry. A complete morphological analysis will require us to check the word's current phonemic and morphemic structure as well as its past and present lexical meanings. Obviously, we can investigate historical alterations simultaneously with a synchronic look at the morphemic components.[2] For purposes of discussion here, however, we will treat the two branches of morphology as separate entities.

Synchronic morphology. A synchronic investigation is asking, basically, what kinds of morphemes are combining in which sorts of ways to form a word. Often, a synchronic analysis of morphemes begins to spill over into an analysis of syntax, for morphology in general often becomes the shared territory of word meaning and sentence structure. We will try here, however, to keep our analysis of morphemes separate from syntax as much as possible.

2. For example, the word "etymology" synchronically analyzed contains three morphemes: {etumo}, {log}, and {y}. Diachronically, the word comes from the Greek *etumos,* true or real, and *logy,* study of. The etymological implication, therefore, is that only the original meanings of words are the true or real ones.

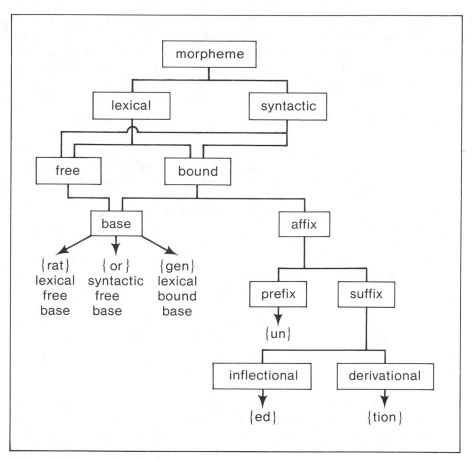

Figure 5.1   Binary Classification in Synchronic Morphology

To begin such a synchronic investigation, we must first discover in what ways morphemes can be synchronically classified. Most useful may be three binary terms, three sets of two words nearly opposite in meaning. One term from each set can be applied to each morpheme as we encounter it (figure 5.1). Each morpheme should be describable by one, but not the other, of the words in each binary set. We have already mentioned the first pair of classifiers: *lexical–syntactic*. Nearly all words in the lexicon can be identified as either lexical or syntactic morphemes.

Free–bound. The second such binary set is free–bound. Morphemes can be classified as either free or bound, that is, either capable of standing by themselves, as words, or not capable of standing by themselves. A free morpheme can be either lexical, like the word {rat}, or syntactic, like the operator {or}. If the free morpheme is syntactic rather than lexical, other morphemes will not combine with it. Lexical morphemes, however, can combine with other morphemes or other words. For example, to the free lexical morpheme {rat}, we can add the bound allomorph {s}, producing the word "rats," or the bound morpheme {ty}, producing "ratty," or another free morpheme {catch}, plus a bound one, {er}, producing "rat-catcher."

Base-affix. The third useful binary set for synchronic analysis of morphemes is base-affix. A morpheme may be classified as a base or as an affix, but not as both—at least, not in the same word. (Like the other terms in the two previous binary sets, "base" and "affix" are relational classifications rather than pure opposites. It is possible for the same morpheme to be free in one use and bound in another, or lexical in one case and syntactic in another.) A base—sometimes called a root—is a morpheme to which other morphemes are attached. The attaching morphemes are called the affixes.

Bases are morphemes that lexically, rather than syntactically, dominate other morphemes. Bases always have more lexical than syntactic meaning, but bases are not always free. There are many bound bases in English as well as free bases. An example of a bound base is {gen}, a morpheme that has more lexical than syntactical meaning (*gen* = beginning), so it is a base rather than an affix; but it cannot stand by itself as a word, so it is bound, not free. Put together with various other attaching morphemes, {gen} gives us words like "generic," "gene," and "engender."

Affixes. The affixes, or attaching morphemes, can be further subdivided by two subsidiary binary sets. The first set, *prefix-suffix,* merely indicates where the attachment occurs. If the affix is attached at the beginning of a base, as {un} is, then the technical term used is *prefix.* Prefixes alter the lexical meaning of a morpheme, but do not change its syntactic function. The prefix {un} and its allomorphs {im} and {in}, for example, turn an affirmative base into a negative one: {un}+{well} means "not well"; {im}+{possible} means "not possible"; {in}+{secure} means "not secure."

If the attachment appears at the end of a base, as does {ed}, then the name for it is *suffix.* It is in connection with suffixes that the second binary subdivision should be applied, for there are two kinds of suffixes: inflections and derivations. As we indicated earlier, inflections alter the syntactic function of a base but do not change the lexical meaning very much. The class of inflections is very small (plural, tense, possession, comparison) and very stable; no new forms are being added. Derivational morphemes, however, having more lexical meaning than do the inflections, belong to a larger and a more open class. New derivations can easily be added. Like inflections, derivations can change a base's syntactic function, but they can also alter the base's lexical meaning somewhat, in a way that the inflections do not.

For example, take the base {friend}. This is a noun of the type called [+ count], that is, having the feature "capable of being counted individually."[3] Such a noun can be made plural by the addition of the plural allomorph {s}: we can speak of one "friend" or of many "friends," and we can count the number of friends if we wish, one by one. The basic lexical meaning of {friend} has not been much altered by the addition of an inflection. But if to the singular base, we add the derivation {ship}, to produce the word "friendship," we have a different sort of change. The syntactic meaning has not been altered, for the word is still a noun, but now the lexical feature shifts from [+ count] to [− count]; "friendship" is ordinarily a mass noun, one that refers to a quality or a concept rather than to a number. Ordinarily, such nouns cannot function as plurals; we say "friendship is" rather than "friendships are."

As another example, if we add the derivational suffix {tion} to the base {derive}, the suffix will change the function of the word from verb to noun. If we then add another suffix, {al}, to the newly produced noun "derivation," we get a second category change: the word "derivational" is an adjective. Add one more, {ly}, and there is a third change in function, to adverb. Derivational suffixes, like {ship}, {tion}, {al}, and {ly}, are added to a base before the inflectional suffixes: inflections always tag along last.

Now let us try a little practice with synchronic analysis. Refer to the binary chart (figure 5.1) and keep in mind that the principle of minimal-pairing applies in morphology as well as in phonology: investigating types of morphemes, we should use morphemes that are as syntactically similar as possible—preferably identical—but are different in lexical meaning. Let us use the word "geography" as a test case, to discover how many morphemes it contains and of what sort they are.

Let us substitute {bio} (life) for {geo} (earth); we get a recognizable word, "biography." So {geo} is a morpheme. Substitute {logy} (study of) for {graphy} (writing about), and the result is another familiar word, "geology." Finally, change {y} (activity or product)[4] to {ic} (characteristic of), and we have a new word, "geographic." Since we cannot change any other part of "geography" and still get a standard English word—that is, we cannot subdivide the meaningful forms of "geography" any more than we already have—these must be the only three morphemes in the word: {geo}, {graph}, {y}.

One of these morphemes never appears by itself as a separate word; therefore, it is not a free morpheme, but a bound one. Is it a bound base or an

3. Features like [± count] are discussed in more detail in chapter 9.
4. The {y} suffix can also mean, depending on context: existence or possession; relationship or resemblance; condition or state of being; smallness or diminutiveness; familiarity or endearment. But none of those meanings seems quite so applicable to "geography" as the one noted.

affix? It has very little lexical meaning, serving mainly to direct traffic, so it must be an affix. Since it appears at the end, it is specifically a suffix. Since it has some lexical meaning of its own, as well as indicating the function—noun—of the word "geography," {y} is a derivational rather than an inflectional suffix.

{Geo} is a bound base. It cannot stand by itself lexically as a word and therefore is not free; in other words, it is bound. But morphemes with even less lexical meaning do attach to {geo}, so it is a base. In fact, other morphemes *must* attach to {geo} in order for there to be anything like a word formed from it, so it has to be a bound base.

Finally, there is {graph}, the most independent morpheme in "geography." It is, we discover, a free base: free, because it can stand by itself as a word; base, because it can accept other, attaching morphemes. Like other free bases, {graph} is unlimited positionally. It can appear at the beginning of a word ("*graph*ology"), in the middle ("geo*graph*y"), or at the end ("photo*graph*").

Around such bases as {graph} is our English lexicon built. One of the reasons for the flexibility of English is that it borrows bases from just about every language there is; {graph} comes from Greek. Another reason for this flexibility is that English constantly uses bases and affixes to produce precise distinctions of lexical meaning. This manipulatability of parts allows for marvelous adaptability to the shifting demands of linguistic contexts, the changes that happen to all languages in response to historical, social, or other pressures. In the next section, we will discuss some specific ways in which morphemes can be manipulated to form different kinds of words.

Diachronic morphology. If we alter our investigative stance from a word's present morphological construction to its historical development, we move from a synchronic to a diachronic analysis. (It is perfectly possible to do both, but we are here keeping them separate.) Diachronically, we would ask where a given word came from and how has it changed its meanings as it has changed its forms.

Not all words do change their lexical meanings over time. For example, "stone" currently, in standard usage, has pretty much the same referent as it did when it was the Old English *stán*. Most function words, such as prepositions (words like "with," "out," "of," "under," or "over"), have remained pretty much unaltered in meaning and in form since they entered the language. But enough words do change to make reading older literature difficult, as you know if you have tried Shakespeare or *Beowulf*. The constancy of change will also make a prowl through the etymologically oriented, many-volumed *Oxford English Dictionary* entertainingly worthwhile; check the O.E.D., for instance, on what has happened to the word "nice."

Occasionally writers will make deliberate use of a change in a word's meaning, playing off an older meaning against a contemporary one, like a historical pun. Blake does that with "appalls" in these lines from the poem "London": "How the Chimney-sweeper's cry / Every blackning Church appalls . . . ." On one level, the word has the contemporary meaning of "horrifies," but on another level, it echoes an archaic meaning, "turns pale." As a contrast with "blackning" (Blake's spelling), "appalls" suggests the terrible plight of the chimney sweep in an industrialized city, so terrible that even the sooty buildings, and the social institutions symbolized by the buildings (the Church), grow pale with alarm.

We can discover general patterns of lexical change in words, trends that the English lexicon as a whole tends to follow over time. Broadly speaking, there are two ways of classifying the trends, as processes and as directions. If we are concerned with etymological processes, we are investigating morphological changes that can occur at any time to alter a word's lexical meaning. Directions, on the other hand, reflect the incremental drifts from one stage to the next stage of specifically historical change in meaning.

Processes

Different etymologists will classfiy the processes and directions in different ways, but this is the one used here for processes:

1. analogy
2. compounding
3. reduplication
4. derivation
5. back-formation
6. base-creation
7. shortening

Analogy. Of these processes, analogy may be the most significant; some linguists have argued that all the processes involve some sort of analogy. (Other linguists disagree.) In any case, analogy in effect matches an already existing pattern with the demands of a new context. The new context produces a new word or a new usage of an old word. For example, "defense" /dɪˈfɛns/ used to be a noun only, but now is commonly also used as a verb /ˈdifɛns/ by sports commentators and fans, as in "to defense against the Cowboys' front four." Everybody uses analogy to some extent, but children in particular are prone to doing so during the overgeneralizing stages. "I *goed* to town" is a common analogy with the regular {ed} past-tense inflectional affix. My daughter, Joni, was once told to "Behave!" (phonetically:

[bi′heiv]). Her answer was, "I'm being have!" (phonetically: [′biŋ heiv]), an analogy with linking-verb–predicate-adjective constructions such as: "Be good!"—"I'm being good!"

Many standard constructions and words have come into Modern English by way of analogy. There was, for example, an Old English verb, *drincan* /drinkɔn/, "to drink," and a noun, *drenč* /drɛnč/, "a drink." The verb *drincan* produced a converted form, the noun *drinc*, which has come down to us as "drink," while the old *drenč* disappeared as a noun. But *drenč* also produced a conversion, the verb *drenčan*, which is now our word "drench." The conversions from verb to noun to verb were made by analogy of the respective noun-verb derivational suffixes. So Modern English has one verb, "drench," and one noun, "drink," as well as the original verb ("drink").

The other processes involve a systematic juggling of morphemes:

> Free + Free: Compounding, Reduplication
> Free + Bound: Derivation
> Free − Bound: Back-formation, Shortening
> + Free: Base-creation

Compounding and reduplication. Compounding, discussed earlier when we were examining free bases, simply combines two or more bases into one new word: {road} + {block} = "roadblock"; {stop} + {light} = "stoplight"; {over} + {see} = "oversee." Note that the resulting compound word means something different from the sum of its parts; it is a new word. Reduplication, the repetition of phonologically similar free morphemes, almost always produces a comic effect because of the near rhyme in key phonemes: "mish-mash," "helter-skelter," "zigzag." Consequently, reduplicated words appear more often in colloquial or slang use than in formal utterance.

Derivation and back-formation. Derivation, possibly the most common etymological process after analogy, and back-formation, which is far less common, are in effect opposites of each other. As we mentioned in the section on bases and affixes, derivation adds affixes to a base, as in {com} (affix) + {pound} (base) + {ing} (affix), "compounding." Where that process derives words by the addition of affixes, back-formation deprives a base of its apparent affixes, producing a new word in the form of an unadorned base. The verb "edit," for instance, comes from the Latin noun *editor,* one who gives out, that is, one who publishes and distributes copies of something. The suffix {or} on the bound base {edit} dropped off, resulting in a back-formed free base. "Sidle," meaning a sort of crablike shuffle, is back-formed from the Middle English adverb *sideling,* beside or alongside of. "Nestle," to cuddle close to, comes from an Old English noun, *nestling,* a creature still young enough to be confined to its nest. In all three instances, the bases—{edit}, {sid<e>l}, and {nestl}—came into existence after a longer word had already been in use.

Shortening. Shortening (sometimes called abbreviation) is like the process called synecdoche in poetry: a part is substituted for a whole. In poetry, it is common to find such substitutions as "the crown" for "the king" or "the monarchy"; in diachronic morphology, we find "cab" substituting for "cabriolet," "extra" for "extraordinary," or "varsity" for "university." In "varsity," the graphic shift from <e> to <a> reflects the common British pronunciation of short <e> as [a], where Americans would say [ɛ].

One of the more socioculturally interesting examples of shortening occurs in connection with the word "mistress." Originally, and sometimes still, "mistress" was a term of courtesy applied to any middle-class woman in a position of some authority, whether she was married or not, as in the phrase "mistress of the house." Since about the eighteenth century, however, the original word has split into four: two shortened forms, now used to indicate marital status: "Miss" and "Mrs."; a new, "neutral" form—"Ms." [mɪz]—that is supposed to signal only gender, not marital status; and the original form, "mistress," which now has acquired connotations of sexual relationship it did not have before.

Base-creation As its name suggests, a base-creation makes up bases, using morphemic relations as guidelines. A base-created word often echoes natural sounds onomatopoetically, as in "hiss," "mumble," "hum," or "drizzle." There is, of course, no such thing as a completely new word, since we are limited generally by the sounds the human speech organs can produce and particularly, by habit as much as anything else, to the sounds with which we are familiar. Thus, while the word "drizzle" (as either noun or verb) is a base-creation, it is also phonologically and etymologically related to the Middle English noun *mizzle,* a fine mist. Even the brand name Kodak, often cited as an example of "pure" base-creation, did not come out of thin air. Whether its creators intended it or not, "Kodak" follows a familiar English phonological pattern. It consists of two syllables with the accent on the first syllable and an alternation of consonant and vowel sounds. Compare ['kowdæk] with these transcriptions of common nouns that follow the same phonetic pattern of first-syllable stress and consonantal-vocalic alternation: ['nowtɪs], ['rɪvɛr], and ['tuwtər].[5]

Directions

As with processes, the directions of etymological change will be classified in different ways by different people; we will use this scheme (the classifications here are not mutually exclusive):

5. Lewis Carroll's famous word "chortle," from his poem "Jabberwocky," comes from "chuckle" and "snort," but is what linguists call a blend word rather then a true base-creation. (Carroll called it a *portmanteau,* or "suitcase," word.)

1. deterioration
2. elevation
3. specialization
4. concretization
5. extension
6. metaphorization
7. radiation

We can divide these seven into three groups according to the direction of change each manifests. Deterioration and elevation are opposites of each other; specialization and concretization develop in similar ways, the approximate opposite of those followed by extension and metaphorization; and radiation's directions include nearly all of those followed by the others. We might suggest their relationship by diagrams like those in figure 5.2.

Deterioration and elevation. When a word deteriorates (in etymology, the term has no bad connotations, such as of decay), it changes from a relatively exalted or at least neutral significance in its first recorded usage to a relatively condemnatory or trivial meaning. "Silly," for instance, originally meant blessed, not its current foolish; "knave" referred to a youth or boy, not to a rascal. The opposite happens when a word's semantic meaning is elevated from something neutral or deprecatory to something more suggestive of approval. "Knight" originally referred to any young man and carried none of its present associations with romantic gallantry and glory. "Fond" first meant foolish, daft, or crazy, not affectionate (although it is easy enough to see how the meaning changed as it did). A "surgeon" began as a barber who also drew blood, applied leeches, and pulled teeth; his sign, incidentally, was a bloody rag, which survives in the red-and-white barber's pole.

Specialization and concretization. In specialization and its analog, concretization, the motion of change is from the general or metaphoric to the specific or concrete. The opposite path is followed by extension and metaphorization, which change from the specific or concrete to the general or metaphoric. A word is said to have become specialized if its application has become narrower over time. "Meat" has come to refer particularly to animal flesh rather than to food generally, and "starve" now means death through failure to ingest food instead of death by any means. But a concretized word has moved from an abstract reference to a more concrete one. "Multitude" now means a crowd, a collection of tangible, individual, countable bodies. It has the feature [+ count] now. Originally, however, it was a mass [− count] noun meaning "many-ness." Similarly, the word "youth," which originally referred only to the abstract, [− count] concept "young-ness," now also has acquired a [+ count] reference to young people, as in "the youth of this nation are its best chance for the future."

Extension and metaphorization. Extension reverses specialization: an extended word now has a wider application than it did at first. For example, "bird" currently is a generic reference to any member of the class *Aves,* rather than its original, specific reference to a young, nesting bird.[6] Similarly, metaphorization reverses concretization: what once had only a specific, concrete reference can now be applied in a metaphoric, nonliteral fashion. "Bright" no longer applies only to a quality of light; we can intelligibly speak of a bright boy. "Sharp" can be applied to tongues or winds, not just to blades; a smile is "cold," not only the temperature. Many words that technically are the products of metaphorization have been in use so long that they have lost their flash of metaphor: "*blanket* of snow," "to *labor* under an illusion," "*casting* aspersions," "the *grasp* of a subject." These are known as dead metaphors.

Radiation. Finally, although radiation is probably most closely related to extension, it actually combines the directions of the last four types. When a word's meanings undergo radiation, they spread or branch out into near-metaphor, in the sense that the meanings are applied in unusual contexts. But unlike extension and metaphorization, the meanings are not derived chronologically from one another, in a sequential alteration of meaning. Rather, the present meanings of a radiated word coexist with the original

6. "Bird" in current British slang is also a common term for a young girl, not to mention the more or less obscene gesture that in America is called "flipping the bird." More extension?

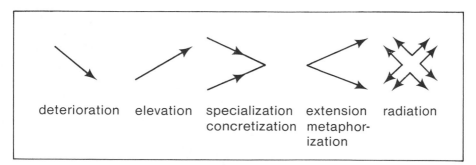

deterioration   elevation   specialization   extension   radiation
                              concretization   metaphor-
                                                ization

Figure 5.2   Relationships among the Etymological Directions

ones, and all meanings, past and present, still refer to essentially the same idea. For instance, all the current applications of the word "paper"—from those referring to an essay or journal to the references to a governmental policy statement—still carry some sense of the original, literal reference to a papyruslike material on which to write. Similarly, "head" still conveys the notion of that part of the body containing the brain, even in such diverse uses as "head of state," "head of the bed," or, in the slang of some drug users, "head" meaning one who uses drugs extensively, as in "He's a real dope head."

Folk etymology. One further pattern in diachronic morphology we have not yet discussed is folk etymology. This is a change in the form of a word or phrase, resulting either from an incorrect popular notion of the term's original meaning or from the influence of more familiar terms mistakenly taken to be analogous. "Sparrow-grass," or "sparrygrass," a regional-dialectic word derived by folk etymology from "asparagus," and "cold slaw," from "cole slaw," reflect mistaken analogies. The Middle Ages were particularly fond of the first type of etymologizing, as can be seen in the common medieval spelling of "abomination" as "abhomination," with an <h> in its middle. The word actually comes from the Latin *ab,* away from, and *omen,* evil sign or portent, and thus means an ill omen to be shunned. But throughout the sixteenth century, the assumption was that it had come from *ab homine,* away from man, that is, something inhuman.

All of these directions and processes of morphological change depend to some degree upon phonological shifts as well. All the changes stem from one of any language's, and therefore one of the English language's, more important traits: its open-ended acceptance of change, particularly lexical change. As we move in the next chapters to the grammars and the history of the English language, bear in mind that the open-endedness in turn depends upon majority rule, or conventionality, which itself is an aspect of language's systematic and sociocultural functions. Languages change because speakers participate in and accept the changes. Those lexical and structural shifts may reflect alterations in the speakers' perceptions of the varying realities around them: social, political, economic, psychological, and so on. Alterations in a language over time probably reflect the alterations in the society of which that language is a part.

Review Questions

1. Why is there no such thing as "morphetics"?
2. What are the two major kinds of meaning dealt with in this chapter?
3. Give some examples of inflections, of operators, of affixes.

4. Distinguish between diachronic and synchronic morphology.
5. What three binary sets do we use in synchronically describing a morpheme?
6. Distinguish between inflectional and derivational suffixes.
7. What are processes in morphology? What are directions in morphology? How does each function?
8. Which of the processes do linguists identify as most significant? Why?
9. What is folk etymology? What is a blend, or portmanteau, word? What is a dead metaphor?
10. Upon what universal trait does etymological function depend?

Selected Reading

Adams, Valerie. *An Introduction to Modern English Word Formation.* London: Longman, 1973.

Arlotto, Anthony. *Introduction to Historical Linguistics.* Boston: Houghton Mifflin Co., 1972.

Bloomfield, Leonard, and Harry Hoijer. *Language History.* New York: Holt, Rinehart and Winston, 1965.

Gleason, Henry A., Jr. *An Introduction to Descriptive Linguistics,* rev. ed. New York: Holt, Rinehart and Winston, 1961.

Hoenigswald, Henry M. *Language Change and Linguistic Reconstruction.* Chicago: University of Chicago Press, 1960.

Householder, Fred W., and Sol Saporta, eds. *Problems in Lexicography.* Bloomington: Indiana University Research Center in Anthropology, Folklore, and Linguistics, 1962.

Langacker, Ronald W. *Fundamentals of Linguistic Analysis.* New York: Harcourt Brace Jovanovich, 1972.

Lehmann, Winfred P. *Historical Linguistics,* 2nd ed. New York: Holt, Rinehart and Winston, 1973.

Marchand, Hans. *The Categories and Types of Present-Day English Word-Formation,* 2nd ed. Munich: C. H. Beck'sche Verlagsbuchhandlung, 1969.

Matthews, P. H. *Morphology: An Introduction to the Theory of Word Structure.* Cambridge: Cambridge University Press, 1976.

Nida, Eugene P. *Morphology: The Descriptive Analysis of Words,* 2nd ed. Ann Arbor: The University of Michigan Press, 1949.

Onions, C. T. *The Oxford Dictionary of English Etymology.* Oxford: Oxford University Press, 1966.

Saltarelli, Mario, and Dieter Wanner, eds. *Diachronic Studies in Romance Linguistics.* The Hague: Mouton Publishing Co., 1975.

Skeat, Walter W. *An Etymological Dictionary of the English Language,* 4th
ed. Oxford: Oxford University Press, 1910.
Stockwell, Robert P., and Ronald S. K. Macaulay, eds. *Linguistic Change
and Generative Theory.* Bloomington: University of Indiana Press, 1971.

Journals   *General Linguistics; International Journal of American Linguistics; Language Sciences; Lingua*

6

The Grammars of English

The definitions of the word "grammar" take up three columns in the O.E.D., so it is clear that the word is used to indicate several different concepts. Probably the three most applicable usages for our purposes are what W. Nelson Francis calls "Grammar 1," "Grammar 2," and "Grammar 3."[1] Grammar 1 Francis describes as "the set of formal patterns in which the words of a language are arranged in order to convey larger meanings"; Grammar 2 refers to "the branch of linguistic science . . . concerned with description, analysis, and formulization of formal language patterns"; and Grammar 3 means "linguistic etiquette." Since these three very different meanings of the word "grammar" are often used interchangeably and therefore confusingly, we shall here substitute different words for the separate meanings.

To make the distinctions clear, we will say that Grammar 1 can usefully be called *syntax,* meaning the actual speech behavior by which people arrange words into sentences, and the resulting arrangement of words. Syntax, then, is what people do to produce linguistic strings. Part of a linguist's task is to describe and analyze this syntax. Francis speaks of such study and analysis as Grammar 2; we will identify it simply as *grammar.* Grammar for us, then, means the study of syntax. Finally, what Francis terms Grammar 3, linguistic etiquette—or the judgment about what is correct or incorrect, good or bad, syntactic behavior according to whether or not it follows "rules"—we shall call *prescriptivism.* Syntax (behavior) really is not the same as prescriptivism (judgment), nor is either of those identical with grammar (analysis). In chapters 8 and 12, in particular, we will deal with the prescriptive approach; in this chapter, we shall be concerned with behavior—syntax—and its study, grammar.

Grammars as Models

That language changes constantly we have seen illustrated on at least three levels: sound, form, and lexical meaning. These changes may occur syn-

---

1. W. Nelson Francis, "Revolution in Grammar," *Quarterly Journal of Speech* 40 (October 1954): 300.

chronically or diachronically or in both ways. In addition, the ways of analyzing those changes in the actual language have altered over the years. Linguists and grammarians have shifted from one method to another in their attempt to investigate, describe, and evaluate what is going on in language. Thus, it is no longer accurate to speak of "English grammar" (singular), for in fact, there now exist several analytical approaches and models. That is why the title of this chapter uses the plural form "grammars," for three such systems of analysis are in wide use today: the Traditional model, the Structuralist model, and the Transformational-Generative model.

Before we begin our survey of the most important principles in each of these analytic systems, however, it is important that we clarify what is required of a satisfactory grammar. Like any scientific theory or model that purports to explain a system (such as syntax), a grammar must meet five criteria or requirements: simplicity, completeness, mutual exclusion, consistency, and predictability.

1. A grammar must be simple, not so elaborate that the model begins to take over from what it intends to represent. The so-called Law of Parsimony, also known as Occam's Razor, is the principle here: the simplest explanation that takes account of all the data is the best one. We must beware of unnecessary elaboration.

2. The categories within the model, the basic definitions, should be complete. Nothing that actually functions as part of the syntax should be omitted from the grammar, for a complete model or theory must match up with the real-world behaviors that the model describes.

3. The categories within the system should be mutually exclusive. One definition should not include two referents, and two definitions should not be applicable to the same referent. As much as possible, the aim should be one-to-one correlation of category and referent. In phonology, for example, the IPA and Trager-Smith symbols are mutually exclusive, for one symbol represents only one phoneme or one phonetic sound.

4. The model must be internally consistent in its applications of categories and principles. Just as the same definition should not be made to apply to two different syntactic units, so also should a principle not be applied one way at one time and another way at another time—at least, not without good and consistent reasons for the exceptions. For example, the plural morphophoneme {Z} discussed in chapter 4 produces consistent morphophonetic variations according to the phonetic environment in which {Z} occurs.

5. Finally, the model or theory must be usable when we need to predict how new data, such as sentences we have not heard before, are likely to fit into the system. A workable theory cannot just describe what we already know; it must also be able to give reliable assessments of what we do not yet know.

Without this feature of predictability, a grammatical model would have to be radically reorganized whenever the syntax changed, as it always does, however slowly.

Each of the three grammatical models we will briefly describe here should be tested against these five criteria. The better each model meets the test, the better a grammar it will be. But, as we have seen in chapter 2, language is intimately tied with the human brain, about which we do not know nearly as much as we would like. So all three of the theories are likely to be deficient in some respects, until we have more information about psycholinguistics and syntax.

Traditional Grammar

As the most ancient of the three grammars, the Traditional system has a good deal of precedent behind it. It has its origins in the fifth century B.C., with Plato and Aristotle in Greece and a Sanskrit scholar named Panini (who knew nothing of the Greeks' work, nor they of his) in India. Various Romans and early-Christian-era writers also made contributions to the system, but the most influential of the Traditional grammarians began writing in the eighteenth century, about the time when English was beginning to be taken seriously as a separate language and not as merely another vernacular. Writers like Daniel Defoe, Jonathan Swift, Samuel Johnson, and John Wallis argued vehemently that English needed to be "regularised" and "improved," its principles spelled out, its discrepancies smoothed out, and its distortions ruled out. Naturally enough (because there was no grammar of English before this time, but several centuries' worth of clear analysis did exist for Latin), the first grammarians modeled their analysis of English on Latin. Also naturally, they found that English did not match the rules of Latin. So they reshaped English to fit. That is why we are sometimes warned, for example, never to split an infinitive in English: Latin infinitives, being part of the verb's base, cannot be split apart as the two-word infinitive of English can. Many such prescriptive rules linger in English Traditional grammar today, as carryovers from Latin grammar.

Even in the earliest days, there were writers who protested that the grammarian's job was to record how the language was used, not to manipulate it and hand down prescriptions, but the voices of men like George Campbell and Joseph Priestley were not loud enough. As a result, nearly every English-speaking person today is self-conscious about "grammar," uncertain about what is "good grammar" and what is not, and anxious about his or her ability to analyze the workings of the native language. As a sadder result, few adults are even interested in their own language, once they learn the basic skills of using it. Perhaps these unhappy consequences can be laid as much to bad teaching as to the inadequacies of the Traditional system, but there is still no denying how awkwardly Traditional grammar has served us as an analytical tool and how much it has confused most of us.

What ultimately happens with Traditional grammar is that the system becomes more important than the syntax. Naming the eight parts of speech, mastering the complicated vocabulary of analysis (such as gerund, participle, transitive-intransitive, subordinating conjunction, independent clause), and—at least in many school situations—becoming familiar with the many different lines one must draw in the sentence diagram: all these tend to take over the spotlight from what a grammar should do, which is to explain how a language's various structures actually work.

To make matters worse, the Traditional system is heavily dependent on notionalism (or naturalism), giving names to things based on one's concept of what those things "naturally" symbolize or *should* be doing. Notionalism shows up in the common, meaning-based definition of nouns, for instance, as being "the names of persons, places, or things," which is fine as far as it goes, but does not consider the fact that other sorts of words and groups of words often behave as nouns do (that is, as actors or receivers of action), but without being names. The sentence diagrammed Traditionally in figure 6.1 is an example. Consequently, the definition of "noun" has to be adjusted so as to read something like this: " . . . or things, or clauses or phrases that serve as multiple-word substitutes for persons, places, or things." After a while, it

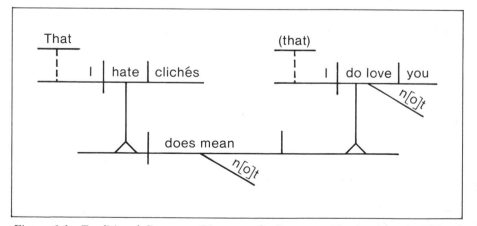

Figure 6.1   Traditional Grammar Diagram of a Sentence. The sentence is: "That I hate clichés doesn't mean I don't love you." The clause "That I hate clichés" is serving as the subject-noun of the sentence, while the clause "(that) I don't love you" is serving as the object-noun. The second, parenthetical "(that)" is said to be "understood."

almost begins to seem as though there are more exceptions to Traditional grammar's rules than there are original rules.

Still, Traditional grammar has two extremely significant points in its favor as an analytical system. The first is precedent: it has been in use for nearly three hundred years; most English-speaking people who have gone to school have had some contact with it; and a great many people still believe that it is a functional, elegant, time-honored way of teaching people what they should know about syntax.

More important, Traditional grammar has given the other grammars the bulk of the terms they use. Both of the major modern grammars, Structural and Transformational, rely heavily on the nomenclature, or classifying names, from Traditional grammar: noun, verb, adjective, adverb, and so on. Much of the work done descriptively, rather than prescriptively, in contemporary grammatical analysis was couched in Traditional-grammar language by scholars like Otto Jespersen, W. Nelson Francis, and Henrik Poutsma. To understand any of the modern grammars, and to understand virtually all discussion about writing or literature at the level of stylistic analysis, one must have an understanding of the terminology drawn from Traditional grammar, if not of the whole system.

Parts of speech. Even though the terminology of Traditional grammar is not always as helpful as it should be—for it is not always complete, the categories are not always mutually exclusive, and it certainly is not consistent in its application of concepts—the basic vocabulary is so fundamental to a discussion of grammars that a very sketchy review of the eight parts of speech is called for here.

1. Noun. A word or word group that names a person, a place, a thing, an attitude, an idea, a quality, or a condition. Examples: brother, rotunda, chair, happiness, truth, clairvoyance, solitude.
2. Pronoun. A word that functions as a substitute for a noun. Examples: it, he, she, we, they, us, ourselves, you, this, them.
3. Verb. A word or word group that expresses activity, condition, or state of being. (The verb's function is sometimes called predication, and the main verb in a sentence is therefore often called the predicate.) Examples: run, sleep, is, feels, believes, promises, write. A verb phrase (a group of words acting like a single part of speech) will usually consist of a main verb plus an auxiliary (helping) verb like "have" or "be": has been going, is walking. A special subclass of auxiliary verbs is the modals: can, may, must, ought, shall, will.
4. Adjective. A word or word group that modifies—limits, defines, characterizes, or describes—a noun. Examples: slovenly, impressive, brocaded, sublime, undeniable, stubborn, wracking.

5. Adverb. A word or word group that modifies a verb, or an adjective, or another adverb. (Adjectives and adverbs together are sometimes called modifiers.) Examples: run *fast,* sleep *deeply, seldom* is; *very* slovenly, *extremely* impressive, *delicately* brocaded; run *extraordinarily* fast, sleep *exceptionally* deeply, *very* seldom is.

6. Preposition. A word or word group that signals relationship of space, time, direction, or association between its object (the object of a preposition is always a noun) and some other word or word group. Examples: *in* the doghouse, *after* 5:00 P.M., *to* the lighthouse, *with* a calendar.

7. Conjunction. A word or word group that connects two or more sentence components. There are three major subtypes: coordinating conjunctions (examples: and, but, for, yet, so); subordinating conjunctions (examples: although, because, if, whether); and correlative conjunctions (examples: either . . . or, neither . . . nor, both . . . and, not only . . . but also).

8. Interjection. Any part of the sentence that is syntactically independent of the rest of the sentence. Examples: well, oh, goodness sakes. Many swear words, incidentally, are interjections.

This quick review merely summarizes the eight parts of speech, as defined by Traditional grammar. We have made no attempt to get into diagramming, much less into any of the subtler relationships between the parts of speech and the syntax of a sentence, and least of all into those prescriptive rules of "correct" usage that most people mean when they think of grammar. Those usage rules are far too complicated, and on the whole too much based on style and taste instead of on linguistic data, to be dealt with here. But any standard handbook can give you fairly standard rules for using "shall" and "will," or "me" and "I," or commas in compound sentences. Those rules, of course, have much more to do with social convention than with syntax.

Structural Grammar

A combination of factors provided the impulse away from Traditional grammar toward something both more objective and more accurately descriptive. Among the factors was the growing research, throughout the late eighteenth and nineteenth centuries, in comparative linguistics, the study of lexical and syntactic relationships among several languages. In the late eighteenth century, Sir William Jones first identified the central connection of Latin and Greek with Sanskrit—not, you will note, with English—an identification that prepared the way for comparative linguistics as we know it today. It is partly because of these studies, and partly because of historical linguistics, or the study of changes over time in a single language (sometimes compared with changes in other languages, too), that we know about language families and the relationships among the world's languages.

As was mentioned in chapter 3, comparative and historical linguistics produced abundant evidence that at least eight to twelve thousand years ago, there was located somewhere, perhaps in north-central Europe or in south-central Russia, people using a language now lost that we call *Indo-European.* From this "ancestral" language, three or four "daughter" languages were derived when the original Indo-European speakers drifted geographically apart. As the centuries went by and the population dispersed even more, their languages became more isolated from one another. Consequently, there are several modern "great-great-many-times-great-granddaughters" of the now extinct Indo-European mother tongue. English and Latin are both Indo-European descendants, but they derive from different "daughters."

As linguists gathered more data about the development of the world's languages, they found it increasingly impossible to justify the attempt to study one language (English) in terms of a grammar derived from a distantly related language (Latin)—just as well try to study Flemish as if it were a debased form of Quechua! Consequently, descriptive linguistics came into being: the nonprescriptive study of a language's phonology, morphology, and syntax. Descriptive linguistics was (and is) used extensively by anthropologists, like Franz Boas, Bronislaw Malinowski, or Margaret Mead, for example, to help them learn the languages of preliterate peoples.

A specialty or subarea of focus in descriptive linguistics is structural linguistics, which attempts to categorize or make structural sense out of the raw data of sounds, forms, and syntactic patterns provided by descriptive data from the field. Structural linguists such as Leonard Bloomfield, Edward Sapir, and Benjamin Whorf studied many other languages besides those in the Indo-European family. From their investigations comes the contemporary emphasis on linguistic principles of phonology, morphology, and syntax as means of analyzing languages, rather than the old naturalistic approaches. It is also from these investigators—and their followers, such as George Trager, Henry Lee Smith, Nelson Francis, Charles Fries, and Zellig Harris—that we ultimately get Structural grammar.

Structural grammar is quite different from Traditional grammar. Instead of focusing on the individual word and its notional meaning or its part-of-speech function in the sentence, Structural grammar focuses on clusters of structures—sounds, forms, word groups, phrases—working from smaller to larger units. Structural grammar does not ignore semantic meaning (although some of its earlier advocates tried to do so), but it tends to emphasize syntactic over semantic meaning. That is, Structural grammar analyzes the meaning carried by the syntactic patterns that morphemes and words make with each other, patterns like those formed by plural morphemes, modifier-verb or modifier-adjective connections, subject-predicate connections, and so on.

Besides the general emphasis on morphology and syntax, Structural grammar developed three particularly useful analytical techniques: test frames, immediate-constituent analysis, and sentence formulas. Test frames especially have been helpful in teaching grammar in the schools.

Test frames. These are blanks in simple sentences that may be filled in with any example of a particular class of word, such as a noun or an adjective. For instance, noun test frames customarily set up any or all of three types of sentence structures:

1. The _____ laughs. ("The" or "A[n]" _____ verb.)
2. He was riding a _____ rapidly. (Subject, predicate, "the" or "a[n]," _____ adverb.)
3. Put it on that _____ . ([Subject], predicate, preposition, [modifier] _____ .)

Each version illustrates a different position, and therefore a different function in the sentence which a noun can fulfill. The first blank calls for a subject, the second for a direct object, and the third for an object of a preposition. (Nouns can also serve other functions in a sentence, but these three will illustrate the technique.)

A test-frame exercise demonstrates two important points about English syntax. The first, of course, is that speakers of English know what goes where; they are competent in the use of the language. Even very small children can put the right kind of words into the blanks, words like "clown," "horse," or "table," or any noun that is not someone's name. Speakers may not know that it is nouns they are inserting—that is, they may not know the jargon of grammatical analysis—but they know what belongs in the noun slots.

The second point is that the English language is quite regular in its signaling of nouns. This signaling is accomplished in two ways: first, by position in the order of words in the sentence (the subject-noun, for instance, nearly always comes at the beginning of the sentence), and second, by use of function words called determiners, words like "the," "a," "an," "this," "those," or "my." (Function words have been discussed in chapter 5.) Determiners will only work with noun test frames, but other kinds of function words can help identify verbs: these are the auxiliary, or helping, verb forms "be" and "have," and the modal verb forms like "may," "will," or "can."

Immediate-constituent analysis. This technique, usually referred to as IC analysis, is like Structural grammar's version of Traditional diagrams. The idea here is that sentences are constructed from groups of words, often paired, rather than from single words added one onto the next. These groups of words in turn cluster with other groups, layer upon layer of word pairs and pair groups, which eventually build a sentence. One can begin the IC analysis at the word level and work one's way up to the sentence, or one can begin with the sentence and work back to the word level. With younger children, starting small and building up seems the most effective technique.

Let us take the sentence "Test frames in particular have been helpful in teaching grammar in the schools." If we work from the smallest constituents to the largest, we get five levels. The first level looks like this:

1. Test frames in particular have been helpful in teaching grammar in the schools . The words in boxes seem naturally to cluster together; we sense a relationship of the words in each box, whether or not we can identify what that relationship is. Some words do not seem so closely connected at this level, but if we take each box as standing for a single cluster and then connect the clusters, the "unboxed" words now fall into groups, too:

2. Test frames in particular have been helpful in teaching grammar in the schools . Now we connect these groups at yet a more inclusive level of clustering, according to how each boxed group relates to the next one, like this:

3. Test frames in particular have been helpful in teaching grammar in the schools . This sentence is arranged in such a way that the third cluster, because of its position, seems to belong more naturally with the second cluster than with the first:

4. Test frames in particular have been helpful in teaching grammar in the schools . Finally, we reach the last level with:

5. Test frames in particular have been helpful in teaching grammar in the schools .

We can do the same procedure in reverse, beginning our division of the sentence by cutting the largest units apart, then the next largest, and so on, down to the level of the word:

1. Test frames in particular have been helpful in teaching grammar in the schools .

2. Test frames in particular have been helpful in teaching grammar in the schools .

3. Test frames in particular have been helpful in teaching grammar in the schools .

4. Test frames in particular have been helpful in teaching grammar in the schools .

5. Test frames in particular have been helpful in teaching grammar in the schools .

Finally, we test the structure of our sentence, and the accuracy of our IC analysis, by making constituent substitutions, putting in a different word of the same class (the new words do not need to be synonyms) for each group of two or more words in the original sentence:

Test frames	in particular	have been helpful	in teaching	grammar
in the schools .				
The drills	especially	help	teach	language
in class.				
Drills		teach		language
there.				
They		teach		language.

IC analysis also demonstrates two important points about English syntax. The first reinforces what we already knew from using test frames: English syntax is highly positional in structure—English is a word-order language—and words placed next to each other are usually semantically connected. The second point is that groups of words in English do indeed function as single units of syntax. In our sentences, the word groups "Test frames," "The drills," and "They" are all subjects. The groups "have been helpful in teaching," "help teach," and "teach" are all predicates. The groups "in teaching grammar in the schools," "language in class," "language there," and "language" are all object-complements.

Sentence formulas. Syntax, rather than parts of speech, gave the Structural grammarians the most trouble in the realm of practical analysis. Working with detailed IC analyses, Structuralists nevertheless derived four basic syntactic patterns, which they called sentence formulas:

Type 1: Noun/Pronoun + Verb
Type 2: Noun/Pronoun + Verb + Adjective
Type 3: Noun/Pronoun + Verb + Noun/Pronoun
Type 4: Noun/Pronoun + Verb + Noun/Pronoun-1 + Noun/Pronoun-2

Interlacing determiners, auxiliaries, prepositions, and other function words and modifiers where we choose, we might apply a Type 4 formula to derive a sentence like this: "Yesterday the boy willingly showed me his blue basketball." In this sentence, N-2 ("basketball") does not refer to N-1 ("me").

But in another sentence from the same formula (N + V + N-1 + N-2), "They chose me president," N-2 ("president") does refer to N-1 ("me"). The formula alone, in other words, cannot account for the semantic distinction that we see clearly in the two sentences. Neither can the formulas explain the underlying connection that holds between these two sentences: "The boy showed me his basketball" and "The basketball was shown to me by the boy," even though, as we saw in chapter 2, very young children can sense that these sentences are somehow alike.

Thus, none of the three Structural techniques—test frames, IC analysis, sentence formulas—will completely answer all the questions that an investigator or a curious student might have about a language. Furthermore, each of the techniques has limited effectiveness for teaching. Test frames will reveal some parts of speech but cannot comment in detail on structural methods in a sentence: coordination, subordination, and so on. Although IC analysis can identify some structural behavior without recourse to a speaker's innate knowledge of the language, nevertheless, intuition, guesswork, and reliance on semantic meaning inevitably are called into play at some point. And sentence formulas can generate only a limited number of very simple sentences without accounting for some important semantic distinctions. In short, although Structural grammar is considerably more objective and consistent than Traditional grammar, it is not equipped to deal either with some major theoretical questions or with many exceptions and contradictions, inherent in the language, which trouble students and teachers at a practical level of grammatical analysis. It is a better model in many respects than the Traditional one, but still not as functionally useful as a grammar should be.

Transformational-Generative Grammar

Good grammarians had of course been struggling for a long time with the problems inherent in both the Traditional and Structural models, attempting to adapt those theories to syntactic reality wherever possible. In 1957, however, Noam Chomsky stepped outside—indeed, specifically rejected—many of the principles of the older models. In his book *Syntactic Structures,* Chomsky proposed a new grammar: the Transformational-Generative model, usually shortened to Transformational or TG.[2]

This new model had grown out of Chomsky's work with his Structuralist teacher, Zellig Harris, but TG also reflected Chomsky's alliance with some aspects of Traditional grammar, notably the belief that syntactic principles

2. Since 1957, Chomsky has much modified his original theories, most notably in *Aspects of the Theory of Syntax* (1965). The material presented in this chapter focuses on the later (modified) versions of TG.

may be universal and innate. Thus, TG is partly new, partly remodeled old, and partly rejected old. Chomsky was especially dissatisfied with the limited predictability of Structuralism, feeling that it focused so much on the gathering of particular data (recording sentences already uttered) that it neglected a general theory that would enable grammarians to describe how sentences will be uttered. Chomsky argued that an adequate grammar must not merely describe the past; it must also be able to predict the future.

Competence and performance. Important in understanding this predictive aspect is the distinction between competence and performance, for Traditionalists and Structuralists had relied almost entirely on performance, whereas Chomsky and other Transformationalists shifted much more toward competence. Performance, as might be expected, refers to what a speaker actually does when he or she talks: the syntactic utterances produced by the act of performing speech behaviors. There are as many levels of performance as there are speakers, for some perform very well, some adequately, and some poorly. It is performance we judge when we make prescriptive statements about the correctness or the incorrectness of someone's speech.

Competence, on the other hand, refers to what a speaker knows about the native language he or she uses. This knowledge, or competence, is not book-learning knowledge, nor is it analytical knowledge; rather, it is the presumably innate, genetically coded, and certainly deeply buried understanding of syntax. A competent speaker knows what the native language will allow in a construction and what is simply not possible. A speaker knows this almost intuitively, without necessarily being able to explain why such and such a construction will or will not work. For example, all speakers of English know that the utterance "Fox over the the brown quick jumps dog lazy" is impossible. The individual words make sense, but the construction does not, because the syntax does not follow any English pattern. In comparison with performance, competence is asserted to be relatively without level: all native speakers are said to possess the same general understanding of linguistic structures and to recognize what is grammatical (that is, competently possible) and what is "ungrammatical" in a syntactic sense. Competence is assumed to hold at the lexical or semantic level, too, but less universally.

The important point about competence is this: if indeed we are all competent speakers, then a grammar can be devised that will explain and predict all possible grammatical sentences and exclude all ungrammatical ones. We would be able to test such a grammar by relying on speakers' competence, that is, on their ability to tell whether or not a sentence is grammatical. Such a complete grammar is not yet available, but TG theory so far seems to come closer to such a model than do either the Traditional or the Structuralist theories.

Let us therefore examine two key points, both mentioned earlier (in chapter 3), which form the foundation of the TG model: first, all languages can produce an infinite series of particular constructions by manipulating a relatively small number of rules; second, all languages have certain basic syntactic units which can be converted or altered in various regular ways.

Generation. The basic unit in TG grammar is not the word, as in Traditional grammar, nor the phrase, as in Structural grammar, but the sentence. And the most basic concern in TG grammar is to describe and predict how a native speaker produces or generates grammatical sentences. (In TG terms, ''grammatical sentences'' are those recognized as being complete and competent by all other native speakers of the language.) The generative processes may not, of course, work exactly as TG grammar describes them. When we speak, we make so many of our selections in a subconscious or unconscious way that we seem to be making no selections at all. We don't think about speaking, we just do it, so any model of the mental processes we go through is bound to be inaccurate in some details. But the TG model has the advantages of being visible, as the mental processes are not, and of being comparatively simple, as the brain's functioning is not. The TG model is simple because, adopting the Structural approach, it works binomially, that is, by setting up a series of selection points at which one of two—and only one—alternatives must be chosen.

TG holds that the two most basic processes involved in generating sentences are phrase-structure derivation (usually shortened to PS derivation, or just derivation) and transformation, which we will take up in the next section. The process of derivation, followed through all its stages, will produce a terminal string, the almost subconscious underlying syntactic arrangement of sentence parts—not words, but categories or constituents—to which various transformations can be applied. When cues for the transformations are added to the terminal string, the result is called the deep structure.

The stages in the derivational process (which will produce a terminal string) are noted by a series of binomial rules, called phrase-structure (PS) or rewrite rules. These PS rules look like mathematical formulas, because they indicate how categories (not words) can be manipulated. Each of the written rules is accompanied by a diagram, often called a tree, which illustrates what that rule means and the choices indicated in the rule. The PS rules are summarized in figure 6.2.

When we work through all of the PS rules, we will produce a terminal string, a list of constituents that looks like no sentence ever uttered by anyone. This terminal string is merely a list of directions, cueing the speaker to insert certain kinds of words. For example, a deep-structure string such as *Pro past Mod have -en be -ing V-t N* (whose derivation we will go through in a moment) could cue us to insert any appropriate word in the constituent slots:

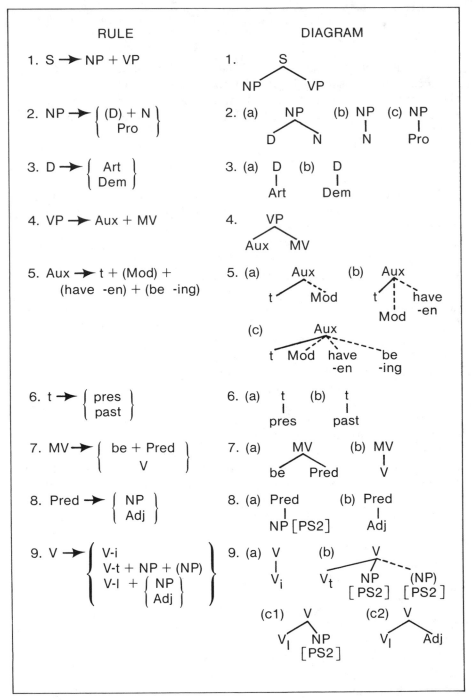

Figure 6.2   Simplified Phrase-Structure (Derivational) Rules and Diagrams (Trees)

Pro (pronoun): I, you, he, she, it, we, they

past (the past-tense form of whatever is the first verb in the string)

Mod (modal auxiliary—a verb form): can, may, must, shall, will

have -en (signals any past-participle verb form)

be -ing (signals any present-participle verb form)

V-t (any transitive-verb form): make, drink, understand, enjoy

N (any noun form): coffee, Coca-Cola, bumblebees, cooperation

This one string, *Pro past Mod have* -en *be* -ing *V-t N,* can produce any number of surface structures, or sentences as we recognize them, because we can use the same string for any words that fit the constituents:

I could have been making coffee.

You might have been drinking Coca-Cola.

He must have been understanding bumblebees.

We should have been enjoying cooperation.

Many, many other combinations are possible, but let us use the first surface structure ("I could have been making coffee.") as our example in working through the derivation of the terminal string.

PS 1 (figure 6.2) is the universal generative rule, applying to all terminal strings. It says, "A sentence *S* consists of or can be rewritten as[3] a noun phrase *NP* and a verb phrase *VP.*" At this point, "noun phrase" and "verb phrase" do not mean anything at all; they are just slots or categories. Thus, we should not anticipate that a phrase necessarily goes under *NP* or *VP,* for *NP* may be one word or many, as may *VP.* We will have to work through a few more PS rules before we can tell how many words are involved.

The tree-diagram for PS 1 says the same thing: "A sentence consists of a noun phrase [branching off to the left, and below the sentence marker *S*] and a verb phrase [below *S* to the right]." The *NP* and *VP* constituents in the tree are lower than the sentence marker because *S* contains *NP* + *VP*; a sentence includes these two and therefore dominates them.

To find out just what the noun phrase *NP* consists of—one word, many words, what kind(s) of word(s)—we must go to PS 2. Here is our first selection point, our first binomial choice, for we must decide among three possibilities for our noun phrase: a determiner plus a noun, a noun alone, or a pronoun. PS 2 translates as: "A noun phrase *NP* consists of (rewrites as) one and only one of these possibilities: a determiner (*D*) plus a noun *N* [PS 2(a)]; or a noun alone [PS 2(b)]; or a pronoun [PS 2(c)]." The curly brackets, or braces, around the constituents to the right of the arrow let us know that we must select only one of the choices listed inside the braces, and the parentheses around the *D* let us know that it is an optional constituent. Since we already know from our terminal string that we are going to choose PS 2(c), *Pro,* we can ignore 2(a) and 2(b). That means we can also

---

3. The single-shafted arrow is called the "rewrite" arrow.

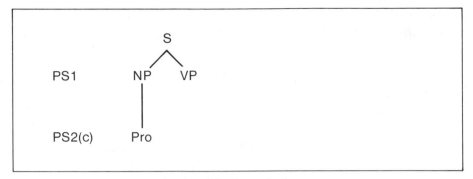

Figure 6.3   Tree for PS Rules 1 and 2, Example Sentence

ignore PS 3 altogether, for we have no determiner in our string. Our tree so far would look like the one shown in figure 6.3.

We do not yet know which pronoun we will use for this slot—it could be "you" or "he" or "they" or any other pronoun—but we do have the first part of the universal rule finished, for we know what the noun phrase is. Now we go on to fill out the verb-phrase part of PS 1.

We do that by moving to PS 4, which—like PS 1—gives us no choice; it merely states a fact: "A verb phrase *VP* consists of an auxiliary *Aux* and a main verb *MV*." Since "auxiliary" is a word used in Traditional grammar to apply only to a special type of verb, it might seem as though PS 4 says that we must always have words like "can" or "must" or "should" in a sentence; but we know from practical experience in using our language that that is not so. There are plenty of sentences without auxiliary forms, like "Richard loves Susan" (that does not say he *might* love her) or "Typewriters cost money" (not that they *will* cost, but that they cost). So we must recognize, by looking ahead for a moment to PS 5, that Transformational grammar is using the word "auxiliary" to mean something more general than what Traditional grammar intended by the same word. (We will return to PS 4 in a moment.)

PS 5, which is called the Auxiliary Rewrite Rule, states that the constituent *Aux* must—no choice in the first part—consist of tense *t* and can also, if we wish, include any or all of the following optional elements (enclosed in parentheses, like the determiner marker *D* in PS 2): a modal *Mod*, a past-participle marker *have -en,* and/or a present-participle marker *be -ing.* These last two constituents are always written as listed, with the *-en* separated from the *have* and the *-ing* separated from the *be,* because these participle markers are only signaling constituents, not the words "have"/"had" or "being."

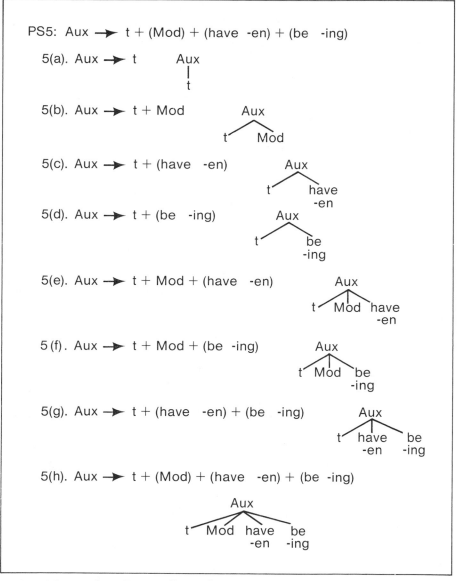

Figure 6.4   Auxiliary-Rewrite Expansion

The eight possible combinations of choices from PS 5 are listed in figure 6.4. Because we are using the string *Pro past Mod have -en be -ing*, we know that ours is the eighth possibility (5h): tense *(past)* plus modal *(Mod)*

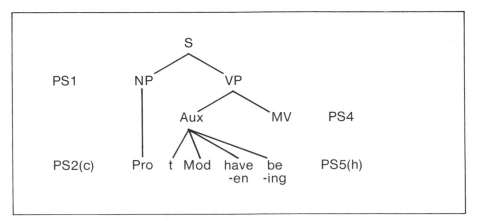

Figure 6.5   Tree for PS Rules 1–5, Example Sentence

plus past participle *(have   -en)* plus present participle *(be   -ing)*. If we had preferred to leave out some constituents, we could certainly have done so—for anything except tense *t*—and so could have produced other surface-structure versions of our sentence, whose main verb is "make." Had we chosen (d), for instance, our surface structure would have read "was making"; (f) would have produced "could be making"; (a) would have given us "made"; and so on.

"Auxiliary" as used in Transformational grammar, then, in PS 4 and PS 5, does not mean that you are always obliged to have an auxiliary-verb form like a modal in your sentence, but rather that you may have one if you wish. Since our deep structure has one, and participles as well, our tree—through PS 4 and its continuation, PS 5—now looks like figure 6.5.

To finish the auxiliary rewrite rule, we need one more piece of information: What is the tense of *t?* To answer that, we check with PS 6, which tells us we have two choices for *t:* present *[pres]* or past *[past]*. We already know that our string requires *past*, so from our chosen modal "can," we will get the surface-structure past-tense form "could." (If we had chosen *pres* here at PS 6, our surface structure would read "I can have" instead of "I could have.") PS 6 will select the tense of the first verb form in the string; it does nothing at all to any forms after the first one.

Our tree for PS 1 through PS 6 now looks like figure 6.6.

Now we must backtrack to the second part of PS4, *VP → Aux + MV*, for we have finished rewriting the auxiliary but have not yet completed the main verb *MV*. PS 7, PS 8, and PS 9 tell us how to do that.

PS 7 tells us that we have two choices here, for the main verb rewrites as either *be + Pred*—that is, some form of the verb "to be" plus a predicative complement—or as any other verb except "to be." (Note that the *be* here,

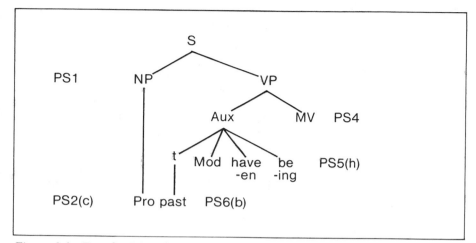

Figure 6.6   Tree for PS Rules 1–6, Example Sentence

in PS 7, is not the same as the *be   -ing* in PS 5. They may look the same, but they are two different constituents performing two different functions.) Our terminal string, *Pro past Mod have   -en be   -ing V-t N,* shows no form of "to be" in the predicate, so we know that we must select *V* here, as in figure 6.7.

Having no *be + Pred* constituents in the main verb, we can skip PS 8, which tells us what kind of predicative complements we could select, and move to the last derivational rule, PS 9.

PS 9 says that we can choose one—and only one—of three kinds of verbs here: 9(a) is an intransitive verb, one that takes no object at all; 9(b) is a transitive verb, taking at least one noun-phrase *NP* object and possibly two; and 9(c) is a linking verb—but not any form of "to be"—taking either a noun phrase *NP* or an adjective *Adj.* Our terminal string, *Pro past Mod have   -en be   -ing V-t N,* shows that we want PS 9(b) with only one noun-phrase object, in other words, a direct object, so our tree now has grown to figure 6.8.

And to finish off our derivation of the terminal string, we must return to PS 2 to rewrite the last noun phrase from PS 9. This noun phrase, we know from the string, is not a pronoun and does not include a determiner, so it is PS 2(b) we want. (See figure 6.9.)

The very bottom line of the tree—*Pro past Mod have   -en be   -ing V-t   N*—will be the same as our terminal string of constituents. The completed tree will show the same sequence of steps that we followed in working through the phrase-structure rules, too, so drawing a tree while you write out the PS selections is a good way of double checking to be sure you have not skipped a step.

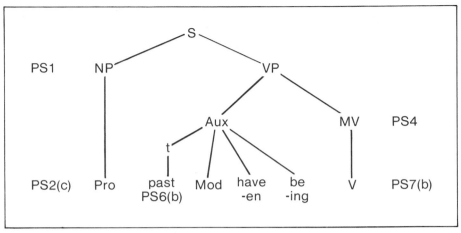

Figure 6.7   Tree for PS Rules 1-7, Example Sentence

Transformations. Various transformations can now be applied to this terminal string, as we shall see in the next section, but an important point must be noted: transformations can only occur if phrase-marker constituents, such as *NEG* (signaling negative), appear in front of the terminal string. Without such phrase markers before the syntactic constituents in the string, a fundamental principle of transformation would be violated: a transformation relates sentences as we know them to their underlying deep structure, but without changing the basic meaning. The basic meaning must also include the phrase markers. Hence, deep structure equals phrase markers (for transformations) plus terminal string.

It is the working out of various transformations which produces sentences as we know them, the kind of utterances that we speak, read, and write. Sentences that have gone through all the necessary transformations are called surface structures, and one of the fascinating results of TG grammar has been to demonstrate why it is that surface structures that seem so different are really related to each other. The reason is that many surface structures can be created out of the same deep structure, as we suggested in chapter 3.

Take, for example, the surface structure suggested for the diagrammed sentence "I could have been making coffee." To get that form, we are required to have in the deep structure the phrase marker *AFF*, signaling the obligatory *Affix* transformation: *AFF Pro past Mod have -en be -ing V-t N.* Sometimes called the "Flip-Flop Transformation," Affix transformation requires that we shift the tense markers with the immediately following verb forms, like castling in chess. In our sentence, there are three tense markers: *past, -en,* and *-ing.* And there are three verb-form markers: *Mod, be,* and

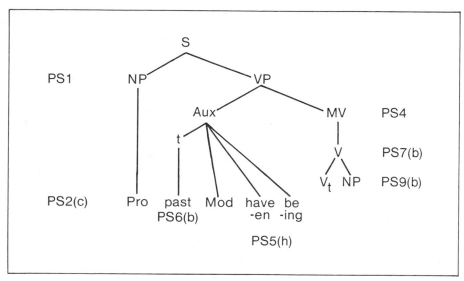

Figure 6.8   Tree for PS Rules 1–9, Example Sentence

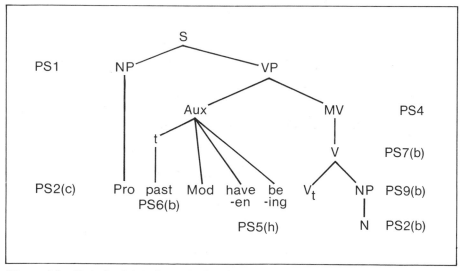

Figure 6.9   Tree for PS Rules 1–9 +2, Example Sentence

make. The verb form *have* is not immediately preceded by a tense marker, so we leave *have* alone and do not apply Affix to it. Switch the markers, and we get *Mod* + *past* (that is, the past tense of the modal "can," which is "could") and *be* + *-en* (that is, the past participle of "be," which is "been") and *V-t* + *-ing* (that is, the present participle of "make," which is "making''). The **Affix flip-flopping** is a required transformation, and if you are not studying TG grammar, you do it without thinking.

We could apply other transformations to our deep structure, which would stay exactly the same; only the surface structure would change. Try, for instance, the Negative transformation, symbolized by this formula:[4] NEG (NP) + t + Mod + X + (Y) $\Rightarrow$ (NP) + t + Mod + *not* + X + (Y). The formula says that to make a negative of a deep structure that includes a modal, you insert the word ''not'' between the modal and whatever follows it, symbolized by X and (Y). In our case, X stands for ''have.'' Transformed, the deep structure we have been using would now read: $\Rightarrow$ *N past Mod not have -en be -ing V-t N.* In surface-structure terms, this would be: ''I could not have been making coffee.'' It is possible to produce other surface structures from this same deep structure, such as ''Julia might not have been painting peonies'' or ''Philodendrons should not have been tattooing Portuguese,'' which does not make lexical sense but is all right in the syntactic sense.

Another common transformation is *Adjective,* which inserts a modifier in front of a noun: ''good coffee,'' ''pink peonies,'' ''Portuguese registrars.''[5] Or we could make our deep structure into a surface-level *Yes-No Question,* the type that can be answered by ''yes'' or ''no.'' This transformation requires that we switch the positions of the first NP (''I'') and the tense-modal cluster (''past-can''), to produce this: $\Rightarrow$*Past Mod Pro have -en be -ing V-t N.* Our particular surface structure would now read: ''Could I have been making coffee?''

A fifth common transformation is *Passive,* in which we exchange the positions of the subject NP (''I'') and the direct object NP (''coffee'') and rearrange the verb structure. This is the formula:

$$\text{PASS}\atop\text{AFF} \quad NP_1 + Aux + V\text{-}t + NP_2 \Rightarrow NP_2 + Aux + be + en + V\text{-}t + by + NP_1.$$

Aux here, as we would expect, means ''anything derived from PS 5,'' which in our case includes modal, past participle, and present participle *(Mod have -en be -ing)* as well as the obligatory tense *(past).* After we have applied the formula, our transformed deep structure reads like this:

	NP$_2$		Aux			be	-en	V-t		by NP$_1$
$\Rightarrow$	coffee	past can have	-en be	-ing		be	-en	make	by	I.[6]

Applying the obligatory Affix, we then get *can + past = could, be + -en = been, be + -ing = being,* and *make + -en = made,* or: ''Coffee could have been being made by me.''

---

4. The double-shafted arrow here is used for transformation rules, to distinguish them from the rewrite arrow.
5. Notice that descriptions of nationality, such as ''Portuguese'' or ''Thai'' or ''Icelandic,'' can function as either adjectives or nouns, depending on their context.
6. Another transformation changes this form to ''me.''

Singulary and recursive transformations. These five examples—Affix, Negative, Adjective, Yes-No Question, and Passive—all illustrate the type of transformation called single-based, or singulary, which means that they are applied to only one terminal string. There are many singulary transformations besides the five noted here, of course, but all of them work in one of three ways: by rearranging the order of the constituents in the string (Affix, Yes-No Question, Passive); by adding some constituents to the string (Adjective, Passive, Negative); or by deleting something from the string (Passive). The Imperative transformation, for instance, produces a surface structure like "Sit down" by deleting the subject NP from the deep structure $\frac{IMP}{AFF}$ *Pro pres V-i Particle,* where *Pro* is "you," *V-i* is "sit," and *Particle* is "down."

But another major category of transformation, the recursive or double-based, works on two or more deep-structure strings, combining them into a single string. This act is called embedding, for one or more secondary deep structures are overlapped with, or embedded into, a primary, or matrix, string. For example, in a recursive surface structure such as "The coffee, which tasted awful, was made of chicory," the words inside the commas have come from an embedded deep structure ("The coffee tasted awful"). The particular double-based transformation applied here is Non-Restrictive Relative Clause; other types include the Restrictive Relative Clause, the Appositive, the Gerund, the Participle, and so on. You would not be expected to work with complicated patterns like these until you were thoroughly familiar with the phrase-structure derivations and the singulary transformations.

Transformational grammar was originally viewed by many people as merely an extension of Structuralist theory, especially in its emphasis on binomial selection for phrase-structure rules of syntax. But although Chomsky's teacher, Zellig Harris, was a Structuralist, Chomsky's grammar goes far beyond Structuralism, for Chomsky and his followers have insisted from the beginning that their grammar is as much a theory of the mind as a theory of the syntax produced.

Transformational grammar thus almost seems to come full circle back to the old Traditional notionalist assumptions about "the nature of things," but with two important differences (besides the advantage of information about linguistics not available to Plato). The first is that TG grammar restricts its examination of "the nature of things" to the nature of language use and the intuitive knowledge of language all speakers have. TG is less concerned with the truth of the universe outside a speaker's head than with mapping the linguistic universe inside. The second difference is that TG grammar is far more systematic than was Traditional grammar. Its "rules" are testable, replicable, and functional. Its rules are much better able to take account of linguistic and semantic exceptions, to identify the reasons underlying discrepancies, and to describe language production in a far more objective fashion than Traditional grammar can.

Most interesting of all, TG is avowedly universalist in stance. Chomsky began his work with the hypothesis that all children were born with an innate drive to learn language; eventually he and his followers postulated—as others had before them—that all languages were strikingly similar in their deep structures, most linguistic variation being on the surface. This hypothesis continues to be substantiated by evidence from phonology, morphology, historical and comparative linguistics, and psycholinguistic studies around the world. This is not to say that all of the world's languages are identical if one looks deep enough, nor that all of the world's languages developed from a single source and diffused into superficially different forms later. Rather, TG appears to be demonstrating that linguistic processes (such as sound production and change, morphemic adaptation, and syntactic patterning) are probably universal, and those processes *may*—emphasis is required here, for the evidence is not clear yet—arise from something coded in our genes, directing us to acquire language.

But of course the surface structures we hear and read every day are not universal. We deal as much with linguistic variation as with similarity, differences in pronunciation, in syntax, and in lexicon. The greater those differences, the wider the gap in understanding: we have little trouble with local dialects, more trouble with British English, and are often stumped by non-English languages, even when they come from the same branch of the Indo-European family. In the next chapter, we will discuss the historical development of English, using it as an example of how one language has so much changed historically that contemporary speakers cannot understand the language of a thousand years ago.

Review Questions

1. What are three different definitions of "grammar"?
2. What is naturalism, or notionalism? How is it related to prescriptivism?
3. Discuss the origins of Traditional grammar.
4. What are the principal advantages and disadvantages of the Traditional system of grammar?
5. Name and define the eight parts of speech.
6. What are comparative, historical, and descriptive linguistics? What do they have to do with grammar?
7. How is Structural grammar different from Traditional grammar?
8. What are test frames, IC analyses, and sentence formulas?

9. How is Transformational grammar different from Structural grammar? From Traditional grammar? How is Transformational grammar related to the other two?

10. Define these terms: generation, transformation, terminal string, deep structure, surface structure, phrase marker.

Selected Reading

Bach, Emmon. *Syntactic Theory.* New York: Holt, Rinehart and Winston, 1974.

Bloomfield, Leonard. *Language.* New York: Holt, Rinehart and Winston, 1933.

Chafe, Wallace. *Meaning and Structure of a Language.* Chicago: University of Chicago Press, 1970.

Chomsky, Noam. *Aspects of the Theory of Syntax.* Cambridge, Mass.: M.I.T. Press, 1965.

———. *Syntactic Structures.* The Hague: Mouton Publishing Co., 1957.

Francis, W. Nelson. *The Structure of American English.* New York: The Ronald Press Company, 1958.

Fries, Charles C. *The Structure of English.* New York: Harcourt, Brace & World, Inc., 1952.

Harris, Zellig S. *Methods in Structural Linguistics.* Chicago: University of Chicago Press, 1951.

Herndon, Jeanne H. *A Survey of Modern Grammars,* 2nd ed. New York: Holt, Rinehart and Winston, 1976.

Jacobs, Roderick A., and Peter S. Rosenbaum, eds. *Readings in English Transformational Grammar.* Boston: Ginn & Co., 1970.

Jespersen, Otto. *Language: Its Nature, Development, and Origin.* New York: W. W. Norton & Co., 1922 (reptd. 1964).

Langendoen, D. Terence. *Essentials of English Grammar.* New York: Holt, Rinehart and Winston, 1970.

LaPalombara, Lyda E. *An Introduction to Grammar: Traditional, Structural, Transformational.* Cambridge, Mass.: Winthrop Publishers, Inc., 1976.

Lester, Mark, ed. *Readings in Applied Transformational Grammar,* 2nd ed. New York: Holt, Rinehart and Winston, Inc., 1973.

Long, Ralph B. *A Grammar of American English.* Austin: University of Texas Press, 1959.

———, and Dorothy Long. *The System of English Grammar.* Glenview, Ill.: Scott, Foresman and Co., 1971.

Lyons, John. *Noam Chomsky.* New York: The Viking Press, 1970.

Newsome, Verna L. *Structural Grammar in the Classroom.* Urbana, Ill.: National Council of Teachers of English, 1961.

Salus, Peter H., ed. *On Language: Plato to von Humboldt.* New York: Holt, Rinehart and Winston, Inc., 1969.

Stockwell, Robert P. *Foundations of Syntactic Theory.* Englewood Cliffs, N.J.: Prentice-Hall, Inc., 1977.

Strang, Barbara M. H. *Modern English Structure.* New York: St. Martin's Press, 1968.

Thomas, Owen, and Eugene Kintgen. *Transformational Grammar and the Teacher of English,* 2nd ed. New York: Holt, Rinehart and Winston, Inc., 1974.

Tufte, Virginia. *Grammar as Style.* New York: Holt, Rinehart and Winston, Inc., 1971.

Whitman, Randall H. *English and English Linguistics.* New York: Holt, Rinehart and Winston, Inc., 1975.

Journals   *College English; English Studies; International Journal of American Linguistics; Lingua*

7
The History of the English Language

The passage in extract 7.1 was written in an English dialect common about a thousand years ago. As you can tell if someone who knows how will read the passage aloud, the words sound more like modern German than like English, a resemblance not at all coincidental.

Fæder ure
þū þē eart on heofonum
sī þīn nāma ğehalgod.
Tōbecume þīn rīče
Gewur e þīn willa
on eorðan swā swā on heofonum.
Ūrne gedæghwāmlīčan
hlāf syle ūs to dæğ.
And forğyfe ūs ūre gyltas
swā swā wē forğyfað ūrum gyltendum.
And ne ğelæde þū ūs on costnunge
ac ālȳs ūs of yfele.
Sōþlīče.

Extract 7.1   A Passage of Old English

Language Families

If you look at the abbreviated chart of languages (figure 7.1),[1] you can trace the taxonomic classification of Modern American English. Follow the trail of bold face words from the lower left-hand corner and up along the left-hand side, through the various levels of increasingly more inclusive linguistic relationships. You will then see that English is indeed Germanic (or Teutonic, as it is sometimes called), from the level of "Group" on down. In its present-day form, English is most closely related to Frisian and then to

1. "Abbreviated" because all of the non-Indo-European families have been omitted, as have all of the non-Western groups. In addition, the subbranches and subgroups on the chart have been somewhat condensed and simplified. Other language families are: Semitic, Uralic, Turkish, Southern Caucasian, East Sudanic, Korean, Japanese, Han Chinese, Bodo-Naga-Kachin, Mayan, and Austronesian.

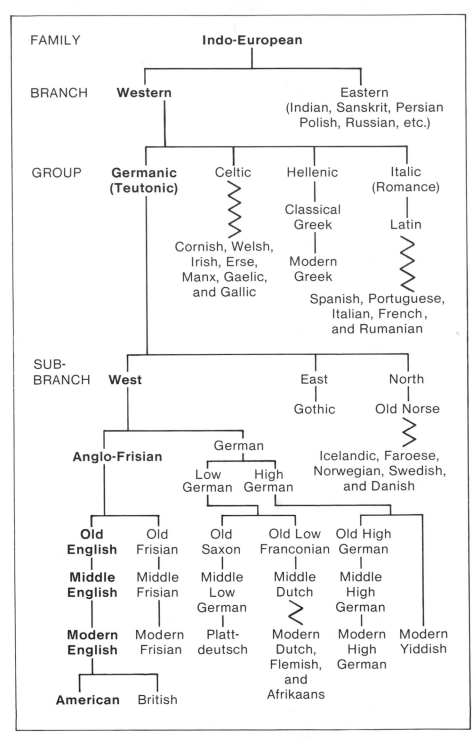

Figure 7.1 Abbreviated Language Chart

the various High and Low German offshoots. You will also discover that although English is a relative of Latin, which is in the Italic, or Romance, group, the relationship is more like fourth cousins twice removed than like that of child to parent.

A third point you will observe from the chart is that English is subdivided into three historical periods:

Old English	A.D. 500–1100
Middle English	1100–1500
Modern English	1500–present
Early Modern	[1500–1800]
Present-Day	[1800–present]

Some language historians would argue for more precision in the dates. Specifically, they offer A.D. 449, when the forerunners of the Vikings began to raid the coasts of Britain, as the starting point for the Old period; 1066 as the end of Old and the beginning of Middle, since that was when William, Duke of Normandy, successfully conquered the English at the Battle of Hastings; and 1485 as the end of Middle and the beginning of Modern. In 1485, two important events occurred: Henry VII, the first Tudor monarch, ascended the British throne and thereby brought to an end the devastating civil war between the Lancaster and York factions called the War of the Roses; and William Caxton printed the first English book in England, Sir Thomas Malory's *Le Morte d'Arthur*. If one already has the specific dates engraved on one's brain, well and good, but it would be foolish to assume that the language stopped being Middle on, say, July 15, 1485, and became Early Modern on July 16. Languages do not change that fast. So the approximate datings are probably more meaningful simply because they are less precise.

Historical Survey

Old English period. Occasionally you will still see the earliest period and its language referred to as "Anglo-Saxon," but that term is not only loaded (as in the acronym WASP: "White *A*nglo-*S*axon *P*rotestant") but also misleading. "Anglo-Saxon" ignores the other linguistic groups contributing to the language then: the native Picts and Celts, for instance, and the Jutes and the Frisians, who—like the Angles (or Engles)[2] and the Saxons—were Germanic tribes coming into England from the north. What eventually became the language we call Old English was actually a coalition of German dialects, more or less mutually intelligible, with some Latin from the Roman occupation of Britain and native Celtic for flavoring.

---

2. Why the name of a single tribe, the Engles (from prehistoric Old English *Angli*), should eventually have come to be adopted as the national name, no one knows. (The asterisk [*] in front of a word or morpheme means that it is reconstructed; we have no recorded use of it.)

That linguistic diversity reflects the social and political turmoil of the times, for the tribes constantly fought with each other as well as with the invaders; the longest peaceful stretch during the period lasted barely a hundred years. It came under the Anglo-Saxon Heptarchy, or alliance of seven kingdoms: Kent, Wessex, Essex, Sussex, East Anglia (that is, Norfolk and Suffolk), Mercia, and Northumbria. When Alfred the Great, the most brilliant and influential of the Heptarchy's rulers, died in 899, his successors took as their title Rex Anglorum, Latin for "King of the English." Despite that title, however, their rule was not monarchic, their people were not nationally unified, and their kingdom was not England. They ruled essentially as tribal chieftains, keeping power largely by force over bands of seminomadic warriors who uneasily dominated only a part of present-day England. Nevertheless, there was more cultural and linguistic unity by the time Alfred's grandsons were ruling in the tenth century than there had been at the beginning of the period.

The comparative uniformity was brought about by force (wars, raids, invasions), by normal assimilation (intermarriage and crossbreeding), by politics (the Heptarchy and other alliances), and by Christianity. This last factor may have been the most influential of all, for when Pope Gregory I sent St. Augustine to bring Christianity to the island's inhabitants in A.D. 597, he introduced them indirectly to Western European civilization as well. The religion was itself a universalizing force, but even more significant was the Church's language: Latin. Latin was the universal scholarly tongue in Europe at that time and for many centuries thereafter. If someone knew Latin, he could communicate with anyone who also spoke and wrote it, regardless of their respective native languages (or vernaculars).

With the clergy, then, came contact with the world beyond England. Since the priests were the only sizable literate population at the time, with them also came the means of survival for the few Old English documents not already destroyed. In the monasteries that soon arose in such towns as Glastonbury, Lindisfarne, Jarrow, Wearmouth, and York, the clerical scribes copied hundreds and hundreds of manuscripts, some in the vernacular and some in Latin, covering all the known fields of discourse and inquiry. Among them were those works on which our literary, linguistic, and general historical research depends, like *Beowulf, The Battle of Maldon, Cædmon's Hymn, The Wanderer, The Dream of the Rood,* or the Venerable Bede's chronicle, *The Ecclesiastical History of the English-Speaking Peoples.*

Middle English period. When the Normans under Duke William won the Battle of Hastings in 1066, they moved in on a culture whose level of sophistication, however crude by our standards, far surpassed the Norman one, as the Norman invaders themselves admitted. The Old English period had produced poets, artisans, and philosophers as well as warriors, hunters, and ravagers. To this flourishing society, the conquering French brought their language (which for a century or so completely superseded English as the language of courtly discourse), some changes in food, clothes, music, litera- ture, art, and architecture (this is the period of French *romances* and Gothic cathedrals), and—especially important—increasing contact with the Conti- nent. What had begun with introduction of the Church in the late sixth century continued with occupation by the Normans in the eleventh: England continued to move closer to the cultures outside her island, closer culturally, commercially, demographically, and linguistically.

In comparison with pre-Norman England, medieval England developed a society more urban, less rural; more nationalistic, less tribal; and more middle class, less simply divided into aristocrats and peasants. The wars continued, to be sure, both overseas (the Hundred Years' War) and at home (Wars of the Roses), but England never again was invaded by foreign armies. As the country became more involved in commercial trade with the Conti- nent, her people became more self-conscious, more sophisticated, and more literate. During this Middle English period, the demand for books of all sorts increased, even though books were hard to get and valuable because they were still being copied by hand.

Old English poetry had been largely oral, read or chanted aloud or recited from memory by a *scop* (bard) in public, to a good-sized audience of aristo- crats assembled in a baronial hall. By contrast, much of the Middle English literature was written (initially or soon thereafter) and was meant to be read by oneself, a private occupation: for instance, the anonymous poems *Sir Gawain and the Green Knight* and *The Pearl,* Langland's *Piers Plowman,* Chaucer's *Canterbury Tales,* Gower's *Confessio Amantis,* or Malory's *Le Morte d'Arthur.*

Modern English period. By the time of the English Renaissance and the beginning of the Modern period in the sixteenth century, English society, although still alien to us in many crucial respects, was nevertheless much more like our own than like the Old English. The center of English power was no longer the countryside and forests, but London, and it was from an urban setting that most English commercial, national, and political interests were developed.

The society was comparatively stable politically, because the institutions of Parliament and common law had developed sufficiently to sometimes counterbalance the whims of the monarchy. Political stability also began to come about because the middle class had acquired more financial, and there- fore more political, control over the government as the years went on. The English were becoming what Napoleon called them, "a nation of shopkeep- ers"; they were also becoming financiers, working for overseas exploration and expansion as much to enrich the coffers of the realm as to advance its glories. Colonization followed swiftly upon exploration, and by the nineteenth century it could be legitimately declared that the sun never set on the British Empire.

Paradoxically, all this expansion into lands with other cultures served to consolidate the British sense of their own cultural uniqueness. Early Modern English, like Early Modern England, was self-conscious, sophisticated, and increasingly more dependent upon the written rather than the spoken word for the transaction of daily business as well as for literary purposes.

Historical-Linguistic Survey

With this necessarily brief and simplified overview of English social history in mind, let us now consider the language of each period in more detail. Since all of our conclusions about Old, Middle, and Early Modern English must be drawn from written sources, we can only be tentative about the spoken language, especially its pronunciation. The description of the languages, then, has to be regarded with patient skepticism, since all research is limited by the scarcity of sources.

Old English. However alien that opening passage of Old English in extract 7.1 may look to our modern eyes, its spoken form actually differed from the present-day language in only four substantial ways: lexicon, pronunciation, gender, and inflections.

Lexicon. Unlike our modern lexicon, which is drawn from a number of languages, the word stock of Old English is heavily Germanic. The four main dialects of Old English (West Saxon, in which most of the literature survives, Kentish, Mercian, and Northumbrian) and the early Scandinavian dialects of the Viking raiders already had many words in common, particularly the workhorse terms of family relationship and seasons, certain verbs, and certain prepositions: "man," "woman," "mother," "folk," "house," "thing," "winter," "summer," "will," "can," "hear," "see," "over," "under." Occasionally the Scandinavian forms brought in by the coastal raiders from Sweden, Denmark, and Norway dominated the native British forms, as in the case of the Old Norse *systir* (sister) instead of the Old English *sweostor,* or the Old Norse *vindauga* (window; literally, "wind-eye") instead of the Old English *eagþyrl* (literally, "eye-hole"). In any event, one of the most notable features of Old English was its stubbornly Teutonic lexicon; not until the Norman Conquest did English allow any significant number of imports from outside the Germanic languages.

Pronunciation. The poems available from Old and Middle English tell us that their pronunciation is closer to that of a present-day Romance language, such as French or Spanish, than to that of modern English. The vowels tend to be pronounced in the Continental way, as /a/, /e/, /i/, /o/, and /u/, rather than in the more diphthongized American way (/ei/, /ij/, /ai/, /ow/, /juw/).

If you look back at extract 7.1, you will see that some vowels carry a short bar, or macron, overhead. This editorial insertion indicates that those vowels are held longer than the unmarked ones, since in Old English, length was a segmental phoneme. *Sōþlīče* (line 13), for instance, carries two long vowels, <ō> <ī>, with the macron as the editorial equivalent of the linguist's /:/, the sign for length. Thus, *sōþlīče* would be pronounced /so:θli:čə/. The other editorial mark in the extract, the small crown over some <g>'s, <f>'s, and <c>'s, indicates that these are to be pronounced /j/, /v/, and /č/, respectively. The Old English graphs <ð> and <þ>, respectively called ash and thorn, were redundant features; each can represent either /ð/ or /θ/ on the IPA chart (table 4.2). Like the macron over certain vowels, a doubled consonant, as in *willa* (line 5), indicated length; a roughly equivalent pronunciation might be achieved if you said that word's <l>'s as we would say them in "wi*ll l*eave." The rest of the consonants are pronounced as on the IPA chart, except for some of the <g>, <h>, and <r> sounds, which in Old English are more complicated than it is worth spending time on here.

Finally, stress in Old English generally fell on the first syllable: */Fæder*, */ure*, */yfele*, except in verbs with certain prefixes. For example, *ǧe/halgod* (line 3), *ge/wurþe* (line 5), and *for/ǧyfe* (line 9) will take the stress on the second syllable, which of course is the first syllable of the base. Modern English shows a tendency toward the same first-syllable stress pattern, although it has been contaminated by the many non-Germanic words that take stress on other syllables, for example, "taboo" (/tə/buw/, from Tongan), "Muskogee" (/məs/kowgi/, American Indian), "retroflection" (/rɛtro/flɛk-šən/, Latin).

Gender. After word stock and pronunciation, a third difference between Old and Modern English appears in their uses of gender. Old English, like many modern European languages, had grammatical gender; Modern English does not. Gender in the grammatical sense has little or nothing to do with sex; it is simply a set of correlations between the inflections of the nouns and the inflections of modifiers or referents (that is, adjectives or pronouns) commonly associated with nouns. Gender is subdivided into three types or sets, masculine, feminine, and neuter, although in most cases, grammatically masculine nouns rarely had physiologically masculine referents. *Wīf* (woman or wife), *mæǧden* (maiden), and *bearn* (son, bairn) are all grammatically neutral, but *strengðu* (strength) is grammatically feminine. Like many Indo-European languages, Old English early began to lose its genders, even before the eleventh century. For example, our most common modifier, "the" (from the Old English *sē, sēo, þæt*), now retains its morphemic identity—does not change form according to gender—regardless of what-

	Singular	*Plural*
Nominative	*sē gylt* [the guilt]	*þā gyltas* [the guilts]
Accusative	*þōne gylt* [the guilt]	*þā gyltas* [the guilts]
Genitive	*þæs gyltes* [of the guilt]	*þāra gylta* [of the guilts]
Dative	*þæm gylte* [to, by, or	*þæm.gyltendum* [to, by,
	þat the guilt]	þor at the guilts]

Table 7.1   Declension of OE gylt

ever noun it modifies. The modern pronouns "he," "she," and "it" now refer to words whose meanings themselves have extralinguistic gender, such as "man," "woman," or the neutral "table."

Inflections. Inflections, the fourth major difference between Old and Modern English, probably give the modern reader as much difficulty as the lexicon, since Old English has so many word endings and Modern English so few. As we mentioned in chapter 5, English has become syntactically more complex as it has become morphologically simpler over the centuries. That is, it has increased its structural patterns and the number of structuring words while dropping inflectional morphemes. Old English nouns, for instance, had from four to seven inflectional forms compared to the three noun forms we retain: our zero-ending form (no inflection, {ø}) for singular nouns, the plural {s} inflection and its allomorphs, and the possessive {s} inflection.

The most common Old English noun-inflection forms, or cases, were the singular and plural of the following:[3]

Nominative: the "name case," most like our zero-ending form (Jim)

Genitive: like our possessive (Jim's)

Accusative: indicating a direct object; this case's inflection was commonly the same as the nominative's (Jim)

Dative: Indicating an indirect object ([to] Jim)

When we run a word through its cases, giving the inflection for each case, we are said to be showing its declensions (or declining it). Declensions will vary according to the noun's gender, so a masculine noun like *gylt* (lines 9 and 10 in extract 7.1) would be declined as shown in table 7.1.

Other nouns with different genders will follow different declensions, but they all change inflections according to the grammatical function—subject, direct object, possessive, indirect object—that they are fulfilling at the time, and they all have to match endings with their referents or modifiers.

---

3. All of the technical terms used in this section—"inflection," "declension," "nominative," "direct object," and so on—are derived from the Traditional, Latin-based approach to English grammar.

	Weak (Regular)	Strong (Irregular)	Anomalous
Infinitive	*syllan*	*lædan*	*bēon, wesan*
Present (first person)	*sylle*	*læde*	*eom, bēo*
Singular preterit			
(first and third person)	*sealde*	*lēd*	*wæs*
Plural preterit	*sealdon*	*lēdon*	*wǣron*
Past participle	*seald*	*lǣden*	[no occurrence]

Table 7.2   Conjugation of three OE verbs

The historical trend in English verbs has been toward leveling or regularity, that is, a consistency in verb endings. There were many more verbs of the type called strong or irregular in Old English than in Modern English, "irregular" because they were conjugated[4] differently from the weak or regular verbs most common in Modern English. Weak (regular) verbs take the familiar {ed} past-tense and {ing} present-participle endings; strong (irregular) verbs take other kinds of inflections. The four principal parts of an Old English verb, from which its other forms can be reconstructed, are:

Present tense, derived from the infinitive: "I walk," "he walks"

Singular preterit, or simple past tense: "I walked"

Plural preterit: "they walked"

Past participle: "had walked"

The various parts will be signaled by various inflectional changes, as was true with nouns, and by changes in the vowel(s) of the verb's base. Depending upon inflectional changes, an Old English verb is categorized as either weak (regular) or strong (irregular); and depending upon the kind of internal changes, a strong verb is further categorized as belonging either to one of the seven classes of strong verbs or to a separate class, called anomalous, of verbs so irregular that they have to be grouped by themselves.

Let us look at the conjugations of three verbs from extract 7.1: the weak verb *syllan* (to give), line 8; the strong verb *lædan* (to lead), line 11; and the anomalous verb *bēon* (to be), line 2. ("To be" in most languages, including Modern English, is wildly irregular.) See table 7.2.

In all three examples, you can see that whatever may happen in the base, or stem, the inflectional changes are fairly consistent. These inflections save a good many extra words, for where Modern English must say "he [or "they"] had given," Old English needs only one word: *seald.*

---

4. "Conjugate" and "parts" are to verbs as "decline" and "cases" are to nouns; that is, they refer to the practice of putting a word through its inflectional paces. For verbs, there is the added necessity of considering tense, mood, and voice.

Synthetic and analytic. A heavily inflected language like Old English, one which linguists call synthetic, derives its structures more from its word endings than from the order in which the words appear in an utterance. Unlike Modern English, which is an analytic, word-order language, a synthetic language need not concern itself overmuch with whether the direct object comes before or after the indirect object. In a synthetic language, the accusative and dative inflections will let the listener or hearer know which word is serving which syntactic function. For example, the sentence appearing in extract 7.1 at lines 7–8 could be rearranged to read *To dæg ūs ūrne hlāf gedæghwāmlīcan syle,* and it would still convey the same sense to one familiar with the language, because each word's inflection has not changed. *Hlāf,* for instance, retains its zero ending, characteristic of the nominative (subject) or accusative (direct object) case, even though we rearranged its position from the third to the fifth word in the sentence. Therefore, *hlāf* is still a singular noun functioning syntactically as either subject or direct object in the sentence, regardless of its linear position.

But with an analytic language like Modern English, whose structural meanings depend almost completely on our keeping the individual words in their place, we make such positional rearrangements at our peril. If we scrambled the modern translation to fit the scrambled Old English, we would come up with this: "Today us our bread daily give." To be sure, we probably could figure out what was meant,[5] but in order to do so, we would again have to rearrange the words into their more familiar pattern: "Give us this day [today] our daily bread." The words themselves are individually, lexically recognizable; but only in the unscrambled form ("Give us this day . . . ") is the structural order recognizable, the pattern in which the words appear. That order holds constant in most Modern English utterances: verb before direct object ("give"/"bread"), adverb close to verb ("[today]"/"give"), adjective close to noun ("daily"/"bread"), indirect object before direct object ("us"/"bread"), direct object ("bread") near the end of the sentence.

Middle English. The shift from a synthetic to an analytic syntax, underway before the Norman Conquest, was by no means completed by 1485. If only for that reason, the whole Middle English period may be regarded linguistically as a time of transition; but there are two other reasons why this Middle period is linguistically transitional, and thus two other distinctions (besides synthesis-analysis) between Old and Modern English. First, the lexicon changed from almost exclusively Germanic to a much more inclusive word stock; and second, the pronunciation changed from the distinctively velar

5. As you have been figuring out, from reading the passage itself and from picking up clues in this chapter, it is an Old English version of the Lord's Prayer.

Old English sounds to the more palatal, "flatter" sounds to which our ears are accustomed.

These two changes were initiated by the defeat of the English at the Battle of Hastings, for when the French came in, the English went out—politically, socially, and linguistically. The conquerors made what some modern historians regard as almost a systematic, and certainly a thoroughly successful, attempt to exterminate both the Old English language and its users. When written English finally resurfaced in the twelfth century, after serving as the underground language of the outcasts,[6] it was vastly altered. Almost overnight, as these things go, reemergent English began to assimilate French words and French pronunciation (just as it had done with the Scandinavians six centuries before) and to drop even more of its inflections. These adaptations probably happened without much conscious intention on the part of the speakers, but happen they did.

How effective that adaptation was may be judged by comparing the passage in extract 7.2, the opening lines of Chaucer's *Canterbury Tales,* printed in 1400, with the passage in extract 7.1, written down about four hundred years earlier. Even though Chaucer's lyrical celebration of springtime must still be read with Continental vowels instead of our American diphthongized ones, and even though in some cases the spelling is still alien to the eye, Chaucer's language is nevertheless much closer to our own than is the language of the Old English prayer. With a little help on pronunciation and vocabulary, in fact, you can probably read the passage quite well.

The consonants are pronounced as on the IPA chart; the vowels are given the Continental pronunication. A doubled vowel, like <ee> or <oo>, is held longer than a single vowel, as in *soote* /soːtə/, line 1. The digraphs <ou> and <ow> also indicate length: *showres,* line 1, is pronounced

Whan that Aprill with his showres soote
The droghte of March hath perced to the roote
And bathed every veine in swich licour,
Of which vertu engendred is the flowr;
Whan Zephyrus eek with his sweete breeth
Inspired hath in every holt and heeth
The tendre croppes, and the yonge sonne
Hath in the Ram his halve cours yronne,
And smale foweles maken melodye
That slepen al the night with open yë—
So priketh hem Nature in hir corages—
Thanne longen folk to goon on pilgrimages . . .

Extract 7.2   Opening lines of The Canterbury Tales

6. Latin, of course, remained the language of learned discourse throughout Europe.

/šu:rəz/. Put the stress on a word where you usually would. Most commonly, stress will be on the first syllable: /ˈtɛndrə/, line 7.

Three exceptions to the rule of stress bear noting:

1. Do not pronounce terminal <e> on a word inside a line if the next word beings with a vowel. *Veine,* line 3, is pronounced /ve:n/, since the next word is *in.* Do, however, pronounce terminal <e> as *schwa,* /ə/, inside a line when the next word begins with a consonant: *smale,* line 9, is /smɑlə/.

2. Always pronounce terminal <e> as *schwa* if a word is at the end of a line: *sonne,* line 7, is /sən:ə/. (Inside or finishing a line, pronouncing the terminal <e> adds a syllable.)

3. Do pronounce these three inflections: the {ed} as /əd/ or /ɪd/, the {en} as /ən/ or /ɪn/, and the {es} as /əz/ or /ɪz/, whichever seems most natural to you. (These inflections also add a syllable.)

All of the above recommendations will help you get the stress and rhythm, and the vocabulary list in table 7.3 will help you get the words. There are three reasons why you will not need much help with the syntax at all. One is that by the beginning of the fifteenth century, the shift from a synthetic to an analytic syntax was very nearly complete. Another reason is that Chaucer's dialect, from the East Midland (specifically, London) area dominated in literary production. Eventually, that dialect superseded all of the other Middle English dialects and became the ancestor of Modern English. The third reason you can read Middle English more easily than you can the Old English is that there are many French and Latin-via-French words in the passage. So the lexicon is much closer to our own in flavor than the Germanic Old English was. Just in the first four lines of Chaucer, we find five French-based words where there were none in Old English: *veine, licour, vertu, engender,* and *flowr,* in their modern counterparts, are all words we use today.

A fascinating side effect of the linguistic assimilation going on during the Middle English period was a phenomenon called pairing. This is the doubling up of words originating in two different languages but, in contemporary usage, having approximately the same referent. Because the outcast English used one language and the conquering French another for so long, the reformed English language that emerged in the twelfth century occasionally overlapped French-based and German-based words. When both versions survived into Modern English, our lexicon will show a curious division along class as well as etymological lines. For example, many of our present words for meat on the table are French in origin, whereas the same words for meat on the hoof are Old English. Like the French aristocrats, we eat "beef," "veal," and "pork," but like the Old English peasants, we tend and butcher a "cow," a "calf," or a "pig." The same sort of pairing shows up in other everyday concerns: furniture ("throne" is French, "stool" Germanic), articles of clothing ("cloak" is French, "shirt" Germanic), even weaponry ("dagger" is French, "sword" Germanic).

Line	Middle English	Modern English
1	whan that	when
1	soote	sweet
3	swich	such
3	licour	liquid
4	vertu	essence, impulse
5	Zephyrus	name of the west wind
6	holt	grove
6	heeth	field
7	croppes	shoots, vegetation
7	sonne	sun
8	Ram	Aries, first sign of the Zodiac
8	halve cours yronne	halfway through the sign of the Ram
9	foweles	birds
11	hem	them
11	hir	their
11	corages	hearts
12	goon	go

Table 7.3   Vocabulary list for The Canterbury Tales *extract*

Latin-based imports. It is important to be aware that nearly all of the Old French words imported into English during this period were ultimately derived from Latin. If you check the language chart (figure 7.1), you will see that French is an Italic, or Romance, language directly descended from Latin. Thus, the high proportion of Latin-based words in Old French is not surprising. The point is raised here because of the common assertion that one of the notable differences between Middle and Modern English is the greater proportion of Latin-based words occurring in Modern English. Specifically, the beginnings of the English Renaissance in the late fifteenth century are said to have created a tidal wave of Classical-language imports into the lexicon, mostly from Latin but a fair proportion from Greek as well. This assertion is true, but the implication—that Latin had been a stranger to English before the Renaissance—is not true. Even Old English had absorbed some Latin during the Roman occupation of Britain in the first and second centuries, and Middle English indirectly (by way of Old French) brought in more.

Because those secondhand, Latin-via-French imports (such as "throne" or "engender") were screened through French, they seem a little less "Latinate" than the direct imports that came in during the Renaissance. The direct imports tend to retain their Latin affixes unadulterated, whereas the secondhand imports often have had their affixes modified by the phonemes and morphemes of Old French.

"Engender," for instance (extract 7.2, line 4), comes originally from the Latin *ingenerare* (to beget, produce, or form), but Old French changes the prefix and suffix to suit its own patterns: *engenderer.* Middle English changes the infinitive inflection again, to *engenderen.* In addition to the affixative changes, French and English added a <d> in the middle, possibly because the shift from /n/ to /ɛ/ was difficult to make without sliding the /n/ through a transitional /d/ first. (Try it with your own tongue and alveolar ridge.) The infinitive inflections, {are} in Latin, {er} in Old French, and {en} in Middle English, are characteristic of each language, as are the sound shifts represented by French <e> instead of Latin <i> and by <d> in the two vernaculars. Thus, *engenderer* and *engenderen,* while recognizably of Latin origin, are also recognizable as, respectively, Old French and Middle English, too, in a way that the later, direct-from-Latin imports into English are not.

Modern English. Let us consider extract 7.3, a passage of heavily Latinate prose from the Early Modern period, by way of comparing the different flavors of the languages that had permeated English by then. John Milton wrote *Areopagitica,* from which the selection is taken, in 1644. It is a famous attack on censorship, and in this section, he is attempting to clarify a distinction between worthy and unworthy virtue.

"Excremental" (line 10) is used in conjunction with "whiteness" in a way that seems peculiar in Modern English. But Milton is counting on his readers' recognizing "excremental" as a Latin word whose original meaning was "to sift out," especially referring to "sifting out" refuse or ordure. Like Blake's etymological pun on "appalls" (p. 57), this one plays a contemporary meaning against an older one by conjuring up a pale and drifted cover of refuse, perhaps like the old bird dung commonly seen splattered over the heads and shoulders of statues raised in honor of noble and virtuous men. Ironically, then, a "youngling" virtue, "blank" (related to the French word *blanc,* "white") rather than "pure," is not at all what we ordinarily think of

He that can apprehend and consider vice with all her baits and
seeming pleasures, and yet abstain, and yet distinguish, and yet
prefer that which is truly better, he is the true wayfaring
Christian. I cannot praise a fugitive and cloistered virtue,
unexercised and unbreathed, that never sallies out and sees
her adversary, but slinks out of the race where that immortal
garland is to be run for, not without dust and heat. . . . That
virtue therefore which is but a youngling in the contemplation
of evil. . . . is but a blank virtue, not a pure; her whiteness is
but an excremental whiteness. . . .

Extract 7.3   Lines from Milton's Areopagitica

as virtue. A youngling virtue, instead, is like a dusty shroud concealing internal corruption.

"Excremental" happens to be one of the two words in the passage which came to Modern English directly from Latin. In fact, although the Germanic words in the passage considerably outnumber the Latinate ones, nearly all of the significant words in one way or another are Latin based.[7] So, ignoring style, Milton's prose rings with notes different from Chaucer's or the early Bible's because Milton makes so much use in crucial places of Latinate words like "excremental."

The other Latin word in the passage, "contemplation," plays as critical a part in establishing Milton's thesis and his tone as did "excremental." "Contemplation" is derived from the Latin *contemplāri,* to observe carefully, with special reference to the observations of augury, divination, and prophecy. The underlying notion of "contemplation," then, is watching the omens for signs of one's fate. Milton's point is that only such a contemplative virtue is truly wise, truly effective, truly worthy. Anything less alert and active is only a show, a fraud, a rather cowardly posture covering up corruption. In a fine display of polylingual, polysyllabic irony, Milton insists that for him, the "true wayfaring Christian" is far from being a hermit, modestly meditating on the virtues of Mary. On the contrary, Milton's true Christian has more in common with the vigorous temple priests, poet-warriors, and philosopher-kings of Classical (that is, pagan) times than with the stereotyped reclusive mystic.

Of course, it is highly unlikely that Milton or any writer ever said to himself one morning, "Well, I think I'll make sure the key words in this article or poem all come from Latin [or French or Urdu or whatever], and the Germanic words can go sulk in a corner." Few creative writers consciously choose words on the basis of their etymologies. Rather, they draw on the words available in the language at the time—or occasionally make up new ones. Consider the opening line of the modern poet T. S. Eliot's "Mr. Eliot's Sunday Morning Service": "Polyphiloprogenitive," it begins; a frighteningly long word which Eliot coined from scraps of Greek and which immediately establishes an intimidating, learned, perhaps even fussy tone. That is exactly what Eliot wants, because he intends to satirize that tone later, using the comic figure of a hippopotamus to achieve his ironic aim.

The point to bear in mind about both Milton and Eliot is that neither they nor anyone else who plays with Latin, Greek, or any imported words could have done so if there had not been an English Renaissance to bring the

---

7. Not all, however, for the Germanic words "better," "wayfaring," "unbreathed," "slinks," "youngling," and "whiteness" play key roles in the passage too, sometimes because they are striking and unusual, like "slinks" in this context, and sometimes because they almost seem to manage a balancing act with the Latinate words.

writings of Classical authors to the attention of English writers. Those imports could not have lasted in the language long enough to become playthings for poets if there had not been a Norman Conquest to bludgeon the language into receptivity. In an historical linguistic sense, Eliot depends on Milton, who depends on Chaucer, who depends on the Venerable Bede or the *Beowulf* poet, who depends on a pugnacious Jute . . . and so on, back to the shadowy, prehistoric first speakers of all.

Review Questions

1. To what branch and group of which language family does English belong?

2. What are the names and approximate dates of the three major historical divisions of the English language?

3. Briefly outline the social and political characteristics of each of those three periods.

4. In what four ways does the earliest version of English differ from our present language?

5. Define these terms as they relate to language: case, declension, conjugation, strong, weak.

6. What are the differences between a synthetic and an analytic language?

7. Which dialect dominated in Chaucer's time? Why is that important?

8. Define and give some examples of pairing.

9. What role do French and Latin play in the shaping of the sounds and the lexicon of our present language?

10. Which universal principle of language is this chapter based upon? Why is that important?

Selected Reading

Algeo, John, and Thomas Pyles. *Problems in the Origins and Development of the English Language.* New York: Harcourt Brace Jovanovich, 1966.

Anttila, Raimo. *An Introduction to Historical and Comparative Linguistics.* New York: The Macmillan Company, 1972.

Arlotto, Anthony. *Introduction to Historical Linguistics.* Boston: Houghton Mifflin Company, 1972.

Baugh, Albert C. *A History of the English Language,* 2nd ed. New York: Appleton-Century-Crofts, 1957.

Bloomfield, Morton W., and Leonard Newmark. *A Linguistic Introduction to the Study of English.* New York: Alfred A. Knopf, 1963.

Brook, G. L. *A History of the English Language.* New York: W. W. Norton & Co., Inc., 1958.

Clark, John W. *Early English: An Introduction to Old and Middle English.* New York: W. W. Norton & Co., Inc., 1957.

Gordon, James D. *The English Language: A Historical Introduction.* New York: Thomas Y. Crowell Company, Inc., 1972.

Haugen, Einar. *The Ecology of Language.* Stanford, Calif.: Stanford University Press, 1972.

Jespersen, Otto. *Growth and Structure of the English Language,* 9th ed. Oxford: Oxford University Press, 1954.

Jones, Richard Foster. *The Triumph of the English Language.* Stanford, Calif.: Stanford University Press, 1953.

Lehmann, Winfred P. *Historical Linguistics,* 2nd ed. New York: Holt, Rinehart and Winston, Inc., 1973.

Lockwood, W. B. *Indo-European Philology.* London: Hutchinson University Library, 1969.

Myers, L. M. *The Roots of Modern English.* Boston: Little, Brown and Company, 1966.

Pyles, Thomas. *The Origins and Development of the English Language,* 2nd ed. New York: Harcourt Brace Jovanovich, 1971.

Scott, Charles T., and Jon L. Erickson, eds. *Readings for the History of the English Language.* Boston: Allyn and Bacon, 1968.

Traugott, Elizabeth Closs. *A History of English Syntax.* New York: Holt, Rinehart and Winston, Inc., 1972.

Williams, Joseph M. *Origins of the English Language: A Social and Linguistic History.* New York: The Free Press/Macmillan, 1975.

Journals   *JEGP: Journal of English and Germanic Philology; The Journal of Indo-European Studies; Romance Philology*

8
The Dialects of American English

Everyone knows that dialects exist, but not everyone knows what dialects are. Most people assume that "dialect" is a negative word, a pejorative description of some language form different from, and worse than, their own language. Comedians still get laughs by telling stories "in dialect," which usually means a heavily exaggerated version of what the comedian and the audience believe to be Irish English, Yiddish English, Black English, Southern English, or whatever is supposed to be funny that season. There may be affection in such "dialect" routines, but there is a good deal of ridicule, too: human beings often make fun of what they do not understand.

The Nature of Dialects

There are two important points to grasp immediately about the nature of dialects, points that have a bearing on everything we shall say about kinds of dialect in this chapter. The first is that everybody speaks a dialect—or rather, many dialects, shifting back and forth from one to another without even being consciously aware of doing so. There is no "pure," "nondialectic" form of any language, and there never has been. A language is composed only of what its users say and write. Since each individual's speech is both unique (idiolectic) and shared with other speakers of the same language, it is inevitable that no one, pure form of a language can exist. Rather, many forms exist. These forms are the dialects.

The second point is that social judgment is not the same as linguistic judgment. Linguistically speaking, no dialect is better or worse than any other; all dialects are linguistically equal. All dialects serve perfectly well as expressive and communicative devices for their users; all are systematic, complex, functional, and creative. Any dialect, therefore, is linguistically as sound, as viable, as "good" as any other. In fact, judgments like "good" and "bad," "better" and "worse," "correct" and "incorrect," are not linguistic evaluations at all, but social ones. The trouble is that nearly everyone has confused the social (prescriptive) and the linguistic (descriptive) levels of judgment for so long that it has become almost impossible to separate the two categories. Language is, after all, a cultural phenomenon, so judgments are bound to be made, in a social sense, about language use. But at least we can try to examine the differences between social pressure and linguistic fact, and try to remember that they are not the same.

Here is how the social pressure works: the "best" people speak in thus and such a fashion, using this pronunciation or that noun-verb construction or whatever. These people have "taste"; they are "well-educated"; they have "good breeding" (and probably money); they have been to "good" schools and hold "good" jobs. They are, in short, socially prestigious. Other people, wishing to acquire that prestige, breeding, education, taste, power, and probably wealth, will often adopt the speech patterns of these "best" people. After a while, the prestige speech behavior comes to be regarded as having such high social value that it is held up as a model to users of other dialects; it is taught in the schools, in the self-help manuals, in the etiquette books; it becomes the standard by which other forms of speech, other dialects, are measured. Eventually the prestige form comes to be widely regarded as the only right, true, pure, correct way to speak or write. If a speaker does not use that dialect, he is often labeled an outsider, not a member of the "right" social group, and probably stupid as well.

The flaw is obvious—social prestige does not equal linguistic adequacy—but it is a long-ingrained flaw, so deeply trained into all of us that we have a hard time even recognizing it, much less accepting it as an error. Linguistically, there is very little "wrong" about any language use. Socially, however, there are zillions of ways to get into trouble: we all know that, and we have all suffered for it. Take the common statement "It's me." The prescriptions of the prestige dialect declare that statement to be "wrong," "incorrect," "bad." With a verb like "is" (a copulative, or linking, verb, which joins two pronouns or a noun and a pronoun), the prestige dialect prescribes that both of the nouns or pronouns should be in the subjective case. The pronoun "it" is subjective, but "me" is not; "me" is objective. We should say, "It is I" (or "It's I") if we wish to be prestigious.

Linguistically, however, that prescription is meaningless. In the first place, "It's me" is quite clear to anyone who speaks English; there is no syntactic or lexical confusion. In the second place, the rule about copulative verbs and objective cases comes from those eighteenth-century grammarians we met in chapter 6, the ones who borrowed Latin grammar to help them sort out English, the ones who were trying to defend the right of English to exist as a language and not as some bastardized form of guttersnipe Latin. They had a vested interest in making up such rules, for the more English could be made to seem like Latin, the more "respectable" (social judgment) it would appear to be. And in the third place, English syntax no longer makes much distinction among cases like objective and subjective; cases are remnants of old inflectional patterns that dropped out of the language centuries ago (chapter 7). In fact, whatever noun comes after the verb in English usually is an object, as in "I saw *him* yesterday," so "me" is much more linguistically consistent than "I" would be. Certainly, the "me"-construction is quite functional.

But knowing that social judgments and linguistic judgments are not equivalent does not relieve the anxiety most of us feel about what is "correct" or "incorrect." The two kinds of judgments have been blended so long that nearly everyone is nervous about the social niceties of language: are you supposed to say "who" or "whom," "her" or "she"? The prestige prescriptions are so complicated that many people just give up or fall into hypercorrections (like the overgeneralizing of children), such as "between she and I" or "Whom gave you that idea?" We will deal later, in chapter 12, with the problems of negotiating between social demands and linguistic reality when it comes to dialect. For now, let us keep in mind that dialect, viewed linguistically, merely means "variant"—not good, not bad, just different. One variant in any language usually acquires prestigious social status; that one (which is always changing, like any other form of language) is defined as the prestige dialect. In America, the prestige dialect is called Standard English, often shortened to S.E. Other kinds of dialect are collectively referred to as nonstandard, varying in some way(s) from the prestige dialect. These nonstandard dialects are not deficient forms (except socially); they are merely different. The study of dialects, and of the convergence of social influences and language behavior, is known as sociolinguistics.

Non-S.E. dialects can be classified in many different ways, but for purposes of simplification, we will focus on six: historical, regional, occupational, ethnic, age, and gender. Age and gender dialects have not been studied extensively yet, so here they will be combined into a single section. Finally, we shall return to a consideration of the social value attached to dialects when we discuss the ways in which speakers alter their linguistic behaviors (their registers) in different social situations.

Historical

Using the word "historical" to name a dialect type is a bit misleading, for dialects ordinarily are not seen as functioning over time (diachronically) but over space (synchronically). Nevertheless, the word is deliberately used here to indicate that American English had a specific historical beginning, as a dialect of British English. Most of the first American colonists spoke the East Midlands variety of Shakespeare's time or shortly thereafter, in the Early Modern period of our language's history.

By the early 1600s, the English language had become essentially analytic in its syntax, but many of the lexical items were different from our contemporary language. Consider the use of the word "let" in these lines from *The Winter's Tale,* which Shakespeare wrote in 1610–11:

> When at Bohemia
> You take my lord, I'll give him my commission
> To let him there a month behind the gest
> Prefix'd for's parting (I.ii.39–42).

Here, "let" does not mean to allow or permit, but to leave behind or not to take away. Another lexical item in that passage has altogether disappeared from current usage, the word "gest," which means the time allotted for a halt or stay.[1]

Similarly, phonological patterns were quite different in Early Modern English, the dialect spoken by the first American Colonists. Stress, for example, often occurred elsewhere than where we are used to. It was on the second syllable of such words as "character," "concentrate," and "contemplate," but on the first syllable of most polysyllabic words ending in {able} or {ible}, such as "commendable." Pronunciation of consonants was fairly stable, but not all of the vowels had completed the Great Vowel Shift. The <a> in "name," for instance, was no longer pronounced with the Middle- and Old-English /ɑ/, nor yet with the modern /e/; it was something closer to /æ/. The Early Modern English-speakers would probably have pronounced "tide" (modern /taɪd/) as /təɪd/ and "fowl" (modern /fæwl/) as /fəul/. Additionally, the semivowel <h> in such French loanwords as "herb," "humble," and "host" was not pronounced, but <r> before sibilants usually was: Early Moderns said /pɛrləsi/ "parlesie," a variant of the earlier "paralisie" (paralysis), whereas a contemporary speaker would probably say /palzi/, "palsy."

Three hundred fifty years and many thousands of miles have separated the British and the American dialects now, so much so that two speakers of the same language from different sides of the Atlantic often have difficulty understanding one another. The most conservative of the three major elements of language, syntax, has not changed much since the Puritans left English shores, but contemporary British pronunciation is different from American—/klɑrk/ for /klɛrk/, /lə'borətri/ for /'læbrətɔri/, and so on—in vivid and distinctive ways. So is the British lexicon. American "kerosene" is British "paraffin"; the British call paraffin "white wax." If an American in Britain asks for a "cake," he will probably get a scone (rather like a sweet English muffin—for which there is no British term). If he wants American-

---

1. This "gest," from Old French *gist,* is not etymologically the same as the {gest} bound base, from Latin, that forms our modern "gestate"/"gestation."

style cakes, he must ask for *gateaux* /gə'to/. Americans usually ask for the restroom, British for the toilet, but an American toilet is a British W.C., or water closet. Lexical differences like these are so striking that during World War II, when many American servicemen were stationed in Great Britain, the U.S. government issued a pamphlet on British English so the Americans would not insult the British by using "bloody"—a taboo word then in British English—nor be offended when a British speaker offered to "knock you up" (come by for a social visit).

Regional

But the differences between British and American English remain the differences only of dialect, for the languages are still basically mutually intelligible. We can hear equally striking differences of dialect in our own country, as we travel from one region to another or as we speak to different groups of people. Southerners do not sound like Northerners, who do not sound like Midwesterners. Regional dialects, however, may be among the least susceptible of wide-ranging study, because America has become such a mobile society. When the population is stable, it is relatively easy to draw up maps of the regions where a clearly distinguishable dialect occurs, but much of the Midwest and West, settled by people from elsewhere, is difficult to map. Thus, the famous linguistic atlases compiled by Hans Kurath and others for areas along the Atlantic coast and littoral (showing the limits of the Northeastern, Middle, and Southern dialects) may not be transferable in such detail to places like California or Colorado. Where regional and other dialectic features are no longer distinctive, dialect leveling is taking place, comparable to the regularizing or leveling of verb forms discussed in chapter 7.

To draw up the dialect maps that make up a linguistic geography, one sets out with a tape recorder, a notebook, and a list of statistically selected contacts in a particular region so that a cross section of the regional population will be involved: all ages, educational levels, occupations, ethnic groups, and so on. Then one asks contacts such questions as: "How do you say this word? What is your word for this object? What construction do you use to get across this idea?" In other words, as with any language, the investigator of a dialect wants to know about phonology and morphology, lexicon, and syntax. Eventually, working through all of his contacts, the investigator is able to draw isogloss lines on a map of the region. Isoglosses indicate the areas within which all contacts pronounce the same words in nearly the same way (allowing for idiolectic allophones, of course) and use the same words to refer to the same object. Outside those isoglossic boundaries, different pronunciations and different lexicons will be used. An exam-

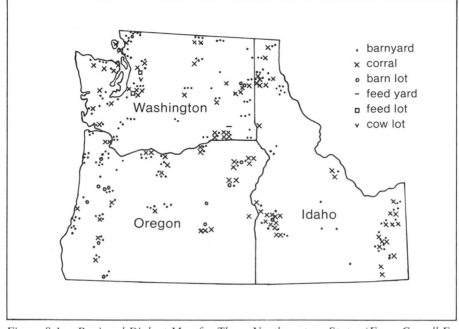

Figure 8.1. Regional Dialect Map for Three Northwestern States (From Carroll E. Reed. Dialects of American English, *rev. ed. [Amherst, Mass.: The University of Massachusetts Press, 1977], p. 118.) Copyright © 1967, 1977 by Carroll E. Reed.*

ple of isoglossic mapping is given in figure 8.1. From these detailed investigations of particular regions, the linguist can draw up component maps, linguistic atlases, which mark the extent of similar dialects throughout wider and wider regions.

Different researchers have marked off different numbers of dialectic regions in the United States as a whole; Kurath says there are four, others say six, but most researchers settle on three major regions in the heavily populated East: Northern, Midland, Southern (figure 8.2.) That very disagreement signals an important point about regional dialects in America: they are blending, leveling, no longer so distinctive as they were even in the 1920s, when the atlases were begun. Geographical mobility, television and other mass media, and social change are all rendering our regional dialects less clearly defined than they used to be. That does not mean that the dialects are not evident, because of course they are; rather, it means that someone who speaks a Southern dialect may no longer live in the South, but perhaps in North Dakota, and as a result, his speech will have become "contaminated" by his North Dakota neighbors. Except for a few pockets of the country

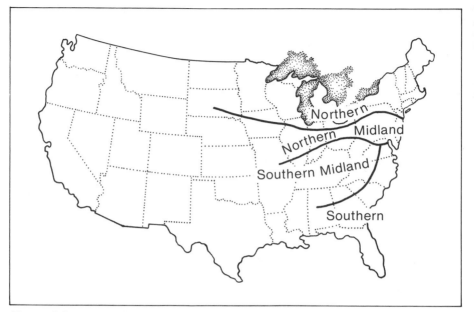

Figure 8.2.   General Regional Map of the United States.

where the population is still relatively stable (the Pennsylvania Dutch area, for example), actual geography serves less and less to mark the lines of a regional dialect.

Nevertheless, general regional differences are still easy to recognize, so easy, in fact, that many people still react negatively to a dialect not their own. Many Northerners think Southerners sound "mushmouthed," while to Southern ears, the speech of people from the North and Midwest has a definite "twang." A lexical regionalism is cause for scorn: "What do you mean, 'stoop'? Everybody knows those are steps!"—or the "veranda," the "porch," or the "platform," all of which are other regionalisms for the same object. Do you breakfast on flapjacks, griddle cakes, or pancakes? Do you use fire dogs or andirons? How about sweet corn, green corn, roasting ears, or corn on the cob? Do you use a skillet, griddle, frying pan, spider? Do you go uptown or downtown? Is something right fancy, mighty fancy, very fancy? Different areas, different terms.

Outside your home region, you may be teased for using the "wrong word," or others from different regions may puzzle you with terms new to you. But if, like many Americans, you have moved your residence often, your speech may be less marked by regionalisms than by other dialectic signs: your choice of job or hobby, your ethnic background, your age, and your sex.

Occupational

Occupational dialects cut across all other types of dialect. The lexicon that comes with a particular job will be pretty much the same from region to region, regardless of any other linguistic factors like ethnic background, age, or gender. All participants in a particular occupation will have much in common linguistically as far as that job is concerned. Regional pronunciation may shape the way the sounds come out, but the lexicon of an occupation will be similar from Florida to Alaska.

When occupational dialect is designed to convey specialized information in a rapid and condensed form from one member of the occupation to another, it is called jargon. (We have used much linguistic jargon in this book.) Although the intention behind the use of jargon is to be concise, and not necessarily to confuse nonmembers of the group, sometimes jargon can be very obscure to those not familiar with it. For example, would you know what a "homer," a "pop fly," a "slide," or a "sidearm toss" were if you did not know baseball? Could you distinguish immediately among "dice," "mince," and "sieve" if you were not a cook? How about "gusset," "dart," and "facing" (sewing) or "blitz," "offside," and "end-around" (football)? Many people are familiar with these jargon terms even if they are not professional baseball or football players, cooks, or tailors, because sports, cooking, and sewing are hobbies as well as occupations. But the fewer the people involved in a task, the less widely familiar the jargon is likely to be.

In some cases, a profession's jargon may be intentionally obscure, designed to keep nonprofessionals from understanding. This intentional obscurity is called cant (or argot). Some children's word games, such as Pig Latin in its various versions, are a form of cant: "Eer-hay omes-cay at-thay it-lay ul-lay irl-gay" is clearly intended to keep "that little girl" from understanding what the speaker is saying. Football playbooks and audibles at the line—"Seven green Charlie left five!"—are cant, deliberately coded so the opposition will not be able to read the signals. All espionage codes are cant, such as the famous "Enigma" during World War II, and various "underground" codes, like the frequently changing terms adopted by many drug sellers and users, are forms of cant as well. Names like "rainbows," "angel dust," "poppers," and so on are meant to sound obscure to the uninitiated (and especially to the narcs). Some of the most colorful terms in a language often come from the underworld: from thieves (booster, fence, kite, dip), from prostitutes (john, trick, old man, around the world), or, in twentieth-century America, from drug dealers (nickel or dime bag, high, get off on, O.D.).

Colorful language like this—not swear words, but new terms or long-used words applied in new ways—is called slang. Slang is easy to recognize, but almost impossible to define in such a specific and predictive way that anyone could determine in advance what a slang word would be. Perhaps that difficulty in definition comes from the fact that slang is intimately tied to social respectability (slang is characteristically viewed as raffish and disreputable), and definitions of "respectability" change from day to day. So does slang. Slang can be differentiated from other dialects, if at all, only because when it is still new and not yet widely used, S.E.-speakers almost invariably regard it with distaste. (They fail to recognize that much of current S.E. was once slang, for instance, "debunk," "scaly," "highbrow.") But S.E. snobbishness toward slang may, in some way, be an appropriate social response. Although many slang terms become part of the mainstream dialects for a while, they were originally intended to divert mainstream, S.E. attention.

The line between slang, cant, and jargon (between intentional and unintentional obscurity) is not always clear. Some groups seem to use jargon deliberately, as if it were cant, in order to cover up meaning; educators, sociologists, and bureaucrats are the groups most often accused. Their language is often marked by polysyllabic, ponderous, roundabout terminology for what seem like simple ideas or things, like "pupil stations" for desks or "sanitation engineers" for garbage collectors. Terminology like this is very high in what has been (mockingly?) referred to as the fog index, a formula for measuring the amount of obscurity in a passage of prose by indicating the number of years of education required to read any passage comfortably.

The formula—the index for "fog"—can be loosely translated as: $0.4(L + H)$, where L = the average number of words per sentence in the passage, and H = the number of hard or obscure words per 100 words in the passage.[2] (Obscure words are those having at least three syllables, not counting inflections or compounding.) Consider this section of a sociologist's report, for example: " . . . the correlation between the residential desirability scale and the continuum of socio-economic status would provide an estimate of the predictive value of aerial photographic data relative to the social ecology of the city."[3] Counting "socio-economic" as one word, we discover that L = 33 and H = 9 (or, roughly, 27 per 100). $L + H = 60$, times $0.4 = 24$: a very high fog index for a passage of this length. (An average fog index for a passage from *True Confessions* is 7; for an advertisement, 8.4.) The passage roughly translates as: "Aerial photographs of the city will show that rich neighborhoods look different from poor ones."

In addition to generalized fog, people writing "official" prose often favor what have been called buzz words, which sound impressive but do not

2. Robert Gunning, *The Technique of Clear Writing*, rev. ed. (New York: McGraw-Hill, 1968), pp. 33, 36–37. Used with permission of the author and copyright holder.
3. Norman E. Green, "Scale Analysis of Urban Structures," *The American Sociological Review* 21:1(1956),9.

always mean much referentially. Like slang, buzz words frequently become fashionable among the general public and are worked to death. "Charisma" and "global" were buzz words of a few years ago; in the late 1970s, computers have provided us with buzzes like "input," "variable," "parameter," and "data base." Any nationwide preoccupation will produce a spate of buzzes, which may outlive fashion and enter into S.E. In the 1960s, many Americans were concerned about the Vietnam War, the civil rights movement, and the youth movement, whose impacts survive in such phrases (now common) as "body count," "bussing," and "hippie." Whether quasi-occupational buzz words like "hippie" and "input" will survive the cultural impetus that produced them, no one can tell. In a few years they may be as embarrassingly quaint as truckers' and citizens' band radio (CB) jargon is already beginning to seem in the 1970s. "Ten-four, good buddy, and keep the hammer down" is still meaningful to those who drive eighteen-wheelers, but has become about as fashionable among nonprofessionals as are technical discussions of the hula hoop.

Ethnic

Next to regional dialects, ethnic dialects are probably the best known and possibly the most ridiculed. They are vulnerably obvious in their differentness from whatever that mythic, "pure" American S.E. is supposed to be, just as the ethnic-group members are obviously different, not "American," somehow, but hybrids: Spanish-American, Italian-American, Afro-American, Irish-American. We have a long history of labeling these ethnic groups—spics, wops, niggers, micks, and so on—all of the labels derogatory and insulting. We have an equally long history of making fun of their speech. Perhaps this ridicule is our version of a practice common among preliterate groups of calling themselves by a word that means "the People" or "the Human Beings" (e.g., Hopi or Cheyenne) and referring to everyone outside the group as "not-people," "not-human," or, at best, "enemy." (In the 1950s a common cant word among some black people for white people was "ofay," or foe.) In any event, when comedians tell dialect jokes, they usually exaggerate the speech patterns—phonological, lexical, syntactic—of the group referred to, and everyone laughs, secure in the shared sense of being on the inside, speaking the "right" language, while "they" are definitely out. It is a very comfortable feeling—unless you happen to be one of the outsiders.

In general, it appears that many ethnic dialects may be distinguished from other dialects because of second-language patterns. New, non-native speakers superimpose their original-language patterns onto English. Thus, those whose native language is Spanish may pronounce English words using

Spanish phonemes (/it/ for /ɪt/, /wɛtər/ for /wɛðər/, and so on). They may apply Spanish suprasegmentals to English morphophonemes (giving, say, /βaka'šon/ instead of /vei'keišən/). They may occasionally use Spanish syntax with English words ("We no can do that here"). Similarly, native French-speakers usually have trouble with the English phonemes /θ/ and /ð/, because that distinction is not phonemic in French. Japanese-speakers often do not make an /l/–/r/ phonemic distinction in English; German-speakers often interchange /v/ and /w/. By the same token, many Americans find the /x/ phoneme, occurring in such words as "Bach" /bax/, "loch" /lox/, or "chutzpah" /xətspa/—respectively, German, Celtic, and Yiddish— impossible to distinguish from /h/. Consequently, Americans speaking German, Celtic, or Yiddish sound just as peculiar in those languages as German (etc.) speakers do in English. Americans develop ethnic dialects when they live overseas.

For a long time, the dialect spoken by many black Americans—it is referred to as Black English, or B.E.—was assumed to be a corrupt or deficient form of English, as all other ethnic dialects were commonly supposed to be. But many studies undertaken in the past two decades have convincingly demonstrated the falsity of that assumption. Black English may or may not—the evidence is not decisive—have its origins in Gullah, a mixture of African languages spoken in parts of Georgia and South Carolina, but it seems clear that B.E. is strikingly different from other ethnic dialects. B.E. apparently had to be built from scratch rather than acquired from an already existent speech community (in contrast with, say, the resident German-American speakers with whom new German-speaking arrivals could talk). Black people who spoke many mutually unintelligible African languages would be thrown onto slave ships, unable to communicate with each other or with the white overseers. Once arrived, the slaves eventually contrived a pidgin (a made-up, compromise language, composed of scraps of this and that language). A pidgin learned as one's native language is called a creole. The creole or pidgin may have been Gullah and may have formed the basis of present-day Black English dialects.

What sets contemporary Black English apart from other nonstandard dialects is that so many of its variant (non-S.E.) features are syntactic. Like other nonstandard dialects, ethnic or otherwise, B.E. differs from S.E. phonemically and lexically.[4] But Black English is striking in its variances of structure; there are comparatively greater differences between the syntax of B.E. and S.E. than between S.E. and other non-S.E. dialects. These syntactic variants are quite regular, of course, as dialectic differences always are.

Characteristic of B.E., for example, is the elision (condensation or omis-

---

4. Indeed, B.E. is so close phonetically to many forms of Southern (white) English that many listeners find it difficult to tell a white Southerner from a black one over the telephone, unless the black speaker consciously uses B.E.

Standard English (S.E.)		Black English (B.E.)	
Past Tense			
Perfect	"I had tasted"	Prerecent	"I been tasted"
Progressive	"I had been tasting"	Recent	"I done tasted"
Simple (Preterit)	"I tasted"	Prepresent	"I did taste"
Progressive	"I was tasting"		
Emphatic	"I did taste"		
Present Tense			
Perfect	"I have tasted"	Inceptive	"I do taste"
Progressive	"I have been tasting"	Immediate	"I tasting"
Simple	"I taste"		
Progressive	"I am tasting"		
Emphatic	"I do taste"		
Future Tense			
Perfect	"I shall/will have tasted"	Immediate	"I'm a-taste"
Progressive	"I shall/will have been tasting"	Postimmediate	"I'm a-gonna taste"
Simple	"I shall/will taste"		
Progressive	"I shall/will be tasting"		
Indefinite Tense			
(no occurrence)			"I gonna taste"

Table 8.1 Tense construction in Standard English and in Black English. (Adapted from Joan G. Fickett, "Tense and Aspect in Black English," Journal of English Linguistics 6 (1972): 18.)

sion) of "be"-verb constructions and plural markers common in S.E., as in B.E.'s "They going," "We cool," and "I hungry" ("be"-form elided), or "five woman(s)," "two brother," and "seven day" (plural inflections). Also characteristic is a different, but equally complex and systematic pattern of tense constructions in B.E. (table 8.1). To say that one will do something within the next thirty seconds, one would use the future-immediate tense; if one wanted to say that one had done something just moments ago (perhaps is still finishing it), the inceptive tense would be used, and so on.

Recursive constructions are also systematic. For example, two common types of relative clauses in Black English, as in Standard English, are regularly developed two different ways. Clause 1 ("Jeannie she be a fox") + Clause 2 ("Jeannie drive that car") ⇒ "Jeannie she a fox drive that car"—in S.E., "Jeannie, who looks really good today, is driving that car." But Clause 2 + Clause 1 tranforms to "Jeannie she be a fox drive that car"—in S.E., "Jeannie, who is driving that car, is a good-looking lady." The first sentence puts the emphasis on Jeannie's driving; the second draws attention to her foxiness, her desirability.

Lexical contributions to Standard English from the many ethnic dialects (such as "fox" from Black English) are so numerous that no one could list them all. Usually, language purists regard such contributions with disdain, occasionally murmuring about how "colorful" they are, but the disdain is both undeserved and misdirected. Many words now regarded as thoroughly respectable (like "fellow," from Hindu) came originally from nonstandard sources, as we have already noted. To deny S.E. respectability to a word or construction because it is not created from S.E. sources is to ignore a universal characteristic of languages: open-endedness, or acceptance of lexical items from external sources.

Age and Gender

Age and gender are primarily biological rather than linguistic circumstances, but people of different ages and different sexes do learn different dialects. Like other dialects, these intersect with each other and with nation, region, occupation, and ethnic background. No idiolect will be solely determined by the speaker's age or gender, since the other four dialect types apparently dominate these two, but age and sex do make a linguistic difference. It is clear, for example, that a male twenty-eight-year-old Midwestern WASP engineer will not always use the same language behaviors as a female forty-two-year-old Midwestern WASP engineer.[5]

Age. Very little study has yet been done on age as a dialectic conditioner. (The psycholinguistic investigations of children's language acquisition are not studies of dialect per se.) But informal observations reveal several differences among the speech patterns of four principal age groups: the very young, up to ± 15 years; the youthful, ± 15 to ± 30; the middle-aged, ± 30 to ± 60; and the older, ± 60 on. These four divisions are more or less arbitrary, for age-dialect distinctions are much less clear than others, and what follows are obviously quite generalized observations.

As we saw in chapter 2, the speech of the very young is marked by many more nonstandard forms than appear in the other three categories (like over-generalized {ed} past-tense verbs, double negatives, and certain lexical-syntactic structures that tend to disappear with age, such as "Boy, are you gonna get it!"). There may still be some difficulty with phonology, for in-

5. Concerning social values attached to age and gender, notice how "natural" the first description seems and how "odd" the second. *Of course,* an engineer would be male and aged twenty-eight, not female and aged forty-two.

stance /θ/-/ð/ distinctions or stress. In addition, this first group has fewer items in its lexicon (a smaller vocabulary) than the other groups; very young speakers tend to use the same word over and over again, frequently a fad word, for many different speech situations. One such recent fad word was "gross," at the moment being supplanted by "weird." Syntax is comparatively simple, with less recursiveness and fewer transformations than appear in older groups. For example, young children will tend to combine sentences with "and" rather than use subordination techniques, as in "I have a cat and her name is Susie and she is black," rather than "I have a black cat whose name is Susie."

At the opposite extreme, the speech of older people (± 60 years on) is fully developed phonologically, lexically, and syntactically, but many older speakers talk more slowly and in shorter utterances than do younger groups. In addition, absorptiveness and adaptability may be diminished, so the speech of this older group tends to be marked by a vocabulary, and sometimes by a syntax, that more resembles the speech of the elders' own youth than the contemporary norms. My grandfather, for example, always referred to automobiles as "motorcars," not as "cars," because "motorcars" was the term he learned when he was young. In addition, some older people may develop a kind of singsong intonation pattern, often regarded as a recreation of similar patterns of youthful speech. This harking back, as we might call it, to linguistic patterns of one's younger days is so striking in the elderly that comics mimic and exaggerate it when they wish to portray old people. Part of the humor in Jonathan Winters's or Johnny Carson's sketches as "Granny" is their juxtaposition of elderly intonation patterns with a lexicon more characteristic of the youthful or middle range. We find it funny that "Granny" should say something like "Far out!"

The two mediate groups, the youthful and the middle range, can be only approximately differentiated from one another, for the dialectic differences between these two age-groups are slight and graduated. Generally speaking, however, it may be said that the middle-range group (± 30 to ± 60) shows more predilection for occupational jargon than the youthful group, whose jargon tends to come from other, nonoccupational obsessions. Also, the middle-range group often is more conscious of the social values inherent in different dialects and will frequently be hyperattentive to the prescriptions of Standard English. In fact, most of the distress voiced against nonstandard usages comes from this group.

The youthful group, on the other hand (± 15 to ± 30), is likely to be less concerned with S.E. prescriptions and more with keeping up with lexical and phonological fashions. The youthful group shows some of the repetitiveness of the very young, but draws the stock of repetitions from other youthful speakers, not from childhood patterns. This group also is marked by its lexical receptivity to words from nonstandard sources, as when, in the 1940s through 1960s, white youngsters adopted many of the speech patterns of blacks, musicians, and social outcasts such as drug dealers. Lexically the liveliest of the four groups, this one also provides most of the fad words for the very young and the middle-range groups—fad words, that is, not drawn from the middle-range occupations—and, thus, in recent years has served as the principal benchmark for what is deemed to be fashionable and therefore desirable. But America's love affair with youth, which has lasted for some twenty-five years now, may be fading: the buzz words from the middle-range group appear to be gaining in social status over the fad words from the youthful group, and the "greening of America" (a phrase popular in the 1960s) may be giving way to the computerization of America.

It will be recognized, I hope, that these descriptions of the traits of age-marked dialects are necessarily oversimplified and incomplete. Nor do they pretend to be accurate for any one person; many ten-year-olds talk as if they were in their thirties, many fifty-year-olds as if they were in their teens. By the same token, the discussion of gender markers in dialect will have to be regarded as simplified and generalized, for not all females use "women's speech" as it will be described here.

Gender. Much has been made recently of "sexism" in language, a topic discussed more fully in chapter 10, along with racism and other forms of linguistic bias. Let us concentrate here on describing the linguistic differences, so far as we can now identify them, between the speech of women and the speech of men. Such dialectic differences between the sexes have nothing to do with biological gender; that is, males and females share identical speech-producing equipment. Rather, dialectical differences arise here, as with the other dialect markers, because of social conditioning from the people who shape the growing child's language. Girls are not born talking differently from boys; girls learn to talk girls' speech.

One of the striking features of English, in all its dialects, is that the norm or standard is male. Women's speech differs from men's—is nonstandard—in several ways, as we shall see in a moment, and those ways also distinguish women's speech from the dialectic standard. Men's speech, however, differs from women's in only two ways, neither of which separates men's language from normative speech. The speech of males *is* the norm, so to differ from that norm or standard is to be nonstandard, in other words, female.

The two factors that most sharply distinguish men's from women's speech—factors prominent in men's speech and noticeably absent in women's—are a carryover of occupational dialect into nonoccupational situations, and the variety of epithets (swear words and rude names) which can be used by males in all but the most circumspect situations. Men often "carry the job home with them" in their speech; it is socially acceptable for them to do so—to speak about "the parameters of" any problem, for example—but women, rarely holding jobs that are socially valued, rarely speak in occupational terms when they are in nonoccupational situations. Until quite recently, women's job has been homemaking more than any other. When a man says "parameter" away from his job, he is assumed to be thoughtful, conscientious, hardworking, respectable, but when a woman mentions curtains or children, she is presumed to have no other thought— almost to be capable of no other thought—than what is encompassed by the four walls of her house. As more and more women take other jobs outside the home, however, it is likely that many of them will become as tiresome as many men are about shoptalk and occupational dialects.

But the second factor marking men's from women's speech, the epithets available to men in most social situations, will probably not be assimilated so easily by women, nor accepted by men as appropriate for women to use. Swear words are strongly identified by males and females alike as masculine prerogatives. Even now, in most circumstances, a woman who uses "Oh, shit!" instead of "Oh, shoot!" alarms nearly everyone, perhaps including herself, no matter how informal the social setting. Nor are men supposed to swear in the company of women. There is an intriguing parallel here between women and children, for young children—male or female—are also not usually allowed to hear swearing or to swear. The child overheard calling a playmate a "mother-fucking sonofabitch" is likely to be punished. A woman who says the same thing may not get her mouth washed out with soap, but chances are that she will be punished some other way, perhaps with an embarrassed silence or giggles or ostracism for her "unfeminine" boldness. A man saying those words might get punched, depending on how and to whom he uttered the phrase, but it would be the extralinguistic context, not merely his utterance of the words, that would determine the reaction from his auditors.

These two qualities distinguish men's speech from women's, by their relative absence in women's speech. Five other devices distinguish women's speech from men's, by their common appearance in women's speech and their rarity in men's. One device is syntactic, one morphophonological, and three lexical.

The syntactic device many women use, but men rarely do, is the tag question, as in "That was a terrible movie, wasn't it?" or "It's raining outside, isn't it?" Tag questions are neither true questions, for they do not really request information (they are really asking for confirmation), nor are they full-fledged declarative statements. They exist somewhere in between statement and question, reluctant, hesitant, uncommitted, waiting to see what the reply will be (or fairly certain there will not be any reply) before they risk a firm opinion.

Accompanying the tag question is the morphophonological device of into- nation: many women utter statements, "tagged" or not, with a question pitch (rising at the end) rather than with the customary declarative falling pitch. Rising pitch is particularly common when a woman is responding to a question, as though she thought an unequivocal reply might jeopardize her: (Q) "How much money do you need?" (A) "Oh, thirty dollars . . . ?" The effect of this question pitching is like that of the tag question: hesitant, awaiting confirmation or denial, not assertive.

Lexically, women's dialect differs from men's in three ways (besides the absence, by and large, of occupational jargon and of profanity): women use more intensifiers than men, make different kinds of fine distinctions, and use more euphemisms and other pleasant words than men do.

Intensifiers are words like "quite," "rather," "very," "such," and so on. One intensifier construction in particular is used by many women but by very few men: the "so"/"such" absolute, as in "It was so beautiful!" or "We had such a good time!" The word "so" or "such," heavily stressed, is the only adverb. (S.E. construction calls for a "so/such X that Y" pattern: "It was *so* beautiful *that* I wanted to buy it.") Intensifiers, as their name suggests, create a feeling of heightened intensity, beyond what the adjective alone connotes: *very* beautiful, *fabulously* wealthy, *outrageously* expensive—emotive rather than (male-approved) logical language, exaggerated rather than realistic, the stereotype of making a fuss about nothing.

Concerning distinctions, it is not that men do not make them, but that many men do not distinguish, in ordinary speaking situations, among the same things in the same way as women do. Color distinctions are the most frequently cited example. The physiology of the human eye is the same in males and females, and the ability to perceive different colors is also the same, but males will not ordinarily use the words that point up fine distinctions between ecru, beige and taupe, or lavender, mauve and fuschia. Men will often be quite knowledgeable about a degree of slope on a particular car's hood or the specific name of a typeface or disease or breed of cattle, but it is rare to hear a man use the word "crimson" except for blood: it's all red, anyway.

Finally, women's dialect is notable for the high proportion of euphemisms, "nice" words for unpleasant conditions, and for the equally high proportion of pleasant words generally, in comparison with the number of such words used by men. Women are much more likely to use words like "nice," "sweet," "kind," and "good" in any conversation than men are—to smoothe things over, to be nurturing or propitiatory, to speak in personal (affective) terms—and are equally likely to speak euphemistically even when they are not adopting the pleasant (nice) role. Many women will ask for "the powder room," "the ladies' room," or even—revealingly— "the little girls' room," rather than for the bathroom or the toilet. Women use diminutives more than men ("tummy," "beddy-bye"). Even women's nicknames tend to be diminutives of their own names ("Marge" for "Marjorie" or "Margaret," "Cher" for "Cheryl"), rather than substitute names, as is common with men: "Bud," "Butch," "Mac," "Red."

All of these characteristics of women's dialect—the absence of swear words and occupational jargon, and the high proportion of tag questions, question pitches, intensifiers, color distinctions, and euphemisms—set off the speech of women from the speech of men, and therefore from "normal" speech. Collectively, these dialect markers suggest that if we use men's speech as the standard, women are regarded—and regard themselves—as immature, frivolous, or irrelevant. Not participating, for the most part, in the "real" world of jobs, sports, or other common focuses of male interaction, women have no "right" (so the language itself implies) to take their own concerns seriously or to intrude on the world of men by using men's—real, grown-up—language. To those who accept the social stereotypes conveyed by language (among other media), it is as disconcerting to hear a woman speak of ohms or rheostats, directorships or management techniques, brokers' fees or plaintiffs, as it would be to hear a Spanish-American born in Arizona speak with a British accent.

These, briefly, are six kinds of English dialects. Each type cross-indexes with the others, so an individual's idiolect may be approximately described in terms of his participation in the six: American or British? Region of the country? Occupation? Ethnic background? Age? Sex? Given the answers to those questions, we can make some predictions about a person's language use, but only in a very general way. To be more specific, we would also have to ask another question: In what context is the speaker behaving? For the dialects a person uses depend to a large extent on his response to the changing circumstances around him; speakers choose, mostly unconsciously, which version of which dialect they will use, according to the social setting. Consequently, a seventh area of dialectology that sociolinguists must consider is social context, or speech situation.

Registers

The varying speech behaviors adopted in response to social contexts are called registers. (If written, such behaviors are called styles.) Every speaker has a repertory of several registers, and most speakers learn, as they acquire language from infancy on, what value society places on each of the registers.

The value attached to any given register will vary from one social group to another; what one group favors, another may regard with distaste. For example, the S.E. admired (and feared) by many WASP speakers is not always so highly regarded by other ethnic groups. "Hello, it's nice to meet you, ma'am" is prestigious white S.E. but may sound drab and stiff-necked to a speaker of B.E., for whom "Hey, what's happ'nin', mama?" carries more prestige. For males, the speech situations in bars, offices, locker rooms, and hunting trips may call for a large vocabulary of swear words, but that register used in church would be frowned upon. Women moving into jobs outside the home are expected to drop their dialect and acquire the "businesslike" jargon of their occupation. American Westerners and Southerners, who sometimes address comparative strangers with terms implying endearment ("honey," "sweetie," "sugar"), may irritate some Easterners and Midwesterners who are not used to the practice. Southerners and Far Westerners, in turn, sometimes find Northern and Midwestern speech habits chilly and standoffish. Most people become more precise in their articulation when they are hunting for a job, for instance, pronouncing the /ŋ/ at the end of words like "having" or "going" where, in more casual speech situations, they are more likely to say /n/. But many speakers of B.E. might find terminal /ŋ/ rather pretentious under any circumstances.

Acknowledging this general pattern of constant, unconscious adaptability to speech situations, we may describe a common classification system for five registers. The classification is based on the experiential awareness all speakers have, in varying degrees, of the appropriateness of this or that linguistic behavior in this or that setting. Broadly speaking, the repertory of sociolinguistic registers ranges from formal to intimate, that is, from the most ceremonious social context calling for the most ceremonial speech to the least guarded and closest context.

Frozen. The most ceremonial register is the oratorical. In writing, it belongs to important public documents such as the Constitution. It is the most conservative style, favoring language patterns "frozen" by centuries of precedent. It never uses slang, fad words, or buzz words. In speech, it is the mode of public address on very ceremonial, ritualized occasions, such as weddings, funerals, or addresses to Congress or the United Nations. Generally, the larger the audience, the more oratorical the speech.

Deliberative. Not quite so formal is the deliberative register. (In writing, this style usually is called "formal.") Professional publications use it in technical articles, and many term papers require this style. In speech, the deliberative register is used in public addresses that are not quite so time-honored in their ceremonial aspects: in commencement speeches, sermons, summing up a case before the Supreme Court, addressing a meeting of company stockholders. This register is a little less polished than the oratorical, but is still directed at an audience too large to speak with face to face. Only rarely will the deliberative register use slang, fad words, or buzz words; if it does so, it will be in a pointed and self-conscious way.

Consultative. In the middle, between frozen and intimate, is the consultative level. Most business letters, newspaper and magazine articles, and reports are written in this style. Spoken consultation typically involves an exchange of dialogue rather than a speech, but it is the sort of exchange that takes place during business meetings, with some attention to ceremony and rules of linguistic and social decorum, rather than the exchange of casual friends. There is still, at this level, a sense of hierarchy: leaders and followers, dominant and subordinate, precedence and rank; speakers still choose their words with some care. Slang, buzz words, and fad words are common here, but within a general framework of standard speech patterns.

Casual. The casual level appears in some written material, but usually as flavoring in an otherwise consultative style. Mostly, this is a spoken register carried on in an informal situation, between speakers of equal or equivalent rank. The acquaintance of the speakers is not necessarily close, but the behaviors are essentially sharing: comments on the weather or taxes or sports in office hallways or on coffee breaks, in classrooms before the bell rings, in elevators, cafeteria lines, air terminals. The regional, ethnic and other dialects and slang, buzz words, and fad words here begin to dominate the concern for correctness; pause markers (like "uh," "you know," or "I mean") begin to show up, too. Casual conversation can occur in groups, but usually only if the group subdivides into two- or three-person clusters.

Intimate. Most informal of all is the intimate register, which rarely shows up in print (except, of course, in fiction or scripts that attempt to recreate it). Intimacy adds to the casual level a closeness of acquaintance between the speakers: family members, roommates, spouses, good friends. There is little if any concern here for ceremony, precedence, rank, or correctness. The emphasis is on personality and individuation, so dialect markers, slang, buzz words, and fad words are strongest here. Many intimate registers include a sort of private language, consisting of phrases or references not shared by outsiders, a kind of two-person or three-person cant. The intimate register is rarely used with groups of people larger than two or three, for its hallmark is a lack of the self-consciousness that almost automatically arises in people in a crowd.

Each of these five registers modulates with the different dialects according to the speaker's perception of the social situation and the linguistic behavior appropriate to it. Consequently, because every individual who speaks English participates in one version or another of six dialects and five registers, it may be said that every English-speaker has at his or her command about 30 (6 × 5) overlapping ways of speaking. Multiply that number by the number of competent adult speakers in the areas where English is spoken—in the

United States alone, this figure is over two billion in the late 1970s—and we get a staggering variety of speech habits. Even granting that some of those habits carry more social prestige than others, no wonder linguists insist that there is no such thing as *a* dialect of English, much less *the* "pure" or "correct" dialectic standard.

Review Questions

1. Give some examples of social judgments about language use. How are these different from linguistic judgments?
2. Define these terms: hypercorrection, isogloss, regionalism, epithet, intensifier, euphemism.
3. Describe the nature of Standard English. What is the opposite of S.E.?
4. What six types of dialect are discussed in this chapter? Why are they dialects?
5. Who compiled the linguistic atlases? What are they for? How are they compiled? Once compiled, what do they tell us?
6. What is dialect leveling? Why does it occur?
7. What is jargon? How is it related to slang, the fog index, and buzz words?
8. How is Black English different from Standard English?
9. How is women's speech different from men's?
10. What are the five registers? In what circumstances might each one be used?

Selected Reading

Abrahams, Roger D. *Talking Black*. Rowley, Mass.: Newbury House, 1975.

Allen, Harold B. *The Linguistic Atlas of the Upper Midwest*. 2 vols. Minneapolis: University of Minnesota Press, 1971-74.

————, and Gary N. Underwood, eds. *Readings in American Dialectology*. New York: Appleton-Century-Crofts, 1971.

Atwood, E. Bagby. *The Regional Vocabulary of Texas*. Austin: University of Texas Press, 1962.

Babcock, C. Merton, ed. *The Ordeal of American English*. Boston: Houghton Mifflin Co., 1961.

Bowen, J. Donald, and Jacob Ornstein, eds. *Studies in Southwest Spanish*. Rowley, Mass.: Newbury House, 1976.

Bright, Elizabeth S. *Word Geography of California and Nevada*. Berkeley: University of California Press, 1971.

Bryant, Margaret M., ed. *Current American Usage.* New York: Funk and Wagnalls, 1962.

Craigie, Sir William A., and J. R. Hulbert, eds. *Dictionary of American English on Historical Principles.* 4 vols. Chicago: University of Chicago Press, 1938–44.

Dillard, J. L. *Black English.* New York: Random House, 1972.

Fishman, Joshua. *Sociolinguistics.* Rowley, Mass.: Newbury House, 1971.

Gumperz, John J. *Language in Social Groups.* Stanford, Calif.: Stanford University Press, 1971.

Hernandez-Chavez, Eduardo, Andrew D. Cohen, and Anthony F. Beltramo, eds. *El Lenguaje de los Chicanos: Regional and Social Characteristics of Language Use by Mexican-Americans.* Arlington, Va.: Center for Applied Linguistics, 1975.

Hymes, Dell. *Foundations in Sociolinguistics.* Philadelphia: University of Pennsylvania Press, 1974.

Joos, Martin. *The Five Clocks.* New York: Harcourt Brace Jovanovich, 1961.

Kurath, Hans. *A Word Geography of the Eastern United States.* Ann Arbor: University of Michigan Press, 1949.

Labov, William. *The Social Stratification of English in New York City.* Arlington, Va.: Center for Applied Linguistics, 1966.

―――. *Sociolinguistic Patterns.* Philadelphia: University of Pennsylvania Press, 1972.

―――. *The Study of Nonstandard English.* Urbana, Ill.: National Council of Teachers of English, 1970.

Leonard, Sterling A. *The Doctrine of Correctness in English Usage.* New York: Russell and Russell, 1962.

Marckwardt, Albert H. *American English.* New York: Oxford University Press, 1958.

McKnight, George H. *The Evolution of the English Language.* New York: Dover Books, 1968.

Mencken, H. L. *The American Language,* 4th ed. New York: Alfred A. Knopf, 1948. Abridged ed.: Knopf, 1963.

Mitford, Mathews M. *The Beginnings of American English.* Chicago: University of Chicago Press, 1961.

Reed, Carroll E. *Dialects of American English.* Cleveland: The World Publishing Company, 1967.

Robertson, Stuart, and Frederick G. Cassidy. *The Development of Modern English.* Englewood Cliffs, N.J.: Prentice-Hall, Inc., 1969.

Shores, David L., ed. *Contemporary English: Change and Variations.* Philadelphia: J. B. Lippincott and Company, 1972.

Shuy, Roger W. *Discovering American Dialects.* Urbana, Ill.: National Council of Teachers of English, 1967.

Stewart, George R. *American Place-Names*. New York: Oxford University Press, 1970.

Teschner, Richard V., Garland Bills, and Jerry Craddock, eds. *Spanish and English of United States Hispanos*. Arlington, Va.: Center for Applied Linguistics, 1975.

Trudgill, Peter. *Sociolinguistics: An Introduction*. Baltimore: Penguin Books, 1974.

Wentworth, Harold, and Stuart Berg Flexner, eds. *Dictionary of American Slang*. New York: Thomas Y. Crowell Co., 1960.

Williamson, Juanita V., and Virginia M. Burke, eds. *A Various Language: Perspectives on American Dialects*. New York: Holt, Rinehart and Winston, 1971.

Wolfram, Walt, and Ralph W. Fasold. *The Study of Social Dialects in American English*. Englewood Cliffs, N.J.: Prentice-Hall, Inc., 1974.

Journals   *American Speech; Dialect Notes; The English Journal; The Florida FL Reporter; Journal of Social Issues; Language; Publications of the American Dialect Society; Quarterly Journal of Speech*

9
The Meanings of Language

It is often assumed that everyone knows of what meaning consists, and in terms of most ordinary, day-by-day language use, nearly everyone probably does. Any speaker of English can use the language. Few of us need to think about "meaning" except in very practical terms: Do I use this word or that? If I memorize a large vocabulary, will I get a better job? What do I need to remember to pass the test? Which meaning of a particular word do I intend to use in this or that context? In these practical senses, "meaning" is seen more or less as a thing, attached to a word like a tail to kite, or perhaps as the thing-itself, meaning (tail) and word (kite) all being one unit. To know the word, then, is to know the meaning, and that's all there is to the problem.

But is it? As with much else about the workings of language, when we look beyond our assumptions, we discover that the issue is more complex. Indeed, it is so difficult to resolve the question of meaning, or even to determine the natures of "meaning", that many linguists have refused to deal with it at all. In the late nineteenth and early twentieth centuries, when language study was first becoming scientific (first turning into linguistics), nearly all of the new science's adherents simply banished meaning from their investigation because they felt so much nonsense had been written about it. They wanted, appropriately enough, to study what could be investigated more objectively: sounds, forms, syntax, historical and regional variations, comparative patterns, and so on. Other language students continued to study meaning from a semantic perspective, not always in the cautious way that suited linguists. The rest of us just kept on keeping on, dealing with the complexities of meaning in the same old pragmatic ways.

Then, in the middle 1960s, it began to be linguistically respectable to grapple with meaning again. Research in Structural and Transformational grammar, in psycholinguistics, in semantics and pragmatics—all of which we shall review in the chapter—is making ever clearer the probability that meaning resides in the brain. The brain itself can deal with the many different meanings of "meaning," but we cannot yet analyze in detail all that the brain does, so our studies of meaning thus far are necessarily limited by what we do not yet know about neurophysiology. But we have more information now than we did fifty years ago about how meaning works, neurologically, psychologically, culturally, and linguistically.

We shall deal in this chapter with three basic questions, knowing that the answers offered are tentative: Where is "meaning" located? What kinds of "meaning" are there? How is "meaning" controlled? We shall approach each of these questions from several perspectives, using whichever one or more seems appropriate: general linguistics (historical, comparative, structural, or psycholinguistics), Structural and TG grammar, psychology, philosophy, and general semantics.

A Review

But first we should review three important characteristics of language that have a bearing on all questions about meaning. First, language is cultural, a spoken medium that exists only in so far as it is used by its speakers. Second, language changes in systematic ways, phonologically, morphologically, syntactically, and semantically; but the changes are usually so gradual, and the received traditions of past usage so strong, that the alterations are not always apparent while they are taking place. Third, and most important, language is symbolic on all of its levels in arbitrary and conventional ways. There is no innate, inherent, "natural" connection between a language pattern, like a word, and the meaning(s) that pattern symbolizes. The connections, whatever they are, between language form and meaning are shaped by custom or convention and by an altogether arbitrary association of ideas with sounds, forms, and structures.

Speakers are both aware and unaware of these linguistic universals. The two antithetical conditions exist side by side; they do not cancel each other out. Speakers are aware of language change, the arbitrary nature of language, and so forth in this sense: users of language can adapt to change, functioning perfectly well in millions of speech situations calling for the manipulation of arbitrary sounds and symbols, because they have stored in their brains billions and billions of information bits about language. All speakers have this linguistic competence first mentioned in chapter 6: the retrievable data that allow human beings to speak. In that sense, all speakers are aware of the complexities of language, because they deal quite competently with those complexities every single day.

But not every speaker uses the stored information as well as every other speaker. We all have pretty much the same data, but we do not all retrieve it and put it into practice in the same way or with the same skill. That is, our linguistic performance is not uniform. And it is in the area of linguistic performance, actual speech situations, where most of us are least aware of how language works: we can do it, but we often have difficulty analyzing what we are doing or why we do it. That analytical gap may also account for the difference in our performance, for why some people seem to be more fluent or more sensitive to nuances of language use than other people are. It may not be that the first group has more language (is more competent), but rather that the first group pays more careful attention to the conscious use (performance) of the linguistic data that we all have.

As we try to answer the three questions about meaning, much of our discourse will consist of attempts to bring up to the surface that stored, unconscious, usually unexamined pool of shared knowledge. But it is extremely difficult to evaluate clearly the environment that one is right in the middle of and takes for granted: difficult to see forest for trees, to think about thinking, to talk about talking. As a result, perhaps any solution of the problems that arise when we try to be thorough and conscientious about the locations, kinds, and control of meaning will have to remain tentative.

Locus of Meaning

It bears repeating here that meaning is *not* located in the external universe but in the connections human beings make between the outside world and whatever is inside their own heads. The objects in the universe have no meaning: human beings give meaning to them. We must reject, again, the naturalistic/notionalist approach and recognize that the ultimate

location of meaning is in the human brain. This object figure

9.1 (not the drawing, but the thing-itself), taken of itself and without fitting it into long established patterns of competence (without immediately identifying it as "tree"), has no meaning whatsoever. It is only when we name it, drawing our competence data up to a conscious level (even if we do not utter the name, that is, do not perform), that the object assumes meaning.

But most of our awareness of meaning, and all of our conscious performance of language acts, involves a connection of the external universe with the internal one. Meaning and language are so interconnected so much of the time that the temptation is strong to identify "meaning" with language itself. The word "tree" *means* that object, or some specific representative of it, does it not? Or the word *arbor* in Latin, *arbe* in French, *arbol* in Spanish, *Baum* in German, and so on? The answer is both Yes and No. Yes, all those words *refer to* the object; but no, they do not *mean* the object. Just as the object has no meaning, neither does the word, except the meaning that human beings attach to both. The point is troublesome but important: meaning exists as a mixture of three entities, object, word-referring-to-object, and connection-of-object-and-word. This connection exists, not in the thing and not in the word, but in the brain.

We have seen already that phonemes have no meaning: /t/, /r/, and /i/ are just sounds. The same is true of most morphophonemes, morphemes, and syllables, although some linguists speculate that there may be a kind of connection in English between certain vowel sounds and basic concepts of size or mass. In English, a stressed *schwa* /ə/—the mid-central vowel—is often associated with "heavy" words like "lump," "bump," "thump"; by contrast, the high-central /i/ often appears in words suggesting smallness: "teeny," "eenie, meenie," "wee." This connection of sound with meaning—a very faint connection indeed—has been called a phonestheme, but there is no suggestion that phonesthemes form the bulk of meanings in English or in any other language. Sound-sense correlations are arbitrary. So are sound-form correlations. The inflectional morphophoneme {ed} refers to the past tense in English, or it signals past tense, or it cues us to recognize the presence of past tense, but it does not *mean* past tense. Speakers indicate the meaning "past tense" when they use that {ed} construction, or its allomorphs {t} and {< >} (spelling change, as in "do"/"did").

Meaning resides in the minds of speakers, then, not in words, syllables, morphemes, or phonemes, and not in the objects to which those language patterns refer. But speakers use words, all the time, in such a way that the words *seem* to have an independent meaning, *seem* to exist as little meaning units all by themselves, without any need for speakers to go around pointing to objects. We are so competent in our grasp of the connections between reference, words, and idea-about-both that we often fail to recognize just how arbitrary these connections are. Ordinary usage of the word "meaning" strongly implies that meaning belongs to the word and is contained in the dictionary. But it is not. The dictionary lists connections that people make among objects, letters (and sounds), and their own brains.

Occasionally two speakers will not have the same connections in mind when they use the same word. Then trouble arises, "noise," confusion. Most of these differences of usage can be worked out on the spot: if I have said to a friend, "You should be more assertive," and her answer is a horrified, "Oh, no, I don't like being rude!" then we can easily clear up the matter by specifying the meaning intended for "assertive" or by acting out the difference between assertion and rudeness or aggression. More complicated or more hidden variances will require more subtle solutions, of course, as we shall see in later sections. The point here is that the variance in connections does not arise from any difference in the word "assertion"—it has the same phonemic and morphemic structure, the same syntactic function, and basically the same denotations when I use it as when my friend does—but rather from a difference in the minds of the speakers.

Words have meanings because human beings attach meanings to words. They do this attaching so often, so regularly, so consistently that the meaning becomes (in the speakers' minds) identified with the word. Such consistency is necessary, else two speakers could not talk with each other for very long; and most words have been so long identified with their meaning-connections that the problem of variable meaning does not arise. Most of the time, it is sufficient to behave as we usually do anyway, performing our speech activities as though words had meaning and a life or force of their own.

Tradition, precedence, history are such powerful forces for continuity that one individual's idiolect rarely makes a widespread impact on the course of language use. Change in language practices comes about because of collective action by many speakers, and when we discuss these changes (as in chapters 5–7), we are actually describing the gradual alteration, over centuries, of millions of speakers' behavior (performance) in using language data stored in their minds.

Kinds of Meaning

We have identified two kinds of meaning already: referential meaning, wherein a word refers to an object in the external universe, and "common," "traditional," "precedential" meaning (the collective associations that allow most speakers to converse comfortably with other speakers most of the time). In earlier chapters, we have referred to still other kinds of meaning, chiefly lexical and lexicostructural, which we will examine in more detail here.

Lexical. In chapter 5, we spoke of lexical versus syntactic meaning, the first having more referential significance than the second. Syntactic or morphophonemic meanings belong to the closed class of nonreferential "traffic directors" like inflections and operators, whereas lexical meanings belong to the open classes of referential nouns or verbs, adjectives or adverbs. We can point to a "cat," we can point out an example of "run," we can point to or demonstrate something that is "tasty" or "slow" or "abruptly"; but we cannot point to an example of "and" or "a" (not the *words* <and> or <a>, but the ideas). We need the words with morphophonemic meaning to make sense of past and present, conjunction and division, spatial relationships and plurality; but it is in the set of lexically meaningful words where most of our interest lies now.

Within that set, as we have also mentioned in chapter 5, lexical meaning is further commonly divided into denotative and connotative meanings. A word's denotations are the "common," "traditional," "precedential" ones referred to above. Denotations are usually the result of centuries of usage; they show up in the dictionary and change very slowly. Connotations, on the other hand, are the emotional responses, often quite personalized, that most lexical words arouse in most users. It is connotation, rather than denotation, that separates "slim" from "thin," "stout" from "fat," "rude" from "aggressive," and "aggressive" from "assertive." Each word in those paired sets carries essentially the same denotation, but the words prompt different responses because of the connotations each has acquired. But even these connotations are still fairly collective. Most people would agree that "slim," for example, is desirable, whereas "thin" suggests scrawniness.

Some words, however, acquire personalized connotations so different from the collective associations that users of these words have to make an effort to connect with the rest of us. If "fly" (verb) has become associated in a speaker's mind only with fear, then that person will likely not appreciate some of the more pleasant connotations of "fly": freedom, vantage point, control, and so on. Similarly, words like "boy" or "girl" are denotatively only descriptions of gender and age; their collective connotations are usually rather pleasant (youth, childhood, happy days); but some specialized connotations, of immaturity and dependence and not-too-brightness, have made these words very unpleasant when they are applied to adults. In the next chapter, we will have more to say on the manipulation of such connotations.

Literal and figurative meanings are related, respectively, to denotation and connotation but are not identical with them. A literal meaning is referential and as accurately descriptive as possible, "descriptive" in the neutral sense as the opposite of "prescriptive": just the facts, without any embroidery. "Machine," for example, literally refers to a mechanical construction, usually of metal and/or plastic, with wheels and levers and blades and whatnot, designed to extend human beings' control over the universe. There are machines that thresh wheat, machines that type, machines that permit me to converse with someone many miles away. If I call a human being a "machine," however, I am using the word figuratively. I am attributing machinelike qualities to that person, characterizing his or her behavior, but I am not intending to suggest literal wheels, levers, blades, and metal.

Figurative language nearly always has a flavor of comparison about it, of pointing out likeness or similarity rather than pure-fact information. Someone using figurative language—which we all do—is drawing attention to the similarities between two referents (such as the psychological traits of rigidity and unimaginativeness which are like the hardness of metal). But figurative language also points, indirectly, to the differences between the compared referents: if a machine literally were the same as a person, we would not be struck by the comparison.

Particular kinds of figurative comparisons, often referred to as "poetic language," are the simile and the metaphor. In a simile, the act of comparing is quite clear because we use the words "like" or "as" to signal what we are doing: we say, "She is machinelike" or "She is like a machine," or "She is as stubborn as a mule" or "as hard as a rock." Metaphors compare, too, but more subtly, for they leave out the signal words. A metaphor can appear as an "is"-statement ("No man is an island"; "My love is a rose"), as a name or name substitute ("You pig!"; "Don't be ridiculous"), or, most commonly, as apparently ordinary words serving various functions: "*grasp* the subject" (verb), "*dead* of night" (noun), "*flashing* imagery" (adjective). Some students of language have suggested that nearly all of our lexical-meaning words are metaphors in one form or another. They propose that language at the lexical level is, metaphorically speaking, nothing but a tissue of these kinds of comparisons.

Semantic features. The habit of association is so strongly embedded in our lexical use of language that some TG grammarians identify association with lexical insertion. That is, they suggest that once we have unconsciously run through the phrase-structure rules and the singulary and recursive transformations, we bring the deep structure up to the surface by selecting words—making lexical insertions—whose associations will fit that syntactic structure. How do we know they will fit? Because our competence in language use has acquainted us with countless categories of relatedness among words. Those categories are not definitions of meaning, but clusters of qualities. For example, words that name colors must be attached to words referring to things that can be colored: red scarf, brown barn, gray lizard. Neither we nor our language can conceive of a "colorless red object." Similarly, if you overhear part of someone's comment, " . . . wet the carpet," you know, because "wet" has certain qualities, that a plant could have done the wetting, or a broken rug-shampooer, or someone spilling a drink. Baking soda, however, would not have produced the effect of wetness. If you overhear " . . . wet on the carpet," the word <on> further restricts the quality clustering and tells you that the agent must be a puppy or perhaps a child.

"Semantic features" (or "properties") is the phrase by which some linguists describe the quality clustering that limits what kind of word will go with what other kinds of words. TG grammarians use lists of such features, for example, to specify which kinds of nouns can serve as subjects with which kinds of verbs (as with " . . . wet the carpet"). Those lists are called feature matrixes (or matrices). Semantic features may be very broad categories ([± human], [± count], [± goal])[1] or very narrow ("changing from motion to rest" [+ settle], "made up of squares and stripes in a particular pattern" [+ plaid]). Obviously, the narrower the restrictions of the features, the closer the features get to dictionary-type definitions. Let us look

1. See chapter 5.

here, however, at three of the broader types of semantic features: [±
human], [± count], and [± goal].

The feature [+ human] includes not only all the varieties of *Homo sapiens*
(boy, girl, man, woman, Australian, Indonesian, actress, philospher, etc.),
but also any quality that belongs only to human beings, not to other living
creatures. A goldfish is not human, but swimming is; a ewe is not human, but
femaleness is; a puppy is not human, but infancy is. We would distinguish
"puppy" from "cherub," then, on the basis of the feature "humanness."
[+ Count], the opposite of the feature [+ mass], indicates the quality of
being individuated, separated into distinct units, as opposed to something
like flour, which is dealt with in a bundle (a cup, a gram, a mass of some
sort). Horses have the [+ count] feature, but a herd of horses does not; a
herd is [− count] or [+ mass]. Human beings are countable, but humanity is
not; lyrics can be counted, but lyrical cannot. Americans tend to favor
[− count/+ mass] abstract nouns, whereas the British usually prefer [+
count] qualities for the same nouns. Where Americans say "the government
is" (one inseparable body: [+ mass]), the British say "the government are"
(separable, plural, acting collectively: [+ count]). [+ Goal] as a feature is
more commonly attached to verbs than to nouns; it distinguishes "depart"
from "arrive," for the goal has not yet been attained in the first word, but
has in the second. "Reach" is like "depart," in that the goal feature is still
imminent, whereas "grasp" is like "arrive": the goal has been attained.

Field analysis. Use of semantic features like [± human], [± count], and
[± goal] gives us ways of distinguishing one lexical-meaning word from
another, or one type of lexical-meaning word from another type. An even
wider-ranging technique, called field analysis, permits us to distinguish relationships among entire classes of words. The most common field relationships are demonstrated by homonyms, antonyms, and synonyms.

Homonyms. Homonyms, also called homophones, share the same field of
sound. They are words whose phonemes are identical, but whose references
are dissimilar: /bɛr/ can be "bare" (uncovered) or "bear" (animal) or
"bear" (carry). Is /pil/ referring to "peel" (strip) or to "peal" (sound)? Do
you eat /flawər/ or wear it? Is /grawnd/ what you walk on, what you base
evidence of suspicion on, or an action of grinding completed in the past?
Spelling will not always help, especially in casual speech: for many people,
there is no phonetic difference between /wɛðər/ "weather" and /wɛðər/
"whether," nor between /wɪč/ "witch" and /wɪč/ "which," nor between
/wai/ "why" (interrogation: Why now?) and /wai/ (exclamation: Why, you
dirty dog!).[2] Context, in all of these cases, has to distinguish between the

---

2. Other speakers do make a phonemic distinction between the plosive and the nonplosive
forms: /wɛðər/ versus /hwɛðər/, /wɪč/ versus /hwɪč/, /hwai/ versus /wai/.

homophonic words; without such a context of surrounding words, the homophone's reference may be unclear. The statement "Jaqueline can't bear children" could mean either she cannot tolerate their presence or she cannot become pregnant (or possibly she is too weak to lift them).

Antonyms. Antonyms are words that have opposite meanings. If word A can be replaced by word Not-A (its opposite in meaning), then the two are called antonyms. The simplest kind of antonym is that of "not"-ness: "bad" equals "not good"; "short" equals "not tall"; "poor" equals "not rich." Most antonyms of this sort have a very generalized referential meaning. The relationship between such A/Not-A pairs is purely two-valued, also called complementary or dichotomous, with no degrees in between A and Not-A. Other antonyms are equally dichotomous but use different words to set up their opposition, rather than the A/Not-A construction. For example, the opposite of "dead" is "alive" (as well as "not dead"); the opposite of "up" is "down"; "front" is the opposite of "back"; and so on.

But the majority of antonymic relationships are not simply complementary or dichotomous; rather, they are gradable and show degrees of opposition. For example, the simple opposite (complement) of "hot" is "cold," but what about "warm," "lukewarm," "chilly," and "freezing"? The opposite of "young" is its complement "old," but there are degrees of "young" ("youthful," "infantile," "puerile," "childish," "babyish") and of "old" ("mature," "middle-aged," "ancient," "decrepit," "antique").

Many of these gradable antonyms show the phenomenon called marking. One of the words in the antonymic set is the preferred or standard, normative, or unmarked form; the other, non-standard form is the marked one. In the pair "wide"/"narrow," the unmarked form is "wide"; we ordinarily do not ask how narrow a room is, but how wide. Similarly, we ask, "How big is it?" not how small it is; how tall someone is, not how short; how high something is, not how low. In terms where masculine and feminine are paired as features, the masculine form is the unmarked, preferred one: "mankind," "chairman," "he."

Antonyms appear in other forms besides complements and gradable sets. There are reciprocal antonyms, like "buy"/"sell," which are opposite in meaning but are also connected functionally: I sell to you, you buy from me. There are relational antonyms, like "employer"/"employee" (and all "-er"/"-ee" words), wherein the "-er" person is the dominant or superior of the "-ee" person: the "-er"/does; the "-ee" is done to. Contraries frequently overlap: "wet" equals "not dry" and is the opposite of "dry," but there are degrees in between the two antonyms: "damp," "moist," and so on. Contrariety also appears in gradations, for how big is a "large" mouse in comparison with a "small" cat? If you mix the color orange by combining red and yellow, then how do you know when you no longer have separate red and separate yellow?

Finally, there is a special kind of antonymy, quite important in scientific nomenclature and in semantic analysis, called hyponymy. Here, one of the paired words is not exactly the opposite of the other (or of the gradable words in between); rather, one includes the other. "Vertebrate" includes fish, reptile, and mammal; "building" includes skyscraper, mansion, house, fire station; "work" includes job, chore, duty, task, construction, painting, and music. The hyponymous, includer term is always more general, less referential, than the other terms.

Synonyms. Like antonyms, most synonyms work on the principle of replaceability, but where antonyms call for the replacement by opposites, synonyms call for the substitution of words very close in meaning to the original. This replacement is probably never one of exact identity (that is, as is often stated, there are probably no exact synonyms), but the connection can be very close indeed. A proper name and its pronoun are as close to identity as may be possible, as in "Marlo Thomas" and a pronoun-noun form, "that girl." Similarly close are the various regional-dialectic terms for identical referents: couch/sofa/davenport, bureau/chest of drawers/chesterfield/chiffarobe, night crawlers/fishing worms/wigglers.

Most synonyms, however, are near but not identical replacements for one another. The closeness of synonymy depends on the number of semantic features shared by the two words. "Curtain" and "drape" are closer synonyms than "curtain" and "shade," for example, because "drape" shares with "curtain"—but not with "shade"—the semantic features [+ loose] and [+ cloth]. But "shade" and "blind" are closer synonyms than "shade" and "curtain," because "shade" and "blind" share the feature [+ comparative rigidity]. The hyponym for all of these terms is "window covering," and if we wished, we could include in the hyponymic set such other window coverings as awnings, reed mats, or shutters.

A thesaurus, or dictionary of synonyms, will list hundreds of such close replacements, like this entry for "exciting": "impressive, telling, warm, glowing, fervid, spirit-stirring, thrilling; soul-stirring, heart-stirring, agonizing, sensational, yellow [*colloq.*], melodramatic, hysterical; overpowering, overwhelming."[3] With such a list as that, how can you tell which of the many synonyms would be appropriate? Context is the answer: In what kind of utterance are you going to use the word? For example, the colloquialism "yellow" to mean excited cannot be used in any other context but journalism ("yellow journalism" means sensational, high-pitched, melodramatic news writing). If you call a person "yellow," you will be delivering an insult to his or her courage, not identifying that person as excitable: "yellow" has

3. C. O. S. Mawson, ed., *Roget's Pocket Thesaurus* (New York: Pocket Books, Inc., 1946), p. 244.

the feature [+ excited] in only one context. Similarly, a story can be impressive, spirit-stirring, or melodramatic, but not hysterical; "hysterical" carries with it the feature [+ human] or at least [+ animate].

As we have already observed, almost every lexical word in English has developed connotations that serve as distinguishing semantic features. Connotations, together with the field analysis of context, will nearly always help sort out one synonym from another. "Warm" and "glowing," for instance, have generally good connotations, whereas "melodramatic" and "hysterical" have generally bad ones. "Fervid" and "agonizing" carry the feature [+ belonging to the doer], whereas "thrilling" and "overpowering" feature the quality [+ belonging to the receiver]. One can speak of a fervid reader or writer, for example, but the effect of a book is not fervid; the effect is overpowering or thrilling.

Ambiguity. When confronted with words that carry multiple meanings, as most words do, one may also run into the problem of ambiguity. An ambiguous word or construction is one whose meaning is not clear for any of three reasons: because the word is homophonic with another word, like /bɛr/ on p. 138; or because one meaning rather than another of a polysemous (multiple-meaning) word is being exploited, like "assertive" on p. 134; or because the word's syntactic function is not specified. Homophonic ambiguity has already been dealt with; let us turn to polysemantic and syntactic ambiguity here.

Consider some simple ambiguities arising from confusion about which feature of a polysemous word is intended in these sentences: "She appealed to him"; "I can do this in an hour"; "Going to the beach is like going to the attic: you are always surprised at what you find in trunks." In the first sentence, the problem is with the word "appealed": does it refer to her action (she made a plea to him) or to his response (he liked her)? In the second, the word "in" is not clear: does it include the hour (I will be able to get to this after I spend an hour on something else), or does it indicate an hour as the outer limit of time (I will have this finished within an hour)? In the third sentence, "trunks" is the culprit—or the source of the wit in the simile—for the trunks one finds in attics are not at all like the trunks one finds at beaches (nor are the contents). The third ambiguous sentence was intentionally so, as most puns are, but the first two probably were not. To clarify the ambiguity in those two, the speakers need to rephrase their sentences so that the features they had in mind are dominant.

The same uncertain dominance of features is true of more complicated polysematic ambiguities, where the lack of clarity does not lie in a single word but in the combinations of words. Syntactic ambiguity, arising from word combinations, appears in several versions, most particularly in two forms. When the function of a word or phrase is not clear, the result is class, or function, ambiguity. When modifiers, especially adjectives, are strung together in such a way that it is difficult to tell which word modifies which, modifier ambiguity is the result.

Class, or function, ambiguity shows in such sentences as these:[4] "You will forget tomorrow"; "Fred looked over her bare shoulder"; "The enormous gorilla back of Walter ambled out the door." In the first sentence, it is not clear whether "tomorrow" is functioning as a member of the class of adverbs or as a member of the class of nouns. If "tomorrow" is an adverb, then the sentence can be paraphrased, or restated in synonymous but clearer terms, like this: "By tomorrow, you will forget." If "tomorrow" is a noun, however, it is functioning as the name of that-which-you-will-forget, like the sentence "You will forget me." Here, the paraphrase might be something like this: "Tomorrow is going to be an awful day, but you will get through it, and then you can put it out of your mind."

In the second sentence, the problem word is "over." Is it classed as a preposition, so she is standing in front of him and he is looking past her shoulder; or is it a particle and part of the verb phrase, as he leers at her shoulder? The ambiguous class word in the third sentence is "back." If it is a noun, then Walter's very large back is leaving, with or without the rest of Walter; but if "back" is a preposition, then a gorilla has been standing behind Walter.

Especially troublesome in English, because of our word-order (analytic) syntax, are modifier ambiguities. In the linear structure of an English sentence, modifiers customarily appear right next to whatever they modify. This linear positioning causes no problem as long as there are only a few modifiers whose semantic features clearly combine only with the noun: "*the green* apple," "*beautiful dappled* mares," "*shiny white* plastic." The plastic is both shiny and white, for instance, and if the whiteness is also shiny (if "shiny" modifies both "plastic" and "white"), there is no real confusion about the meaning of the phrase.

But how about the modifier—in this case, an adverb construction—in the sentence "She sang, danced, and tumbled very expertly"? Is she expert only at tumbling or at all three activities? Does the adverb modify one or all three of the verbs? In the sentence "Nelson was a champion cow owner," what is "champion" modifying, Nelson or the cow? "Give me the dark brown sugar bowl" does not make clear whether the bowl is dark brown (and the sugar any color) or the sugar is dark brown (in a bowl of any color).

Present participles, which function partly as verbs and partly as adjectives, can often cause syntactic ambiguity of a particularly subtle type, as in

4. Examples from Norman C. Stageberg, "Ambiguity in College Writing," in *Introductory Readings on Language,* 4th ed., Wallace L. Anderson and Norman C. Stageberg, eds. (New York: Holt, Rinehart and Winston, Inc., 1975), p. 314.

this sentence: "My job was keeping him alive." What is the relationship between "job" (noun), "keeping" (participle), and "him" (pronoun)? Read one way, this sentence paraphrases as: "It was my job to keep him alive" (I am a doctor, say, and "job" and "keeping" refer to the same concept). Read another way, however, the paraphrase becomes "Only my job kept him from starving" (he needed my income, and the connection here is between "was" and "keeping"). In the first version, "keeping" is functioning like a noun, the name of the job; in the second, it is part of the verb phrase "was keeping."

You will have noted, in this section on field analysis, how often two concepts or techniques have come up in our discussion of homonyms, antonyms, synonyms, and ambiguity. One is paraphrase; the other, context. Both are techniques for discovering the relationships of meanings among two or more words, and both require that the word or construction be tested in terms of its feasible connections, lexical or syntactic, with other words. Relationship or connection is the key here, for although nearly every word has a kind of self-contained set of associations that belong to the word regardless of how it is used, nevertheless, most words do not exist in isolation. Speakers string words together, and hearers sort out the several meanings from the string: that multiplicity of word groupings constitutes the vast majority of language use.

The influence that words exert on each other when they are combined in linear strings is bound to be even more complicated than the patterns we have already observed. In a string of words, all of the isolated associations and fields of influences are combining, not in a simple $1 + 1 + 1 \ldots$ fashion (word A influences the next word, B, which connects with the third in the string, C, and so on), but in a more dispersed way. When words combine, each word has some influence over every other word in the string (A on B, C, D; B on A, C, D; C on A, B, D; and so on). Furthermore, the syntactic function and the position of each word produce influences of their own as well.

Lexicostructural meanings. In an analysis of these multiple relationships, we move into a middle area between lexicon and syntax. Rather like morphophonemes (part sound, part form), this area of lexicostructural meaning is where structure begins to have lexical implications and vice versa. Lexical context, as with the word "yellow" on p. 140, begins to merge with syntactic context, as with the "trunks" sentence on p. 141. We will therefore have to extend our field analysis to include words-in-combinations in order to understand the kinds and the locations of meaning. Three lexicostructural combinations will be examined here: associative fields, collocations, and deep-structure syntax.

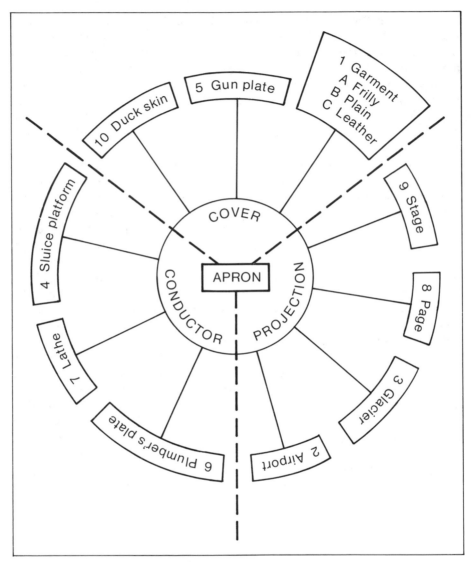

Figure 9.2   Associative Field of "Apron"

Associative fields. The simplest of these word combinations are the associative fields set up by a single word with many referents. Essentially, this is the same grouping we saw in radiation (etymology, chapter 5), but the idea here is not so much change in meaning over time as, rather, multiplicity of connotations or references. This abundance of association cannot always be limited and clarified unless the word is placed in a particular context.

For example, all of the references of the word "apron" are marked by the semantic feature [+ attached to and /or extending beyond], but the associative field dispersing out from that feature includes many different object-referents. Probably the most common referent is the garment worn over one's clothes to protect them from spatters, but there are ruffled hostess aprons worn by women, some of the garments going over the shoulders and some only from the waist; there are plain cooking aprons of various materials, some used by men (e.g., canvas or duck cloth); and there are rubber-coated laboratory aprons or leather shop aprons worn by either gender. Even the most common meaning, then, disperses into a subfield of at least three referents.

We may call these #1-A (frilly), #1-B (plain), and #1-C (rubber or leather). In addition, there are at least nine other referents for "apron":

2. A packed, paved strip around airport hangers and terminals.
3. An area covered by sand and gravel deposited in front of a glacial moraine.
4. A platform placed at the bottom of a sluice or the entrance to a dock, so as to intercept the flow of water and prevent a digout of the bottom.
5. A square piece of lead laid over the touchhole of a large gun.
6. A strip of lead that plumbers position so as to conduct the drip of a wall into a gutter.
7. The part of a lathe that controls the rate of feed.
8. The blank part of a printed foldout in which text and illustration stick out beyond the edge of the book.
9. The part of the stage that projects beyond the edge of the curtain when the curtain is down.
10. The skin covering the belly of a duck or a goose, which is cut to get at the stuffing.

See figure 9.2 for an illustration of the associative field for "apron." Each of the ten referents is located within one of three general features: [+ cover], [+ conductor], or [+ projection]. It is possible to set up such fields for any number of words with more or less concrete references: "horn," "table," "bag," and so on. Unless one wants to conjure up all the referents in the associative field when one uses a word like "apron," one must collocate the word with other terms that limit that field.

Collocation. A second kind of lexicostructural combination is called collocation. A collocation is close to a cliché, but not quite identical. (A cliché is a stock expression, shopworn and overused, frequently derived from a metaphor or simile: "hotter than hell" or "than the hinges of Hades," "a pig in a poke," "warm as toast," "snug as a bug," etc.) Collocations are based on an arbitrary association of one word with another, for no connotative or other associational reason at all. For example, one "*does* one's duty," but one "*performs* good works," "*builds* a skyscraper" (or a nation or a career), and "*produces* a show" (or a masterpiece or a soufflé). All of the italicized words have the same general denotation and much the same connotations, but they cannot be used interchangeably with the various contexts. Something in our stored data about language use, our competence, insists that good works are performed, not produced. Those two concepts collocate with one another and do not ordinarily allow replacement of one element by another.

An even more rigid collocative construction appears in idioms; word groups that make conventional sense only if taken as a whole. You cannot work out the meaning of an idiom by adding up each word's individual meaning(s) and totaling the whole. (That is why idioms are extremely difficult to translate from one language to another.) "How are you?" is a modified S.E. idiom—modified by pitch and register—because most of the time, its users know that it is not to be taken literally, but more like an expanded version of "Hello." B.E.'s "What's happ'nin', baby?" is the same kind of construction: one does not run through a list of the day's news items in response to that greeting. Most true idioms have a metaphor, long since dead, as their foundation: "eat your words," "carry a torch (for)," "cut it out," "snap out of it." No longer, if ever, are such expressions to be taken in any but a figurative way—no forlorn lover literally burns a torch at the altar of his lost lady's image—but their idiomatic meaning rests on the whole expression, not on the individual words.

Deep-structure syntax. Finally, there are some combinations from deep-structure syntax which are structurally rather than lexically connected with one another (chapter 6). It appears that at some levels, syntax itself, without regard to semantics, may shape meaning. One example of this kind of influencing appears in the different surface structures that result from different transformations of the same terminal string, as we saw in chapter 6. "The police chased the suspect" emphasizes the action of the police, but a passive transformation—"The suspect was chased by the police"—emphasizes the suspect and the action being taken upon him. The two surface structures mean two different things. So do these two: "I can do that."/"Can I do that?" The first is an affirmative, declarative statement, connoting self-confidence and self-assurance. The second is hesitant, possibly doubtful (Can I really pull that off?), possibly an implicit, polite, tentative command (Will you let me do that, please!), or possibly a request for information (Do you think that I am capable of doing that?). The second sentences in each of these pairs—the negative and the question—are radically different from the first sentences, not because the lexicon has changed, but because the syntax has been manipulated, resulting in an alteration of meaning.

A second and more complicated way in which deep structure seems to limit lexicon occurs when syntactic structures restrict semantic features. For example, if a deep structure reads *N t V-t N N,* that first noun has to refer to something alive (it has to be an animate noun, in TG jargon) or at least to something capable of producing activity. Such a structure will not allow, in English, a surface structure like "Rocks showed me dandelions," because rocks [− animate] cannot conjoin as subjects with [+ animate] verbs, such as "show." But the *N t V-t N N* string will permit "Cheese gave him heartburn." Immediately, however, we are confronted by a question: Does the permission or allowance of associations—rocks showing, no; cheese giving, yes—lie in the syntax, that is, in the deep structure itself, or does it lie in the lexicon and the lexical relationship of one word to another word? Is it the construction *N t V-t N N* that limits whether rocks can show and cheese can give, or is it the lexical combinations of "rocks" and "showing," "cheese" and "giving" that do the limiting? The answer is that it may be both structure and lexicon, but we do not yet have enough information on how the brain stores and retrieves these bits of competence to be sure.

Lexicosyntactic theories. Three different theories from TG grammar, collectively referred to as interpretive semantics, have been proposed to explain the influence of syntax on lexicon. Standard theory consigns all lexical meaning to a sentence's deep structure; the syntax is therefore said to contain all of the elements necessary for lexical insertion. Extended standard theory tries to establish a kind of midpoint between deep structure and surface structure, where lexical-insertion rules (such as feature matrices) are applied before the deep structure becomes a surface structure. A third proposal, the revised extended standard theory, is in effect the opposite of the standard theory, for it consigns all semantic or lexical meaning to the surface structure. Lexical concerns, this theory holds, actually come before any syntactic considerations, and it is lexicon that shapes syntax rather than the other way around.

In addition to TG's theories, case relationship, a product of Structural grammar, attempts to describe how certain kinds of words are cued by syntactic structure to fulfill certain kinds of functions. The four major cases are: agent, that which performs the action expressed by a verb of action; patient, that which is affected by the verb's action as performed by the agent; experiencer, that which undergoes the experience expressed by a nonactive verb; and instrument, that which provides the means of bringing about the action or the experience.

Notice that the four cases all refer to nouns of one sort or another. Distinctions among the types of nouns depend on each noun's relationship to one of two kinds of verb: the sort that expresses activity or the sort that expresses experiencing of activity. For example, in the sentence "Angela drew a picture with her pencil," the verb expresses activity. Therefore, there must be an agent (Angela), and there may also be a patient (picture) and an instrument (pencil). If we change the sentence to "Angela loved the picture," the verb tells us about Angela's experience, not her action; consequently, "Angela" is the experiencer, and "the picture" is the object of her affections, the patient.

The same noun may fulfill several different functions for the words around it, but the type of case which any noun can assume is limited by the noun's semantic features. For example, rarely will an inanimate noun be an agent, and an animate noun is seldom an instrument (*"Angela drew a picture with a guppy"). To put it affirmatively, if an animate noun, such as "Angela," is linked with an active verb, such as "drew," that noun is likeliest to be either the agent or the patient. Similarly, an animate noun with a nonactive verb ("love") will most commonly be the experiencer, whereas an inanimate noun ("pencil") with either kind of verb will most likely be patient or instrument rather than agent or experiencer. The syntactic relationships are limited by lexical features, and lexical insertions are in turn limited by syntactic patterns.

More investigation will be needed of this kind of cross influencing before we can be certain of how syntax and lexicon control the meaning(s) of an utterance. Although meaning of all sorts ultimately resides in the brain, nevertheless, words and syntactic combinations can acquire a kind of force of their own over time. Tradition controls our competence and our performance in various ways, whether we like it or not—whether we are even aware of the shaping or not. The manipulation of meaning which any one speaker makes is always limited to a certain extent by those linguistic forces over which no one person ordinarily has much control.

Or does he? That question brings us to the third basic issue in this chapter.

Control of Meaning

We must keep in mind that language is so much mixed up with everything we do—feeling, thinking, yelling, ordering tacos—that sometimes it is difficult to sort out the division between language use and other activities. Furthermore, as you are well aware by now, it is not easy to sort out the divisions within language itself. Sounds blend into forms, forms into syllables, syllables into words, and words into phrases and sentences. Where in that chain is meaning located? And what kind of meaning is located where? Once we have some answers to those two questions, we still must deal with a third: How can we, as alert users of language, begin to behave attentively toward that meaning chain, using it instead of being used by it? How can we bring competence up to the surface and turn it into enlightened performance?

We shall begin our response by returning, with a more technical and formal perspective, to some material already mentioned. Before we can approach the question of how we, as language users, can control language, we must first reexamine some important concepts about how language systems appear to control themselves. In this section, we will look first at semiotic theory, then at pragmatics, and finally at semantics, all three of which touch on the question of how meaning can be controlled.

Semiotics. An emerging discipline, semiotics is a general theory of signs. It includes language as a prime—but not as the only—medium by which symbolism is expressed and understood. Codified by Ferdinand de Saussure in the early twentieth century, semiotics includes in its field anything that carries meaning. Thus, followers of Saussure, like Roman Jakobson, Roland Barthes, or Claude Lévi-Strauss, have applied semiotic theory to fields as apparently diverse as kinship systems and mythology, advertisements and history, music and computers, economics and biology. Partly combining with general semantics (which we shall discuss in a later section), semiotic theory has filtered indirectly into psychology and psychotherapy through the writings of Erich Fromm and Jean Piaget and has appeared in the works of philosophers like Ernst Cassirer, Rudolph Carnap, and Bertrand Russell.

Semiotics focuses on the relationship between the object referred to (called the signified by Saussure), the word or name-of-object (called the signifier), and the connection-between-signifier-and-signified, or the whole that exists in the brain (the sign). In semiotic terms, language is a series of signs, strung together linearly on a stream of air or on a printed page. Like all other signs, linguistic ones are arbitrary. They are also structured, through convention and through time. But because language permeates everything else, linguistic signs never exist apart from their use by communities of speakers in all conceivable situations. And that use, as we have seen, is conditioned in large measure by precedent. In this stream of time, an individual sign may be said to have value, but since language consists of words strung together, the collocative effect, or signification, of a group of signs as used by a community of speakers over time is what we grapple with when we discuss "meaning."

To repeat: signs are arbitrary, in that the signifier has no inherent, innate connection with the signified; but each sign by its nature does have value. Value—and its collective form, significance—comes about through the association in the human mind of object (signified) with representation-of-object (signifier). Signification, or the collocation and interrelationships of signs, thus rests on the interaction of the human mind with both the external and the internal universe.

As we have repeatedly observed, signification does not occur in a vacuum, but involves connotation and denotation, idiolect and dialect and language,[5] variation and stability, contemporary usage and the pressure of

---

5. Saussure and other semiologists usually group idiolect and dialect together, as versions of language in actual use, in other words, speech performance. Actual performance is called *la parole*. Its complement, language as collective competence, is *la langue*.

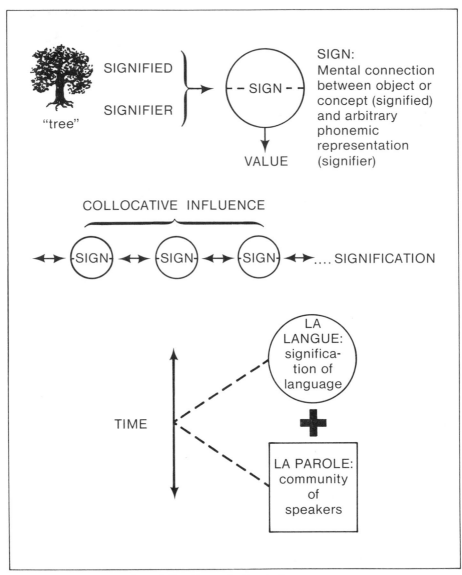

Figure 9.3   Relationship of Key Terms in Semiotics

precedent. Thus, although the signifier is arbitrary, the sign does have "meaning" (significance), because the sign always exists within a network of relationships. The perception and use of that relational network, or structure—be it culture, kinship, music, politics, or the complex common denominator of all social structures, language—give rise to significance. To be accurate in an analysis of any given sign or series of signs, then, one must study the whole structural complex of which that sign or series is one part. (See figure 9.3 for a schematic representation, much simplified, of these key terms in semiotics.)

The whole structure of language consists of two major and constantly interacting parts, each with many subdivisions. The first part is the internal system of phonemes, morphemes, syntax, lexical fields, and collocations, all operating in time. The second part is the extralinguistic system, specifically the multiplicity of connections that language makes with the world. Language both receives the imprint of its culture and puts its imprint onto that culture. Cultural and linguistic interactions always flow in both directions, just as single speakers' idiolects are both individualized (*la parole*) and yet still part of the general speech community (*la langue*).

Any given linguistic sign, then—whether tone of voice, gesture, word, or phrase—shares in those two major parts: internal linguistic systems and external (nonlinguistic) systems. Consequently, every linguistic sign exists in at least three dimensions and must be analyzed or evaluated in terms of all three: as an isolatable unit, as a structural member, and as an index of change. The first two belong to synchronic linguistics; the third, to diachronic linguistics.

First, a sign is a unit that can be isolated and that is used by a definable person or group, at a particular "frozen" point in the ongoing stream of time. It is a unit in daily exchange within *la parole*. Considering it this way, we should properly speak of the sign's value rather than of its significance, since "value" in semiotics refers only to the more or less isolatable quality, which is necessarily artificial and incomplete. Full significance does not appear until one sign is recognized as being part of the larger sociolinguistic structure. It is possible, and we have done so, to deal with a particular word's multiple values, such as homonymy, antonomy, synonymy, case, referent, connotation, or syntactic function. But those values have only become part of any sign in *la langue,* and therefore can be isolated and evaluated, because the sign connects with others in the linguistic and social networks.

The second dimension of any sign or series of signs is its participation in the larger networks of *la parole*. A sign acquires multiple values from its structural connections, such as function in a phrase, use in a dialect or register, particular pronunciation, appearance in this or that social context: on a billboard, in a doctoral thesis, at a bank teller's window. Like the first dimension, this second one involves both the internal system of language and the external system of the world outside. The second dimension must also deal with speakers and their sociocultural contexts as well as with phonemes, morphemes, and syntax. It is in this dimension that we can properly begin to speak of the significance rather than the value of signs.

The third dimension any sign occupies is change over time. Like language, time permeates everything we do; therefore, it also permeates language. We can attempt to stop time (as when we deal with signs in the first dimension, of value), but that cessation is analytical only; we, not time itself, have willed its momentary suspension in order to examine a particular event, a sign and its value as it exists then. When we investigate significance rather than value, we usually perceive time as moving hardly at all, for we seldom notice any but the most blisteringly obvious changes in a language, like fad words or quarrels over usage. Regardless of how perceptive any one observer is of the immediate effects of change, time is always an important factor in the evolving significance of signs. Diachronic linguistics indicates many examples of such change in significance, as we saw in chapter 5.

But it is important to remember that words do not change meanings over time just because it is in the "nature" of language to change. It is "natural," to a certain extent—and that is a language universal—but the particular kinds of diachronic alteration of significance are shaped by the connections in time (past and present) among language, language users, and the general sociocultural structure of which language is a part.

Control of meaning (value or significance) in any language, then, must be acknowledged to be at once impossible and quite possible. We may call it partly impossible because no one speaker can ordinarily expect to have much effect on *la langue* as a whole, which is by nature collective and derived from precedent. But we may with equal accuracy and justification say that control of meaning is partly possible as well, on two counts. First, we can become aware of and can try to understand the many aspects of *la langue*'s collective, precedential tendency; we can recognize what language does (regardless of what any individual speaker or speech community says or does), what it does not do, and how those forces affect *la parole*. Second, as a consequence of that awareness, that raising of competence up to the forefront of our attention, we may be able to sharpen and refine our performance, our day-by-day idiolectic participation in language, our own use—or abuse—of signifiers and signs.

Pragmatics. Value and significance change as speakers change. In discussing diachronic and synchronic types of change, we have seen that change can be manifested in any (or all) of three ways: it can be historical, over time, so that yesterday's meanings are not tomorrow's; it can be dialectic (region, occupation, etc.), so even in the same "frozen" moment of time, Montana's significance may not be Minnesota's; and it can be sociocultural, from one class or group to another, from jiving on the street to brooding in a bar, from intoning in a courtroom to rejoicing in a church. Change always exists as a factor in *la langue,* then, but for each language user, time's influence on *la parole* rarely seems obvious. In day-by-day, practical or pragmatic concerns, the historical context of language has relatively little effect on a speaker's awareness of how he uses his language or how he interprets the speech behaviors of other speakers. The actual performance of language is much determined by historical pressures, of course, but we are concerned here with conscious attention to language use. In this sense, other contexts than history become more forceful.

The study of those other contexts, besides the internally linguistic and the historical, is called pragmatics. This field of study deals with particular utterances in particular situations and is especially concerned with the various ways in which the many social contexts of language performance can influence interpretation. Pragmatics goes beyond such influences as suprasegmental phonemes, dialects, and registers (all of which also shape interpretation) and looks at speech performance as primarily a social act ruled by various social conventions.

Anyone who is not a hermit lives in daily contact with other human beings, learns the explicit and implicit codes by which human beings usually manage to keep from doing violence to one another, and responds to alterations in those codes with greater or lesser good nature and skill. We drive on the right-hand side of the road and expect other drivers to do so. When we write checks, we have the money to cover them, and we expect the bank to honor them. We assume that food will be forthcoming in a restaurant, haircuts in a barber shop, gasoline—maybe—from a service station. We know these contexts so well that we do not think much about them, nor do we often stop to list the expectations we have about the behavior of people in such contexts. Ordinarily, there is no need to be explicit, because ordinarily, everybody else is behaving as we would expect them to. The "unspoken rules" governing behavior work very well, most of the time.

Occasionally, however, they do not work, or someone is not aware of them, or they are deliberately violated. Then it becomes important to be explicit about the "rules," the silent expectations and conventions, in order to discover what they ask of us and whether they are worth saving or not. For example, many people in the past decade or so have come to question certain "rules" about what gentlemen should do for ladies (open doors, light cigarettes, carry packages, etc.), asking whether those behaviors are fixed for all time by generic requirements or perhaps are signs, in the semiotic sense, of role-playing and strategies for coping with conflict. Similarly, pragmatics attempts to identify the "rules" underlying the performance of speech acts, or language as it is uttered in conjunction with the many social conventions controlling what speaker and auditor expect from one another.

Pragmatics theorists have identified three kinds of speech-act principles: illocutionary force, referring to the speaker as interpreted pragmatically by his auditors; conversational principles, referring to the auditors' expectations of the speaker; and presuppositions, referring to assumptions held by both the speaker and the auditors. Each of the three principles, of course, influences the others and therefore influences the significance of the speech act as a whole.

Illocutionary force. This is the speaker's intention, so far as the auditors can discern it from the context. There are two major kinds of illocutionary force: implicit, below the surface and unstated, and explicit, on the surface and stated. The implicit forces are three: assertion, imperative, and question (sometimes called interrogative). Assertion is a statement about action or attitude ("He loves you," "He does not love you"). An imperative is a command for action ("Shut up!" "Will you please shut up!"). An interrogative is a request for information ("How much is that tie?" "What time is it?"). It is important to identify these implicit forces not only theoretically, but also as they appear in their various social contexts, for frequently the apparent intention of the speaker is not the same as the actual intent.

Social convention and good manners usually dictate, for instance, that a speaker will not use imperatives in polite company, perhaps at a party, at dinner, or when he is courting someone's favor. We are taught very early to say "please" as a way of disguising the illocutionary force of a command: "Please pass the biscuits"; "Give me the salt, please." It is even more polite to phrase the imperative as a question: "May I [or Can I] get through here?" "Would you like to go home now?" Most of us recognize that the implicit illocutionary force of these apparent questions is imperative, not interrogative, and we send the salt down or open a passageway without demur. We do not ordinarily respond to such implied commands by saying, "No" or by saying, "Yes" and not handing along the biscuits. We all understand that "May I have the biscuits?" is not a request for information, to be answered by "Yes" or "No," which would then have to be followed by another request for information—"Will you send them down here?"—which could then also be answered "Yes" or "No," and on and on while the biscuits stayed where they were and got cold.

Sometimes, however, the implicit illocutionary force of an utterance is not so clear, for it is often disguised by the surface-structure phrasing. When someone sitting outdoors on a cool evening says, "I'm cold," that is phrased as a statement; it apparently requires neither information nor action. But if there is a wrap in the house, brought along for just this chilliness, and if the speaker's companion is attentive, the simple statement will probably be recognized as an implied command to bring the wrap out. Similarly, the statement "You're driving too fast" (assertion) may often carry the implicit illocutionary force of a command to slow down. "Do you love me?"—an apparent question—may carry many different implicit illocutionary forces: really a question, to be answered "Yes" or "No"; an assertion (perhaps "I love you" or perhaps "I am uncertain about your love for me"); or a command ("Tell me you love me"). Only context, linguistic or otherwise, will clarify this complex utterance.

It may be tentatively suggested that the more intimate the register, the more disguised the implicit illocutionary force in any given speech act. Conversely, the more formal is the register, the less disguised the force. Drill instructors in the armed forces do not suggest; they command. Their audience is presumed to be unfamiliar with the nuances of social convention that would instantaneously translate "Why don't we go for a walk?" into "Fifty-mile forced march, full packs, on the double!" Formalized situations tend to call for formalized utterances, so that an audience of varied backgrounds does not have to fumble with unfamiliar codes and levels of implied illocutions.

The other major kind of illocutionary force is explicit. Explicit illocutionary forces in speech acts take the form of statements in which the utterance itself is an action. "I tell you, it was awful!" performs the act of telling which the verb names. "I pronounce you man and wife" performs the act of pronouncing. "I promise I'll break your head" constitutes the act of promising. Statements like these, promising or pronouncing or telling (or asking or commanding), are called performative utterances; the utterance itself is the deed. There is an understood contract in such utterances, for assertions like these always carry the force of an unspoken command. The unspoken (implicit) command is that the auditor should believe the assertions to be true (should accept their truth value): it is true that something was awful; you are man and wife; your head will get broken.

Most of the time, we do accept such assertions as true, or we pretend to do so, but if the context is intimate enough, the implicit truth value may be questioned even here: "Oh, yeah? Who says it was awful? You wouldn't know 'awful' if it bit you!" Or "Oh, yeah? You and what army gonna break my head?" (But rarely "Oh, yeah? Who says you're married?" for the context here is formal, not intimate.) When explicit and implicit intentions clash over a performative utterance, the auditors are challenging the speaker's capacity, not to *tell* the truth, but to *verify* the truth of the statements. The speaker is challenged to match the truth value of the utterance to some external referent or some action.

Conversational principles. This brings us to what the auditor can expect from a speaker, as opposed to the interpretive skills that a speaker can expect from his audience. In any speech act, the audience generally assumes that at least four conversational principles will apply to what a speaker says. The audience's first assumption is that the speaker is sincere, not saying one thing and meaning another, at least with no greater discrepancy between phrasing and intention than what we expect in the exercise of various illocutionary forces. The second assumption is that the speaker is telling the truth so far as he understands it, not deliberately telling lies. Third, the audience assumes that what the speaker has to say is relevant to the topic or general areas of concern. The final assumption is that the speaker will contribute the appropriate amount of information or commentary, not withhold anything important and not rattle on for an undue amount of time.

For example, if someone (speaker) asks, "What time is it?" we (auditors) usually assume that he does not know what the time is and that his request is a sincere one for information about the time. When we (now speakers) begin to reply, he (now auditor) will usually assume that we will answer with the correct time, not with a rambling discourse on the price of hamburger, nor with a scream of rage, nor with a lie. If any of those four assumptions prove incorrect, then discord immediately appears and one or the other of the conversants has to make a quick test of the assumptions, to discover which one has been violated and what the appropriate response should now be.

For example, should people be hurrying out of a burning building, a request for the correct time is presumed to be insincere and will elicit irritation or disgust: "You crazy? Keep moving!" But if someone begins a prepared speech on tax reform to the Lions Club with a joke about peanut butter, the audience will unconsciously recognize that the relevance of the joke is less to taxes than to the reduction of stress between strangers. It is understood here that the context of speech giving requires some preliminary establishment of shared concerns, even a sort of shared companionship, between the orator and the audience. Such a speaker is not expected to launch immediately into the technical points of his topic. But if that speaker's boss asks for a short telephone conversation on the same topic of tax reform, a joke would not be appropriate as an opening; it would be irrelevant in the context of a business discussion.

Presuppositions. Here, we move into what both speakers and auditors can expect of the content or information contained in an utterance,[6] that is, what a speaker and an auditor can suppose each other to know before a given speech act begins. For example, if I say, "But Jenny has never gone out with a married man before!" I presuppose (before I utter the sentence) that my listener knows at least these content items:

1. There is a person named Jenny.
2. Speaker and listener are both acquainted with Jenny.
3. Jenny goes out with men.
4. Jenny has just recently gone out with a married man.

6. Since each of the three speech-act principles influences the other, it will be recognized that to separate presupposition from the other two is to be somewhat arbitrary. Presupposition about content will vary from one speech situation to another, depending on the influence of intention and expectation.

Presumably, too, the listener and speaker both share the following bits of information, although these presuppositions are not so obvious nor so demonstrable from the utterance alone:

5. Jenny is female.
6. Jenny is not married.
7. Jenny does not usually go out with married men.
8. Jenny is adult.
9. Jenny is not so dependent upon speaker or listener that her behavior can be regulated by either of them.
10. Speaker and listener are surprised by Jenny's behavior.

Presupposition underlies a good deal of the unthinking adjustment we make from one speech situation to another, adjustment that helps ensure we are not (as speech-communication teachers say) "talking over our audience's head" or not "insulting our audience's intelligence." Presupposition is operating when we mutter secrets in hallways so that outsiders will not understand. All codes, jargons, cants, and deliberate use of elliptical or confusing language make use of presupposition.

It is very easy to misjudge presupposition when one does not know one's audience well, or when one thinks one knows them all too well. A good many people seem to sense this principle, as evidenced by the frequency with which they intersperse phrases like "You know," "I mean," or "Know what I mean?" in their conversation. For instance, if I tell you that I will meet you on the corner of Third and Main at noon today, I assume that you know what noon is, where Third Street makes a corner with Main Street, and which of the four points of that intersection I will be waiting on. If you are new in town, I may wait a long time. Conversely, if my husband tells me he wants his favorite meal for dinner and presupposes I will cook it, because we have been married a long time and I always know and cook what he asks for, then he may wait a long time. Presuppositions always require testing from time to time, to be sure that what the speaker and what the auditor assume or know are really the same.

An attentiveness to the unspoken and often unconscious "rules" or expectations inherent in speech acts can help to sharpen our awareness of what is really going on as we speak. The illocutionary force implicit in certain contexts, the active nature of performative statements, the conversational principles applicable to most speech situations, and the presuppositions all of us bring to conversations: these pragmatic contexts of language use shape our performance all the time. The more we understand them, perhaps the better we can control them. The same may be said of our control over individual meanings as well. The practical, as opposed to the theoretical (semiotic), study of such individual meanings is semantics.

Semantics. In semiotics, the concern was with the nature and function of signs in general and of linguistic signs in particular. In pragmatics, the focus was on a systematic analysis of extralinguistic contexts that, to some extent, shape the functioning of signs. In semantics, the principal attention is given to the manipulation of signs within various contexts. Semanticists are particularly occupied with identifying the difference between appropriate and inappropriate manipulation. As semiotics tends to blend with synchronic linguistics and pragmatics to shade into sociolinguistics, so does semantics tend to lap over into psycholinguistics. All three specialties, of course, approach language as a cultural phenomenon, part of society, shaping it and shaped by it. We may oversimplify a bit and propose that from this perspective of cultural symbolism (chapter 6), semiotics deals with language as one cultural symbol among others; pragmatics, as one cultural ritual among others; and semantics, as one cultural tactic among others.

"Tactic" is an intentionally militaristic, manipulative metaphor here, for the central premise of semantics is that language is above all a means of approaching and ordering—manipulating—the universe. That premise is closely related to the Whorfian Principle, discussed in chapter 3, but semantics makes language use more active than the Whorfian Principle appeared to indicate. Its practitioners suggest that the discipline of semantics is a means of sorting out not only linguistic truths, but ethical and psychological ones as well, so that someone attuned to semantics can also become attuned to truth in other realms. Because the connections between mind and language are so interpenetrating and so indissoluble, many semanticists believe that to use language appropriately is to behave appropriately as well.

The foremost proponents of semantics were Count Alfred Korzybski and S. I. Hayakawa, beginning in the 1930s and 1940s, who built on earlier work by C. K. Ogden and I. A. Richards. Other advocates included writers like Stuart Chase, anthropologists like Bronislaw Malinowski, educators like Ralph Philip Boas, and psychologists like Abraham Maslow and Carl Rogers. The influence of semantics has been especially strong in language teaching, in analysis of propaganda of many types, and in nondirective psychotherapy and counseling.

The central question in semantics is this: Given that language is a series of arbitrary signs, and given that language always functions in the context of cultural pressures, what is it that language users do with those signs under those pressures? In other words, what kinds of pressure do the signs exert in return, and how is the language user to discover truth when he is caught between those two forces? In response, semantics points to two important distinctions that language users must understand (become competent at) and then must put into practice (perform) in their own speech: a distinction between extensional and intensional meaning, and a distinction between Aristotelian and non-Aristotelian logic. As a corrective, semantics offers the principle of indexing.

Extensional versus intensional meaning. The extensional meaning of a word is its externally verifiable, referential significance, something that can be checked by pointing to an example: "July," "sneeze," "tea." In semiotics, these would be the signifieds—not denotations but referents, extending outside the self or mind of the individual speaker. They are factual; they are what formal logicians call "hard evidence"; on the whole, they do not change much in any person's lifetime or from one person's perception to another's. Extensional meaning is "real-world" oriented, not overly weighted with connotations or associations of any kind, as close to uninvolved objectivity as human beings can get. A word's extensional meaning is the source of what some psychologists call cognitive, or information-learning, response. "Add 2 cups of sugar to 2 cups of flour" is a statement heavy in extensional meaning and cognitive information.

Intensional meaning, on the other hand, comes from nonreferential sources. These sources, too, are signifieds, but of a different sort. The sources of intensional meaning cannot usually be checked or verified by pointing to something, for such meaning derives from the feelings of the speaker or auditor. Intensional meaning might be thought of as the collocation of all pragmatics contexts, all associative fields, and all general and individual connotations that cluster around a word or phrase. Formal logicians recognize intensional statements as "soft evidence," changeable, true in some circumstances but not in others. Intensional meaning gives rise to affective (feeling) responses rather than to cognitive ones: What do you feel about or associate with "July," "sneeze," and "tea"? A statement like "You always burn anything you bake!" is heavy with intensional meaning and affective information.

Extensional statements can be verified; they have or have not a more or less identifiable truth value (p. 155). It is, or it is not, true that the mean temperature in Afghanistan is 108°F., that the average life span in Western countries has increased three years in each generation for the last one hundred years, or that the smoking of cigarettes has a high probability of inducing cancer in human beings. Intensional statements do not have that kind of truth value, for they do not refer to issues that can be resolved by looking up a fact or pointing to a referent. Their truth is just as true, but it is a different kind of truth, the truth of emotions, of resemblances, of indirection, and (above all) of gradation, distinction, and variability.

The statement "You always burn anything you bake!" is an example of that different kind of truth. The baker addressed might well reply, with some (extensional) truth, that the statement is false, because last week's cookies were perfect. But the speaker's intensional meaning may have had little to do with baking and much more with his feelings: that the baker is clumsy or does not follow the recipe or dawdles over a TV show and does not get the cookies out of the oven before they burn. Even more important intensionally, the speaker may have been protesting that he feels uncomfortable about the baker, not about the act of baking. Perhaps the speaker does not trust her, or perhaps he is angry at her for cooking better than he does, or perhaps he feels threatened by her in some way and wishes to attack her in an area where he knows she is vulnerable. A statement such as "You always burn anything you bake!" is loaded with affective information, which, if it is clearly understood, may be just as true as the truth value and the cognitive information.

The trouble is that affective/intentional statements are often presented *as if* they were cognitive/extensional ones. Confusing the two—disguising intension as extension—can raise difficulties on at least two counts. First, such a confusion may obscure the point of reference: a disguised intensional statement seems to be making an assertion about verifiable data (How many times has the baker burned something?), but it is not really doing that. The reference really is internal, in the speaker's feelings about . . . something. It may not always be clear exactly what that internal something is, and so the discussion may not be able to focus on the real problem.

Second, disguising intension as extension nearly always leads to hard but abstract generalizations. That is, words like "never" and "always"—very firm in their assertion of frequency—tend to crop up in intensional assertions, so the discussion is no longer focused on a particular source of conflict but becomes generalized to include all conflicts: "You *always* burn anything you bake!" Notice, too, that in addition to taking a hard line and generalizing, the topic no longer is *this* batch of cookies, but "anything you bake": all pastry, all casseroles, all food, maybe even all symbolic affection. Disguised intensional statements frequently seem to get out of hand, moving from referential/cognitive, specific, and verifiable assertion to nonreferential/affective, generalized, and unverifiable assertion. This latter tendency Korzybski called "moving up the ladder of abstraction," from specific things like cookies to less and less specific (more abstract) concepts like pastry, food, and symbols for love.

A key point in semantics, then, is to refrain from confusing intensional statements with extensional ones and rather to recognize that the two are different kinds of observations, with different kinds of sources or referents. In sorting out the two types of statements and learning to use them appropriately, we can draw on much of what we have already discovered about language. For example, as noted above, denotation collocates more functionally with extensional statements, connotation more often with intensional ones: "A raven is a bird" is extensional, but "Ravens are creepy" is intensional. Similarly, a slight change in synonymy can alter a statement from extensional to intensional, as in *"His judgment* suggests that we choose this course of action" as opposed to *"Her prejudice* suggests that we choose this course of action."

As another example, consider the performative statement "I declare, you look just lovely today!" This assertion has a verifiable truth value: it is true that the speaker just declared something. In another sense, however, *what* she declared—"You look just lovely today!"—may or may not be equally verifiable. The act of declaring is extensional, but the declaration in the subordinate clause is intensional, since loveliness is not true or false but a condition about which people have perceptions or feelings. Conventional presupposition about such a statement dictates that the auditor should respond with an equivalent affective/intensional reply, like "Thank you" (for expressing the complimentary feeling), and not with a cognitive/extensional remark, like "Yes, you did just declare that."

Aristotelian versus non-Aristotelian logic. The second important distinction that semantics asks speakers to observe occurs between a two-valued (Aristotelian) logic and a gradable (non-Aristotelian) logic. Do not be misled by the word "logic" here, for the application of this concept goes far beyond formal syllogisms to include just about everything that human beings can think about or respond to, linguistically or otherwise. Korzybski's observation here is like Whorf's: If our language is full of two-valued terms, like "up"/"down," "black"/"white," "good"/"bad," "either"/"or," "always"/"never," then will we not inevitably begin to think in such terms? Will we not come to perceive the universe itself, and human beings, and values, as being this *or* that, yes *or* no, A *or* Not-A, with only two choices possible? And—the universe, human beings, and values being rather more slippery and less divisible than that—will we not inevitably come to misunderstand, oversimplify, and reduce what we perceive?

That list of complementary antonyms from our earlier field analysis was deliberately selected to demonstrate a simple kind of two-valued logic. If the problem of dichotomizing were only that simple, we could dismiss it; we could say the list was exceptional, not normative, or we could say that nearly all such pairs have gradable terms in a subset of the field, as "always"/"never" includes "sometimes," "often," "seldom," "frequently," and so forth. But from the perspective of semantics, the point is that two-valued logic goes much deeper than the lexicon.

Along with some Structuralists like Lévi-Strauss, many semanticists suggest that dichotomizing permeates much of our pre-, sub-, or extralinguistic thinking, in such a way that we often cannot even recognize it. For example, if Standard English is preferred, prestigious, "good," then anything nonstandard is "bad." If the unmarked form "man" is good, then anything marked—like "woman"—is not-good. If winning is good, then everything else is losing, which is bad. And so on and so on: A is all right, so Not-A must be not all right. The insidiousness of this kind of reasoning, according to semantics, lies in the indentification of only two possibilities, A or Not-A, and therefore of only two values, good or not-good (bad). There is no gradation, no shading, no degree in between.

We know cognitively/extensionally that such reasoning is false; we are quite aware intellectually or rationally that there are many degrees of good and bad mixed into everything; but affectively/intensionally, we may not always abide by that awareness. And therein lies the danger: intension not only becomes confused with extension, but it often combines with dichotomizing as well. The temptation to create order and impose it on a universe so apparently disorderly, random, and nonsensical must be very strong in human beings, for we do it often in many different ways.

Unfortunately, the order thereby created may not match what actual order there is. Many psychotherapists have pointed out, for example, that the condition called schizophrenia is often characterized by a quite logical perception of the universe by the sufferer, in which everything makes sense, everything is orderly, if only one accepts a two-valued assumption of persecution by enemies or invasion by androids or the hostility of popcorn. But suppose the enemies are not extensional but intensional? Then we must say that the perception is skewed, and the sufferer is drawing illegitimate inferences that do not stand up under testing.

Something of the same pattern seems to appear when people fall into two-valued logic and extensional-intensional confusion in their use of language. Stating values as if they were literally referential and had a quantifiable truth is an example. It is very common to hear a statement such as "Homosexuality is immoral" uttered as if it were absolutely, utterly, universally true—that is, extensional. There are at least three implications of a statement phrased in that manner: that "morality," presupposed to have a "good" value, is referential, which it is not; that morality has only one opposite, immorality, which it does not; and that everyone agrees on what immorality consists of, which they do not. It is quite common for people to argue heatedly for a long time about value statements like that, without ever resolving anything or learning anything and without anyone's changing his or her mind.

Indexing. As a corrective for our tendency to slip unthinkingly into extensional-intensional confusion, laden with two-valued logic, semanticists propose a technique called indexing. The tactic consists in adopting devices that permit one to stay constantly alert to the two important distinctions already discussed. These devices use a memory-jogging (mnemonic) capacity that frees us from the necessity of constantly murmuring, "Intensional or extensional? Two-valued or gradable? Cognitive or affective?" Three catch-phrases in particular are advanced in this service: the *is* of identity versus the *is* of existence; the map is not the territory; and cow_1 is not cow_2. All three mnemonic devices help us control our use of meaning by helping us control our understanding of meaning.

The "is" of identity versus the "is" of existence. This distinguishes the two parts of a syntactic pattern, whose inappropriate blending leads to semantic confusion. Unlike most Indo-European languages, which have two different verbs for the two circumstances noted (such as *ser* versus *estar* in Spanish), English uses only one. The single word "is" (or any form of the verb "to be") must serve two different functions in English.

One function of "is" is extensional and establishes referential identity, a permanent condition, between subject and predicate adjective or subject and predicate nominative, as in statements like: "The walls are thin" (they can be measured); "His· hair is brown" (a color chart will verify this); or "There are fifteen Cub Scouts here" (count them). The other function of "to be" is intensional and establishes a temporary and inferential condition of existence as identified by the subject and the predicative completers: "The walls are ugly"; "His hair is tangled"; "There is a crowd here." Because the two "is"s look the the same, and because the subject-predicate-completer syntactic structure is the same, the tendency is to assume that the two kinds of statements are the same. But they are not. "Ugly" is a value judgment (someone else might think the walls were pretty); "tangled" is momentary, not a permanent condition (five minutes ago, the hair might have been immaculate); what is a "crowd" in one person's view may be quite cozy in another's. Identity (permanent) and existence (changing) are not the same.

The map is not the territory. This catch-phrase is the semanticist's way of pointing out that signs are arbitrary, not innate, just as a map uses arbitrary symbols to represent churches or isotherms or the height of a hill. The phrase also, and more tellingly, points out that the name of something (the signifier) is not the same as the something-itself (the signified): the map only represents the territory; it is not identical with the territory. Closely identifying words and referents, as most of us do, we often forget that the word "pain" is not the feeling of pain, and we sometimes respond to "pain" as if it were pain itself. Furthermore, the mere statement of a non-performative utterance does not usually make the statement true, just as the act of drawing a map does not recreate the turf. The map/statement is always slightly different from, slightly less inclusive than, and slightly removed from referential reality. The statement "You look like a mess" does not signify that I do, but only that the speaker thinks I do.

Cow$_1$ is not cow$_2$. This mnemonic device aims to help us remember that even the "is"-of-existence is subject to change. The walls may not be thin tomorrow (they may be gone), and they may not have been thin yesterday (before we cut them in half). Furthermore, just because *this* man's hair is brown is no reason to conclude that *that* man's or *all* men's will be brown. Even "brown" may be subject to intensional interpretation: I might call it "mud-colored," whereas you might prefer "sable."

The point here is that similarity of language constructions, like the two "is"s, the names of colors, or the syntax of subject-verb-completer, tends to lead us into assuming that references themselves are equally similar. A classic violation of this "cow" principle occurs in the assertion "If you've seen one redwood tree, you've seen them all." Of course, you have not, but to phrase the statement that way is to come perilously close to acting that way, to letting speech acts control other acts.

The aim in this chapter has been to get as good a grasp as is currently possible on the elusive term "meaning." We have seen that "meaning" has many possible meanings itself, so many that holding them all separate for examination is sometimes difficult. We have seen, too, that linguistic meaning often spills over into nonlinguistic areas, such as sociocultural structures, etiquette, and psychology. Given the general elusiveness of "meaning" (and sometimes of meaning), we have nevertheless attempted to answer three key questions about the topic: Where does meaning reside? What are the kinds of meaning? How can we control meaning? Throughout the discussion, we have suggested in various ways that understanding (competence) is at least half the task; the other half is performance—doing something, for good or for ill, with the insights of understanding. It is assumed that the performance will be not only informed, but also conscientious and honorable: saying what we really mean, as fairly and as accurately as possible. In the next chapter, we shall look at some uses of language that, consciously or not, are not so honorable or conscientious in their manipulation of the ways language works.

Review Questions

1. Where is meaning located?
2. Identify and discuss the four major types of lexical meaning.
3. What are the three major types of field relationships? How can they be compared with one another?
4. What are the three principal types of ambiguity? How is each derived?
5. What is an associative field? How is it related to lexicostructural meaning?
6. What are interpretive semantics and case relationships?
7. Discuss the relationships among these terms: sign, signifier, signified, signification, value.
8. What are the three major components of speech acts?
9. What is indexing? How is it related to the major problems identified by semantics?

10. Define and give examples of the following: collocation, feature matrix, antonym, performative utterance, extensional meaning, two-valued logic.

Selected Reading

Bolinger, Dwight. *Degree Words*. The Hague: Mouton Publishing Co., 1973.

Carnap, Rudolph. *Meaning and Necessity: A Study in Semantics and Modal Logic*. Chicago: University of Chicago Press, 1956.

DeGeorge, Richard T., and Fernande M. DeGeorge, eds. *The Structuralists: From Marx to Lévi-Strauss*. New York: Doubleday/Anchor Books, 1972.

Dillon, G. L. *Introduction to Contemporary Linguistic Semantics*. Englewood Cliffs, N.J.: Prentice-Hall, Inc., 1977.

Eco, Umberto. *A Theory of Semiotics*. Bloomington: Indiana University Press, 1976.

Fillmore, Charles D., and D. Terence Langendoen, eds. *Studies in Linguistic Semantics*. New York: Holt, Rinehart and Winston, 1971.

Fodor, J. D. *Semantics: Theories of Meaning in Generative Grammar*. New York: Thomas Y. Crowell Co., 1977.

Hayakawa, S. I. *Language in Thought and Action*, 4th ed. New York: Harcourt Brace Jovanovich, 1978.

————, ed. *The Use and Misuse of Language*. New York: Fawcett Press, 1962.

Jakobson, Roman, and Morris Halle. *The Fundamentals of Language*. The Hague: Mouton Publishing Co., 1956.

Katz, Jerrold J. *Semantic Theory*. New York: Harper & Row, 1972.

Korzybski, Alfred. *Science and Sanity: An Introduction to Non-Aristotelian Systems and General Semantics*. Lancaster, Pa.: Science Press, 1933.

Leech, Geoffrey. *Semantics*. Baltimore: Penguin Books, 1974.

Macksey, Richard, and Eugenio Donato, eds. *The Language of Criticism and the Sciences of Man: The Structuralist Controversy*. Baltimore: The Johns Hopkins Press, 1970.

Morris, Charles. *Signs, Language, and Behavior*. Englewood Cliffs, N.J.: Prentice-Hall, Inc., 1946.

Nilsen, Don L. F., and Aileen Pace Nilsen. *Semantic Theory: A Linguistic Perspective*. Rowley, Mass.: Newbury House, 1975.

Ogden, C. K., and I. A. Richards. *The Meaning of Meaning*, 9th ed. New York: Harcourt, Brace and World, 1953.

Osgood, Charles E., George J. Suci, and Percy H. Tannenbaum. *The Measurement of Meaning*. Urbana, Ill.: University of Illinois Press, 1957.

Quine, W. V. *Word and Object*. New York: John Wiley & Sons, 1960.

Rapoport, Anatol. *Semantics*. New York: Thomas Y. Crowell Co., 1975.

Russell, Bertrand. *Problems of Philosophy*. Oxford: Oxford University Press, 1946.

Saussure, Ferdinand de. *Course in General Linguistics*. Ed. Charles Bally and Albert Sechehaye. Trans. Wade Baskin. New York: Philosophical Library, 1959 (1916).

Searle, John. *Speech Acts*. Cambridge: Cambridge University Press, 1969.

Thurman, Kelly, ed. *Semantics*. Boston: Houghton Mifflin Co., 1960.

Wallis, Mieczyslaw. *Arts and Signs*. Ed. Thomas A. Sebeok. Bloomington; Indiana University Research Center, 1976.

Wimsatt, William K., Jr. *The Verbal Icon*. Lexington, Ky.: University of Kentucky Press, 1954.

Journals   *Education; ETC.: A Review of General Semantics; Quarterly Journal of Speech; Semiotica*

10
The Politics of Language

As with many of the aspects of language we have examined, the subject of this chapter is a paradox. On the one hand, language signs are arbitrary. The significance of any sign derives from the relationship of the sign to other elements of the structural network: from antonymy or synonymy, from collocations, from speech acts, from society and culture in general. On the other hand, the force of precedence may seem as strong as the force of arbitrariness. Once signification has evolved around a sign, it is extremely difficult to separate the sign into its components (signifier and signified). It is therefore extremely difficult in ordinary usage to recognize that signs are arbitrary. Meaning, for most of us, is part and parcel of words. As a result, in ordinary usage there is virtually no such thing as a purely denotative, extensional, value-free lexical item. The sign is arbitrary, but the power of signification, the intensional impact of most words, does not feel arbitrary.

The phrase "politics of language" refers to the uses of that impact, power, or force of signification. Power may be used wisely and well, but it may also be used unwisely and with ill effects. The intention of power users, or politicians (in the broadest sense of the term), may be honorable and conscientious or dishonorable and exploitative. In this chapter, we will investigate some of the broad areas of social contact where the political (power-using) aspect of signs seems to be most clearly exploitative. Word politicians may not be conscious of what they are doing with language, may not intend the effects they produce, and may be irritated at being accused of exploitative behavior. But just as competence and performance are not always the same, so neither are intention and behavior necessarily identical.

In particular, we shall focus on the use of loaded words, those lexical items or phrases with strong emotional (affective) overtones. The connotations are so strong, in fact, that the emotions they arouse may be said to get in the way of extensional (cognitive) communication. Loaded words are weapons and are used as such by word-politicians to control the responses of auditors by manipulating certain words to achieve an emotive, rather than a rational, effect (if we may metaphorically split the brain in that fashion for a moment). Thus, a political use of language is not so much a communication of information as an evocation of emotion, which the word politician wants, consciously or otherwise, to use for his or her own purposes.

We shall begin with politics itself and advertising, the most clearly self-serving uses of language; then we shall move to more subtly political manipulations: in racial/ethnic language, in sexist language, in taboo and euphemistic language, and in propaganda. The basic purpose of these kinds of word politics is the acquisition or the display of power: dominance or control of one group by another group, through the use of language.

Political Language

Unnerved by Vietnam and Watergate, governmental cost overruns and inflation, in the last few decades Americans have become more than usually suspicious of politicians. Fewer and fewer Americans believe that politicians tell the truth or that their language is extensionally reliable. To be sure, any political figure is bound to be controversial simply because he or she is seeking the power of office or already has that power and does not want to give it up. Any officeholder must make or participate in decisions that some people will find controversial; the greater the polarizing of interests during the controversy, the more suspicious the losing side is likely to be. In that sense, politicians are easy to attack, as easy as advertisers. Indeed, any of us is vulnerable to suspicions of self-aggrandizement and power plays any time we shade the truth to make ourselves or some project of ours more appealing. We aim here, however, not so much to shoot at an easy target as to discover why the target is so easy. What sorts of language exploitation do politicians indulge in?

Good feelings. One of the most obvious kinds of political language is the evocation of patriotism. The two-valued implication in such an evocation is that a vote for Senator Phogbound is patriotic, good, while a vote for his opponent is not-patriotic, treacherous. The same phrases keep appearing, loaded with sentiment: "this great country," "our great nation," "this great land." The scope of history and the sweep of geography are magically conjured up by such phrases, as the listeners are intensionally invited to believe that America has always been "great" and will always be "great," but only if we elect Phogbound. What "great" means is seldom defined extensionally or even intensionally—big? wise? healthy?—nor, for the candidate's purposes, should the word be defined. If it were, what Phogbound means by "great" might turn out to be different from what his auditors mean. Better to wave the word and let it be presupposed that everyone agrees: "great," whatever it is, is good.

Another timeworn tactic is to flatter the audience, but rarely directly. Rhetoricians call this "establishing consubstantiality"—common ground—with the audience. Phogbound may refer to "the sensible voters," "the public good," "my well-informed listeners," leaving each person to conclude that he or she particularly is being referred to as sensible, knowledgeable, and informed. Of *course,* we are sensible: we are the public. *Naturally,* we are well-informed: Phogbound has told us so. Flattery of this sort can also be used second-hand, as Phogbound associates himself in our mind with other people we already admire. Long-dead presidents are particularly favored here, for the incumbent president may be going through a spell of unpopularity. John F. Kennedy spoke of Lincoln; Lyndon B. Johnson referred to both Kennedy and Harry S Truman; Richard Nixon sometimes evoked Dwight Eisenhower and sometimes Woodrow Wilson. A shrewd candidate will change his mentor to suit the audience, for at a banquet sponsored by Americans for Democratic Action, Phogbound would not get many votes by claiming a close friendship with Richard Nixon.

A third technique for evoking positive feelings is to refer to "the record." An incumbent seeking reelection will "point" (always "with pride") to his voting record, its impeccable reflection of wisdom and skill, its invariable benefits for his audience. He may often "stand on" his record as well. A candidate looking for office for the first time will also point, frequently with scorn, to his opponent's record: the opponent's votes are self-serving; he has ignored his constituents; he has been absent half the time or under the sway of "lobbyists" and "special-interest groups," neither of whom is in the audience, of course. "The record"—so we are allowed to assume—is an infallible and independent source of ultimate truth, and truth is something with which—we are also allowed to assume—every member of the audience is familiar.

Bad feelings. When a politician switches from assurance to attack, the loaded words swing to the negative. Fear and scorn, rather than comfortable certitude, are the emotions called up here. The trick is first to identify a fear the audience will share, and then to turn that fear into scorn and anger against Phogbound's opponents, who are made to signify the fear. Since everyone is afraid of many things, the candidate need only discover which of those fears is uppermost at the moment.

In the 1950s, Communism was a good bugbear to work on; the threat of "Communist encroachment" got a great many military-aid bills passed, books banned, and civil-defense shelters built. The 1960s grappled with two big fears. On one side, there was the "military-industrial complex" (including a "conspiracy" of "Big Business," "Big Brother," and "the Establishment"), whose collective aim was identified as the "oppression" of the "people." On the other side, there were assorted "radicals" and "extremists" supposedly determined to "destroy" everything that had "made America great." In the 1970s, government itself became a principal cue for fear or rage: a politician had only to mutter against "taxes," "waste," or "government interference" in the lives of the "people" (who might or might not have been the 1960s "people"), and he or she was virtually assured of office.

Specific fears besides these rather broad ones will appear in particular regions or in response to some local circumstances. For example, in the 1970s, the counterpulls of technology and natural resources tugged at voters' feelings. Consequently, "job security" and "industrial growth" alternated with "ecology" and "respect for the land" as factors to be defended, one set of factors serving as the other's dichotomous antonym. As the economic situation grows less stable, the tugging occurs between "taxes," "welfare," and "the high cost of living" on one side, versus "compassion," "the disadvantaged," and "social services" on the other. Here, too, the exploitative tactic is to arouse fear that something the audience values is in jeopardy, and then to turn that fear into scorn against the values of the opposition.

Fog. In addition to affirmation and negation, politicians can use a third linguistic technique: buzz or fad words with a high fog index, that is, abstract, nonreferential, and often polysemous signs (chapter 8). This technique appears most often when a politician is in trouble and trying to justify his behavior to "the folks back home." The fog gets particularly thick when the senator has voted in a way he knows his constituents will not like or, because of some pressure, is proposing an action that even he may feel is outrageous.

George Orwell has declared, in a famous essay on "Politics and the English Language," that politics is largely "the defense of the indefensible." Orwell parodies politicians' inflated and pompous language in this passage, translated into fog from *Ecclesiastes:*

> Objective consideration of contemporary phenomena compels the conclusion that success or failure in competitive activities exhibits no tendency to be commensurate with innate capacity, but that a considerable element of the unpredictable must invariably be taken into account.[1]

By the time Phogbound has finished a passage like this, no one will care what he was talking about anyway, which is the purpose of this distractive technique. The stratagem is so effective that it has even acquired several names of its own: officialese, baffle-gab, polybabble.

1. George Orwell, "Politics and the English Language," from *Shooting an Elephant and Other Essays* (New York: Harcourt, Brace and Company, 1950), p. 84. The original (*Ecclesiastes* 9:11) reads: "I returned and saw under the sun, that the race is not to the swift, nor the battle to the strong, neither yet bread to the wise, nor yet riches to men of understanding, nor yet favour to men of skill; but time and chance happeneth to them all."

One does not have to be a politician to use baffle-gab, however, because one does not have to be a politician to wish, sometimes, to cover one's tracks in a maze of words. If people do not understand what one is talking about—especially if the subject is of deep concern to them—then one has a sort of power over them. The fog makes it nearly impossible to assign responsibility to anyone, least of all to the speaker. Small children sometimes play this game of fogging the issue when, in answer to a question like "Who broke the vase?" they say innocently, "I don't know. It just got broken."

The other techniques (reassurance, attack) and their variants are not confined to politicians, either. Indeed, the purr, the snarl, and the side step form the basis for all word-political manipulation, from the subtlest advertising to the most flagrant propaganda. In every case, the technique is to manipulate the auditors' emotions rather than their ideas, in such a way that they will do what the speaker wants: vote for him or buy something, disparage his enemy or boycott a competitor, go to war or sign a treaty, or just keep some groups of people "in their place"—in other words, submissive to whoever has the power.

The Language of Advertising

Like politicians, advertisers use language in an obvious way, but their manipulations continue because consumers, like voters, keep responding to the manipulations anyway. Like politicians, too, advertisers must be obvious: they have to get our attention somehow, in the middle of all the other advertisers/politicians clamoring for it, and they have to do so in such a way that we will vote or buy. In both areas, an audience's disinclination to act is as good as its outright "No." Politicians are not reelected if everyone stays home, nor are products sold if no one goes to the store. Thus, also in both areas, it is more important to reach the voters/consumers than it is to deal with them as intelligent creatures. And most voters/consumers are neither reached nor stirred to action by appeals to reason. Intensional, loaded appeals work better at getting us to vote or buy than do extensional, cognitive ones. Sophisticated advertising will mix reason, wit, and style with the "hard sell" of emotive appeals, but it is feeling that does the basic selling.

As with political language, there are three basic tactics: arouse good feelings, arouse bad feelings, or blur the issues altogether. Often the tactics are combined. The particular forms of advertising tactics are slightly different from the political ones, for Phogbound did not always have to be so focused as an ad does. Sometimes he wanted election or reelection (buying, metaphorically), but sometimes he wanted support for a bill or justification in a stance. These latter attitude-responses are less measurable than the totaling of dollar figures in product sales, so in a sense, advertisers have it easier than politicians: they know very quickly whether their manipulations were successful or not.

Anxieties.   It is important that the arousal of feelings, good or not so good, is often mixed in advertisements. If the basic purpose is to get consumers to buy, then an advertiser must attempt to create in the consumers a feeling that buying Product X will solve some problem or other. This is referred to as "creating a need for the product" or product need, and is similar to Phogbound's evocation of fear. In order to develop a product need in the consumer, the advertiser often has to create the problem that Product X will supposedly solve. (In advertising, most problems can be solved with a purchase of something.) There are many ways to accomplish this, all hinging on a subtle, frequently unstated appeal to our anxious feelings of inadequacy.

For example, take the common testimonial advertisement. Some famous person appears in an ad to declare that he or she uses Product X, recommends it, and hopes you'll buy it, too. On the surface, this is a quite straightforward appeal to our faith in the famous person's credibility: if Celebrity says X is all right, then it must be all right. But an implicit fear attaches itself to the testimonial's appeal in the audience's mind: "I am not a celebrity and never will be; therefore, in two-valued terms, I am a failure. But perhaps if I buy X, I will take on some of Celebrity's aura."

If, in addition to the evoked fear, the product itself appeals to an already existent fear—which it usually does—then the need for that product becomes doubly strong. Consider some of these common sources of anxiety and the cue words that soothe the fears:

1. "Magic," "miracle," "quick," "time-saving": I'm wasting time that I could better spend on . . . something.
2. "How to," "easy," "introduction to," "simple": I'm not very good at doing some chore or other.
3. "Now," "introducing," "revolutionary," "startling": I'm not keeping up with fashion or trends; I'm turning into a fuddy-duddy and a stick-in-the-mud.
4. Toilet paper that is softer than soft, cars that are safe and economical (or unsafe and expensive), floors that shine without being mopped, snowmobiles that do cartwheels, cereals that supply the minimum daily requirements for vitamins and sugar: I'm a poor provider for my family's needs, which are endless.
5. Most important of all, I'm inadequate physically, especially sexually: I have gray hair, a pantyhose bulge, a ring around the collar, denture breath, body odor, sagging breasts, a sore throat, diarrhea, and a headache.

Participatory invitations. We are subtly invited to participate in the ads, not merely to read or hear them but to become emotionally involved with them. We *are* (or wish we were) that long-limbed girl in the green glen, hair blowing out behind us; we *are* (or fantasize that we could be) the rugged cowboy in Stetson and bruised Levis, cigarette smoke trailing behind us. It is *our* car that needs tires, oil additives, super-powered gasoline, liability insurance; it is *our* grimy kitchen floor, drab laundry, dull dishes, droopy selves. When the girl in the shaving-cream ad purrs, it is we who feel flattered. Even if we cannot remember what she was selling, we will remember the momentary glow, the semiseduction she brought with her, and we will buy the shaving cream that makes pretty girls purr at us.

In snaring our attention and inviting us to participate in the ad, copywriters manipulate language in various ways. For example, they will often violate the conversational principle of relevance—not to mention truth—in order to jar us. What does that girl have to do with the car she is leering at? Why is that man leaping out of a window? Why are those women talking to rolls of toilet paper? Copywriters will also shade the illocutionary force from time to time, phrasing an assertion or a command in the form of questions that draw us into the ad, as we silently answer them: "Does she . . . or doesn't she?" "Which twin has the Toni?" Sometimes quite wittily, ads will exploit the polysematic ambiguity of words or phrases: "If gas pains persist, try Volkswagen"; "There is no such thing as a xerox"; "9 out of 10 thousand people drink Campari." The language is often striking, but it is also comparatively simple: the average fog index for advertising is around 8, about the same as that of the *Reader's Digest*.

Advertisements are simply and strikingly written, sometimes memorably so, but they do not communicate information, no matter how many extensional facts they purport to give. Consumers no doubt would lose much if there were no advertisements to point out different products and prices, and advertisements can be a real stimulus to the Gross National Product Index. They can also powerfully distort perceptions and values as well as present information and cognition, so that buying something seems the solution to any pain, any distress, any feeling of guilt or inadequacy. The world of advertising, like the world of politics, not only is two-valued; it subtly suggests that consumers are two-valued, too.

Racist Language

Like politics and advertising, racist language is both simple and complicated. The individual words are not difficult to understand, but the effects of using such language can be troublesome to identify and worse to live with. Racist speech behavior draws on assumptions so deeply buried that it is hard to root them out into the light. Politicians want us to elect them; advertisers want us to buy what they are selling; but what do racists want from us, and how does their language manipulate both us and themselves? What is the power being exerted here?

It is fairly clear that the power is of one group over another, and that the powerful group is usually white, or Caucasian (and frequently male as well), while the subordinate group is everybody else: blacks, chicanos, Amerindians (Native Americans), Puerto Ricans, Italians, Swedes, whoever. We can identify as a racist anyone who argues, explicitly or implicitly, for the supremacy of one racial or ethnic group over another. Racist language, then, is any linguistic behavior that supports racial "superiority"/"inferiority" and the concomitant imbalance of power that results from such concepts.

"Superiority" and "inferiority" are here in quotation marks to make a particular point: those words are so ambiguous, so loaded, and so intensional in meaning that an objective definition of them may not exist. But "inferiority" and "superiority" are the terms most people think in when it comes to racist issues, rather like the response to dialects. If one racial or ethnic group has come to be socially desirable and prestigious, then all others somehow are commonly regarded as being, not just different, but inferior. It is in the interests of those who already enjoy a prestigious (and therefore powerful) position to keep the status quo, to maintain these notions of "superiority" and "inferiority" whether they have any extensional validity or not.

Consequently, racism is nearly universal, so pervasive and common that at times it seems invisible as well—except to those on the receiving end. And since those on the receiving end do not, by and large, have much financial or political power, they also do not have much power to change the racism or even to bring it to the attention of the dominant group. The issue we must grapple with here is the contribution to racism of language practices. Having identified racist language practices, we may then be able to avoid them, as we would try also to avoid any other distortion and confusion we might have permitted language to impose on our perception, such as between extension and intension, or signifier and signified, or gradable and complementary antonyms.

Epithets. When racist language is blunt, there is no mistaking its intention and effects. The racist epithets (abusive or contemptuous names) that we all know are bluntly and straightforwardly meant to insult, to dehumanize, and to humiliate. Such epithets are terms like "jig," "nigger," "spic," "greaser," "wop," "yid," "kike," "gook," or "slopehead." Equally epithetic are pseudojoking references to food habits or national origins, such as "mackerel-snapper," "potato-eater," "bean-eater," "frog," "Mick," "Polack," "Canuck," and so on. People who are called names like these are treated as if they were things or objects, lacking in value, in dignity, and in decency of any kind. If I label someone with such an epithet, I intend to turn that person into a nonperson or at least something subhuman, who lacks the delicate sensitivity and regard for manners, morals, and ethics which I find in myself.

In times of declared war, it is convenient to label the enemy by some such epithet ("Jap" or "Kraut," for example) in order that he may be killed like the nonhuman species he is described as being. But a war need not be declared to be painful, and the very existence of racial epithets serves as a kind of reservoir of hostility. The dehumanizing, war-declaring connotations implicit in the epithets may be the key to the power that such a process wields. If one group of people consciously, overtly, and systematically refers to another group with epithets, as the Nazis did of the Jews throughout the 1920s, 1930s, and 1940s—calling them "parasites," "bacilli," "pestilence," and other forms of disease—then, after a while, it may seem perfectly plausible, reasonable, and humane to exterminate these creatures like "vermin." And that was exactly Hitler's Final Solution to the "problem" of the Jews: extermination—by starvation, by shooting, by cremation—as remorselessly performed as if the human beings were lice or grubworms.

Euphemistic epithets. One need not literally kill people in the process of dehumanizing them. The "vermin" effect can stop short of slaughter and still be terribly painful and humiliating. That is what the epithets in casual use do: they manipulate both the epithet users and the named group so as to convince them both that "frogs" or "mexes" or "honkeys"[2] are disgusting, indecent, stupid creatures, not really human beings at all. Most people know better than to use names like "spic" and "jig" and "wop" in polite company. Only in intimate conversation are the hard-core epithets likely to appear, unless the speaker is very sure of his audience's bias. But the tensions between racial-ethnic groups do not always disappear when the epithets do, so a lot of racist language has become euphemistic, displacing the hard-core term with something less denotatively offensive. Racial euphemisms, however, carry connotatively the same insulting impact and the same implicit intention to persuade the auditors that "we" are good and should stay in power, while "they" are bad and deserve no power at all.

Consider the connotations of the words "black" and "white." Some people have argued that these two words are racist no matter in what associative field or collocation they might be used. That is probably carrying consciousness of political linguistics to extremes, since there are undeniably

2. Most ethnic-racial epithets are applied by the dominant group to those who have less power. The less dominant group does develop names for those in power (like "honkey," "ofay," "white-eyes"), but those epithets ordinarily are not in such wide circulation as are the names for less prestigious groups.

nonracist usages of both terms. "Blackmail" and "whitewash," for instance, both predate racial tensions in America, coming into the English language even before the United States did: the O.E.D. lists the first recorded usage of "blackmail" in 1552, of "whitewash" in 1591. Nevertheless, most of the connotations of "black" in English are unpleasant (night, death, evil, sin) and most of the connotations of "white" are good (purity, virginity, clarity, truth). Much of the time, these connotations are exploited for racist ends.

For instance, observe the implications of the idioms, stock phrases, and clichés that American English has developed from the two words: "free, white, and twenty-one"; "That's white of you"; "He's a real white man." Clearly, the phrases are compliments; it is good to be white. Not so with "black as sin," "blackguard," "blackball." And when "black" becomes a skin color, not just a color generally, it is invariably insulting, as in the now taboo collocations using "nigger."[3] To have "a nigger in the woodpile" is to have hidden problems. To "work like a nigger" is to exhaust oneself at physical labor that no "decent" (white) person would ordinarily touch. To "catch a nigger by the toe" is to play with a toy, not a person.

Even when the word is not "black" or "nigger," but "colored," the insult still stings. For example, because of their construction, the phrases "my colored girl" (a housekeeper or maidservant) and "our colored boys" (in the armed services, usually, but also on a civilian job) do not refer to grown-ups, but to children, no matter how mature the referential persons might be. And the people are implicitly possessions of the speaker, like a can-opener, a plow, or a slave—not a person. "Colored" and "darkie" were both formerly polite versions of "nigger." "Negro" held sway as their successor until the 1960s, when it too became regarded as racist. "Black" appeared to be the acceptable sign in the 1970s, as in "Black is beautiful!" or "Black Power." The value of any other sign but "black" is now usually regarded as too loaded, too condescending, to serve as a referential term.

When used in certain constructions, however—and this is true of all racial designators, whether they are epithets or not—even the neutral sign "black" carries intensional significance. Two such collocations are particularly notable: "You don't look/act/sound/think/drive like a black person [or an Italian, or whatever]," and the use of labels of primary potency.

"You don't look/act/sound like a. . . ." This type of utterance, apparently a statement, has the illocutionary force of a question: "Everything I have ever learned about you people[4] has informed me that all of you behave the same

---

3. The word "nigger" is probably derived from variant pronunciations of "negro," "niger," or "nigre" (all from the Latin *niger,* meaning black in color).
4. "You people" is another classic example of bigotry and stereotyping, by the way.

way [you all dance well, or you love tacos, or you cry a lot], but this particular individual does not behave in a typical fashion: why not?" In other words, when a speaker is jolted out of his complacent assumptions about stereotypes, he is likely to react with surprise and probably also with dismay or irritation. The presupposition is that the person addressed somehow is at fault for not conforming to the speaker's expectations. Even more deeply buried than the illocutionary question may be a sort of half wish, half command that the "deviant" kindly reshape himself to fit the prejudicial mold.

Another equally curious presupposition occurs here, too, for the speaker of such a remark as "You don't look/act/sound like . . . " seems to assume that the auditor will, or should, take it as a compliment. (That the compliment-presupposition directly contradicts the command-presupposition is the sort of paradox that is not resolvable on the linguistic level.) In other words, even the holder of the stereotype seems to recognize that the prejudicial expectations are limited and constrictive. In effect, he compliments the "deviant" on being better, and therefore more powerful and more worthy of respect, than the mold has allowed—which is to say, more like the speaker or like what the speaker values. "You don't look, etc." is a remarkably intensional, one might even say a remarkably egocentric, observation to make. But dominant groups, who are used to power, can define "good" and "bad" in terms they are used to, by descriptions of themselves.

Labels of primary potency. These labels are signs whose intensional significance is so strong that it dilutes or obliterates the value of any other nearby sign. These labels are so potent that they become the primary signs in any collocation. They can appear in any context, but in a racial/ethnic one, the primary labels are of course the racial/ethnic signs: "*Black* lawyer," "*Chicano* doctor," "*Indian* linebacker," "*French* pipe-fitter," "*Irish* cook." As with all two-valued antonymy, use of a marking sign like these labels focuses the attention on the marked term (the label) and not on the unmarked (normative) term. Thus, a "black lawyer" is a qualified lawyer, a limited lawyer, a modified lawyer, not a "real" lawyer, for a "real" (i.e., white male) lawyer would just be called a lawyer, the unmarked or normative term. Many users of these labels believe they are behaving in a purely extensional manner when they apply the labels, conveying only cognitive information—not *this* lawyer, but *that* lawyer—and in a strictly syntactic sense, that is true. The labels do occupy the same kind of position in a sentence as does any other adjective, usually right in front of the noun. If the adjective were only extensional, however, then why choose the racial/ethnic sign? Why not speak, just as often, of the "short lawyer," the "tall doctor," the "linebacker from Philadelphia"?

All of the racist language used about black people is also used about any other subordinate group. Only the particular details of the terms are different. For example, white people have a stockpile of clichés about Amerindian people: "Indian-giver" (someone who extends a gift and then takes it back); "Give it back to the Indians" (it wasn't worth anything anyway, so they might as well have it); "The only good Indian is a dead Indian." Black people are supposed to be subhuman animals, with an animal's natural rhythm and endurance, who can perform extraordinary physical labor, but native Americans are not supposed to be capable of any decently human work at all: "lazy Indians," "drunken Indians," "savages," "prairie niggers." As another example, Spanish-Americans are often referred to as "lazy," too, as in the stereotype of the happy Mexican peasant in big hat and *serape* dozing under a cactus. In the Southwest, drivers sometimes speak of "Mexican overdrive" (lazily coasting in neutral gear) and of the "Mexican [Aztec, Tijuana] two-step" or "Montezuma's revenge" (diarrhea, from the "uncivilized" food a tourist eats in Mexico).

The cumulative effect of epithets, stereotypes, and labeling—examples of which are far more numerous than what appears here—is to identify those labeled groups not merely as different, but specifically as bad. It follows, in this two-valued kind of reasoning, that the dominant group has the moral right to use unpleasant language and behavior toward the subordinate group and especially deserves to retain its social, political, and financial power.

Why change racist language? Since language overlaps with so much else in human life—with thoughts and feelings, with beliefs and behavior—it sometimes may seem almost impossible to separate language from other kinds of behavior. Therefore, it may seem impossibly naive to propose that an alteration in language behavior might help bring about changes in other kinds of behavior. Few social problems are so simple that merely using another word here, a different one there, will solve the problem, whether the conflict be a clash between individuals or an undeclared war between groups. No politician becomes a better person simply by declining to use the traditionally baffling and fuzzy language of politics. Nor do products become safer or more sensible just because we ease the language used about them. Neither do hostilities between racial or ethnic groups disappear if we decline to use the ugly epithets.

We must recognize, however, that although language use does not by itself cause or rectify social problems, nevertheless, language always does play a greater or lesser part in these conflicts. It would be too narrowly two-valued to say that because changing the sign will not by itself change the behavior the sign evokes, we therefore need not bother with the language at all. On the contrary, changing language behavior is an excellent place to start, as was demonstrated in the 1960s with the widespread insistence that epithets like "nigger" and condescending terms like "boy" must not be used any more in certain contexts. Other behaviors of white people toward black people did, in fact, change: not solely because of the changed language, but at least partly because of it.

Once speakers become consciously aware of the psychological and political implications of some terms, it is possible—not inevitable, but possible—to think and behave in different, less two-valued, less condemnatory ways. A buzz phrase in the 1960s and 1970s for the process was consciousness raising: bringing formerly subconscious assumptions, implications, and condemnations up to the surface. Once made visible, they could be tested, referentially and extensionally, to see whether they had any real merit. Then, if they did not, other, less assumptive and loaded terms might be offered and used, and other, less prejudiced attitudes and behaviors might develop.

To oversimplify the process, we might say that there are four stages involved:

1. Identification. Identify the specific terms that are loaded and identify why they are loaded rather than referential.
2. Extinction. Eliminate or extinguish the use of the loaded language, the epithets, the euphemisms.
3. Substitution. Discover and reinforce the use of neutral, "unloaded," extensional terms that do not encourage racism or two-valued interpretation.
4. Reinforcement. Encourage other behaviors that reinforce the use of neutral language; extend language behavior into all the realms of social interactions: playing, working, dating, watching TV, driving a car, studying, whatever.

In other words, if you decide not to call someone a "jerk," then you try not to behave toward him as if he were a jerk. You try to act toward him as if he were just as valuable as you are. And maybe he is.

Sexist Language

Like racism, sexism means always favoring one group (one gender—nearly always male) at the expense of another. Also like racism, sexism is frequently subtle in its manifestations, is pervasive throughout all of the many behaviors human beings indulge in, and is extremely difficult to identify, neutralize, and change. The imbalance of power between males and females is so strong and seems, by now, so "natural" and "inevitable" that until very recently, every institution in our society, including language, supported it. The power was not seen as unevenly distributed, but as balanced, inevitable, right and proper. Gender, like race, "naturally" (so the presupposition went) determines behavior, and behavior determines reward or power. Language use still supports that deterministic notion.

The marked gender. We have already noted in chapter 8 that the English language is male. The unmarked, or dominant, terms are male ("man" or "mankind" means human beings of either gender); the marked terms are female. To indicate the singular pronominal form for any given person of unspecified gender, one uses "he," as in the last two sentences in the section on racism. Many observers have proposed that this kind of sexism could be obliterated by the introduction of new pronoun forms that do not convey a label of gender, like "gen" for "man" (in its generic sense) or "tey" for either "he" or "she" where the sex difference is not important. Thus, one would say "the politician . . . tey" instead of "the politician . . . he" or instead of the admittedly awkward "the politician . . . he or she." Many observers feel that combination words, like "chairman," carry the same sexist bias as the pronouns do. Some people attempt to remove the bias by saying "chairman" of or to a male and "chairwoman" of or to a female, but other people insist that because "chair" itself is supposedly a title and not a designation of gender, then to include either "man" or "woman" after "chair" is sexist. Two alternatives have been proposed: either use "chair" alone, as in "May I address the chair?" or use "chairperson," regardless of the sex of the person holding that office. But those who adopt the second choice, "chairperson," often apply it only to a woman, so that "-person" has become a curious euphemism for "women."[5]

The male orientation of English carries two complementary implications: being male is normative and natural; and therefore, not being male is abnormal and unnatural. Terms for occupations illustrate the point. Except for a few occupations like homemaking, nursing, and teaching, which are assumed to be proper work for women, the labels of primary potency are always appended when a female is doing the job, but not when a male is: "woman (or lady) doctor," "woman lawyer," "woman telephone-installer," or "woman linebacker." (A male who becomes a nurse or a kindergarten teacher or a homemaker undergoes labeling in reverse—"male nurse"—because, in our culture, it is so odd for males to do these things.) The labeling here produces the same effect as does the racial-ethnic labeling: a suggestion that the lawyer is limited or qualified, not a "real" lawyer, but a "lady" lawyer. In a related manner, women are frequently identified by physical labels, although men usually are not, as in "the charming, red-

5. The same thing appears to be happening with the courtesy title "Ms.," referred to in chapter 7. "Ms." was initially supposed to be a neutral term like "Mr.," which did not identify the marital status of the individual, but in many cases "Ms." is coming to be used in place of "Miss," particularly to identify a divorced woman.

haired skydiver" or "the perky, shapely cellist." Anyone reading descriptions like that knows they refer to women, not to men.

Because value and therefore power attaches to maleness in our culture and our language, females are basically limited to two kinds of power. One source is men, the residual or second-hand status and power women acquire through their attachment to men. The more legal the association, the more powerful, of course: being somebody's "wife" is better than being somebody's "mistress," "paramour," "concubine," "shack-job," or even "common-law wife." But, it would seem, any association at all is better than none: "Mrs." carries much more status than does "Miss" or "Ms.," and a "spinster" is much less valuable than a "bachelor," although both these terms refer to the condition of being unmarried. Our language use clearly suggests that an unmarried man is perhaps a peculiar creature, but an unmarried woman is repellent. But even the residual power a woman gets from being married is still subject to interpretation, for her status and value may sometimes be reinforced, as when she is (mockingly?) called "the better half"; but they may also be denigrated, as when she is called "the ball and chain."

Ambivalence and classification. Perhaps this ambivalence, or two-way response, derives from a woman's other source of power, which is, expectably, her sex. Something so powerful, so important, and so potentially confusing as sex and sexuality always produces confused and inconsistent reactions, sometimes favorable but just as often unfavorable. Ambivalence toward the sexuality of women shows up in the tendency in English to classify them in loaded and two-valued terms: as devil or goddess, seductress or virgin, poison queen or princess. Although males can be referred to as "guys," there are very few neutrally valued terms with which to describe females.

Mostly, the lexicon favors the "devil" implication in such hostile, and taboo, epithets as "bitch," "slut," "tramp," "round-heels," "cock [or prick] teaser," "piece of tail [or ass]," "twat," "snatch," or "cunt." (No equivalently hostile terms exist for males taken exclusively as sexual creatures; words like "stud" or "ballsy" are compliments.) Note that these epithets locate the hostility specifically in sexual terms: a woman is defined by her genitals, summed up by her gender, identified by her sex, as a black-skinned or brown-skinned person is labeled solely by color. The sexual connotations are "bad" here, and so, intensionally, is the possessor of that sexuality, the female. But even the supposedly more polite terms for women frequently focus on some aspect of sexuality: "broad," "bimbo," "dame" (this last, a shortened version of "madame," ironically applied). As another example, the word "hysteria," a term almost never applied to males, is etymologically derived from the Greek word *hysteros,* uterus.

When the emphasis shifts from one side of the dichotomy to the other, from woman as devil to woman as goddess, the loading is still intensional and still focused on sexuality and the roles thought appropriate to the female gender. "She's a good wife and mother" used to be the highest compliment a woman could be paid, and "The hand that rocks the cradle rules the world" used to identify a woman's true (biological) function—and value—in life. Mild epithets merely dodge the issue of gender by reducing women to toys ("chick," "doll"), to food ("sweetie," "honey," "sugar"), or to infants ("baby"). Such terms do not identify women as adults, symbolically not even as human beings. Even when the labels are supposedly complimentary, the point is that women are *identified* as sexual creatures, whereas men are described as *participating* in sexuality. In other words, men do other things, more valuable things.

Should a woman attempt any of those other things that men do, she is likely to be punished. The two-valued system carries over here as well, for whereas "womanliness" signifies serenity, passivity, supportiveness, sweetness, and domesticity, "manliness" carries the signification of assertiveness, independence, aggressiveness, stout-heartedness, and activity. Any woman who does not behave in "womanly" ways is often viewed as "trying to act like a man," as if assertiveness belonged only to men. Such a woman may be seen as a threat, a castrator, a traitor to her "proper" role. The very same actions or attitudes will be described in negatively loaded terms for women, positively loaded ones for men, as this humorous but serious list shows:

> A businessman is aggressive; a businesswoman is pushy. He is good on details; she is picky. He loses his temper because he's so involved in his job; she's bitchy. He follows through; she doesn't know when to quit. His judgments are her prejudices. He is a man of the world; she's been around. He climbed the ladder of success; she slept her way to the top.[6]

That last item, about a woman's sleeping her way to the top, shows how murkily intensional are the judgments made about women, and how likely sex is to be identified as a factor in any aspect of her behavior.

Sexism toward males. Let us acknowledge, however, that men also are frequently constricted by the roles that their gender imposes on them. The language, and the force of the social judgments contained in language, is often just as harsh toward "unmanly" men as toward "unwomanly" women. A passive, supportive, unaggressive male may be called by epithets

---

6. The list has appeared in many forms in many places, from *Woman's Day* to *Ms.* to *Reader's Digest*. See Alma Jacobs, *Views from Women Achievers* (New York: American Telephone and Telegraph Company, 1977), p. 88.

as nasty as any applied to women, in a poorly disguised attempt to exercise power over his behavior by making it conform to the rigidly two-valued stereotype of "masculinity." The parallels of attack are striking. An "un-womanly" woman is labeled a lesbian or lez(zy), a dyke, a ball-cutter or ball-breaker (a castrating female); an "unmanly" man may be called a pansy, a fairy, a faggot, a queer, a nance, a punk (a castrated male).[7]

Less overtly but just as powerfully, a man's "masculinity" is constantly appealed to—and therefore constantly tested—with advertisements that depict "real" men as always being potent, dominant, in control: colognes with names like "Macho," in bottles shaped like erect phalluses; cars that promise (or threaten?) to "make weak men strong, stong men invincible"; cigarettes or beer or shaving cream that will magically turn him into the rugged superhero he is supposed to be. To be trapped inside the cage of perpetual potency, sexual or otherwise, and always expected to perform, to be active, to be right, can be just as harmful as being caged inside the image of passivity, nurturance, and a craving for the perfect floor wax.

So, as with racism, we need to identify the sexist language, extinguish it, substitute less loaded terminology, and reinforce other "neutralizing" behaviors. If we continue to speak and act in ways that perpetuate the power of the old presuppositions and collocations, we shall continue to do an injustice to the complexity of the universe and the human beings therein. We limit and diminish males and females alike when we use sexist language, for we thereby give up one of our principal human qualities: the capacity to distinguish, to discriminate, to compare, to evaluate. In doing that, we abandon our control of language and let ourselves become its prisoners.

Taboos and Euphemisms

As we noted in chapter 7, the word "taboo" comes from the Tonga language; it meant "forbidden by the gods" and even now retains something of its original connotation of sin. Things that are taboo are sinful, perhaps no longer against an immortal, superhuman, omnipotent divinity, but at least against the mortal, human, and extraordinarily powerful dictates of society. Some actions seem to be very nearly universal taboos, regardless of the culture involved—for example, random, nonritualized murder of one's family members—but usually, the taboos change from society to society. Incest and cannibalism are regarded with horror in most Western cultures, but both

---

7. The word "punk" has undergone some interesting changes, according to the *O.E.D.* From the sixteenth to the late nineteenth century, "punk" was one of several slang terms for whores of either gender, particularly catamites; then it began radiating to refer to anything deviant, especially to extra- or nonlegal deviance; in the late 1970s, it specialized again, to refer either to a particular kind of rock musician or to a hyper-masculine male homosexual.

have been seen as honorable elsewhere. Egyptian pharoahs regularly married and bred by their sisters or daughters, and Aztec priests ritually ate the hearts of some sacrificial victims.[8] That we now hold cannibalism and incest taboo does not mean that they are or were universally forbidden, for taboos seem to be nearly as arbitrary as other signs are.

Generally speaking, we may say that whatever a society fears will be labeled taboo. Thus, any action that is frightening—not merely those literally forbidden—can come to be regarded as taboo. For example, death is not forbidden, but it is frightening enough that talking about death may not be allowed. When the act is fearsome, it is very common for the name of that act to become equally fearsome and therefore forbidden. Thus, some signifiers have taboos at least as powerful as those against certain signified referents. The word becomes so identified with the act that to say the word seems almost as bad as doing the deed. The deed is not allowed, so the word is disallowed as well. It is hoped that, by a curious kind of magic, banishing the word may also drive away the forbidden act.

Levels of taboo. But the act never really goes away, so tabooed words retain the "forbidden" flavor of what they signify. It is so dangerous to use them that most members of any society learn very early what can be said sometimes, what can be hinted at or joked about, and what must never, never be mentioned. American children, for example, learn early that money and mutilation are mild taboos, death and anatomy are middle-level taboos, and excretion and sex are "never-never" taboos. The "never-nevers" always generate a rash of euphemisms and humor as strategems for displacing the fear. Always there is a tug between the power of the taboo (the repression, the fear, the imposed silence) and the power of the act (which will not go away). So strong is the connection between signifier and signified that using a taboo sign deliberately—as an intentionally harsh or provocative dysphemism—is almost guaranteed to jolt, shock, and upset one's audience. Children often take great delight in this sort of power game, trotting out the "dirty" words just to hear the uproar raised by the adults.

Money and mutilation. It's "not nice" to talk about how much money you (or your parents) have or don't have, "not nice" to point at or ask loud questions about people with disfigurements or missing parts. The child who does any of these mildly forbidden acts will probably be told not to do so here, in front of the neighbors, and may be scolded or given a lecture on being polite. That money and mutilation are comparatively mild taboos is

---

8. Indeed, eating the brains of one's enemy to gain his wisdom is a very old and widespread custom among many preliterate peoples, and a vestige of that practice may have survived in the custom, observed in Europe as late as the seventeenth century, of putting one's victims' heads up on stakes over the town gates.

signaled linguistically by the relative paucity of euphemisms for them; there are eupehmisms, but not so many as for other taboos. The many slang words for money—"moolah," "gelt," "dough," "green," "lettuce," and so on—are not substitutes for the forbidden word itself. The mildness is also signaled by the popularity of joke words about money, for having no money, or not enough, produces many grim but perfectly acceptable jokes and euphemisms ("broke," "busted," "down on my luck"). Mutilation words, however, such as "feeb," "crip," "gimpy," or "lame," tend to be called "sick" by most people and to flourish only in secret, intimate, or casual conversation. The presupposition is that "spastic" jokes will be heard in school hallways or be told from behind the hand, not in front of the Rotary Club luncheon.

Death. Death is a stronger taboo, as is apparent from the greater number of euphemistic words used to avoid the facts. Death and dying are called "passing away," "passing beyond," "going to sleep," "taking the last bow," "going to one's reward," "going to heaven"—all implying a painless, even a pleasant transition, not frightening or repugnant. Or death will be translated, in a nervous, joking, dysphemistic manner, into something almost humorously exaggerated: "croaking," "crashing," "kicking the bucket," "bombing." Even with the recent interest in the facts of death and the process of dying (thanatology), ordinary language continues to reflect the fear we feel about death as we attempt to make it nicer or less frightening than it really is.

Anatomy. The same processes of joking, euphemising, and dysphemizing occur with the body, but more taboo substitutes appear for anatomy. Anything above the shoulders or at the farthest extremities is generally all right, but anything between the collarbone and the knees is getting dangerous. "Head" and "hands" are the joking exceptions: for head, one sometimes hears "bean," "squash," "noggin"; for hands, we have "meathooks," "paws," "mitts." Perhaps—this is speculative—these regions are exceptional because both head and hands are subliminally recognized as particularly human and particularly vulnerable, and therefore evoke a certain protective fear.

The fear of anatomy used to be much stronger than it is now. Polite Victorians would not refer to legs, but only to "limbs," and our contemporary distinction between the white (or light) and the dark meat of fowl comes from the Victorian refusal to say "breast" and "thigh." Magazine advertisers now occasionally use both of these words, but just as often they will dodge away into euphemisms like "bosom" or "bust." Some nervousness still lingers in conversation about women's breasts, as is apparent from the joke words for them: "boobs" or "boobies," "bazooms," "headlights," "knockers," "balloons," and all kinds of fruit or vegetable comparisons, like "cantaloupes" or "pears." (This last type is analogous to the food epithets men often apply to women, like "honey.") In general, advertisers are very aware of the vague distaste we feel toward our bodies, else why would there be so many exhortations to buy deodorants, avoid "B.O." (body odor), get rid of "denture breath," and stock up on mouthwash to keep our breath "kissing sweet"?

Sexual and excretory organs. The most dangerous anatomical taboos of all, however, are the sexual and excretory organs. Like racial epithets, the number of words (either euphemistic or dysphemistic) for both male and female genitalia is virtually impossible to catalogue. A male has a "cock," a "peter," a "dick," a "dong" (a penis); he has "balls," "nuts," "family jewels" (testicles). A female has a "twat," a "slit," a "muff," a "cunt" (a vulva and vagina—interestingly, these are not always given separate distinctiveness, as the male genitalia are); she may also have a "clit" (clitoris), though there are many fewer euphemisms or joke words for that than for the male's penis. Although most people know these words, they are rarely uttered in "polite company," which usually means any speech situation more formal than the casual or, with much circumspection, the consultative. When we are minding our sociolinguistic manners and attending to the pragmatics of a speech situation, we customarily fend off the danger with any of four stratagems: avoid speaking of these anatomical parts altogether, contrive vague euphemisms (like "privates" or "private parts"), use childish euphemisms (like "wee-wee" or "wienie" for penis), or take refuge in the chilly safety of Latin words (like *pudendum*).

But to the dismay and confusion of the easily embarrassed, human anatomy is so arranged that the sexual organs and the sites of excretion— urination and defecation—are located very closely together. It is often difficult to speak of excretion without also conjuring up sex, and vice versa. Whether our fear of sex and sexual anatomy is causally related to our fear of excretion or not, the two functions and their physiology prompt much the same kind of linguistic evasiveness. Sometimes we speak of excretory functions in children's euphemisms: "pee-pee," "wee-wee," "tinkle," "doo-doo," "pooh-pooh," "ka-ka." (Notice the high proportion of reduplicative and thus half comic words here.) More often, however, the alternatives are the ancient, so-called "Anglo-Saxon" or "four-letter" words that are generally regarded as taboo: "piss" for urinate (actually, Old French, not Old English); for defecate, either "crap" (probably derived from an Old French word for dregs, residue, dirt) or "shit" (probably from an Old Norse word meaning dung). Slightly less taboo alternatives occur in "dump" and "leak," but the most acceptable references are those—like the references to sex and sexual anatomy—which euphemistically avoid any specific terms altogether. We speak of going to the "bathroom," the "powder room," or the "john," "powdering our noses," "washing our hands," or "freshening up." Everybody knows what these constructions mean, and almost everybody secretly acknowledges the hypocrisy of the terms, but not many of us will say otherwise except in very trusted company. We need these substitutes, even when we know they are substitutes, to help us keep a little bit of distance from the unpleasantness of reality.

The same kind of distancing shows up in the euphemisms and dysphemisms for other functions of the excretory-sexual organs, such as disease or menstruation (often treated, in the language, as if it were a disease). "Crotch rot" covers almost every localized disease from herpes to syphilis, but we also speak of "crabs" (they are not) and "the clap." Dysphemisms about menstruation are particularly abundant, in the language of both women and men. It is referred to as "having the rag on" or "having the curse," as "red-letter days" or "the cramps," as "being sick" or "being visited." Sometimes one still hears older euphemisms like "the flower(s)," but about the only nondysphemistic substitute in wide use now is "period." Everything else suggests a pain and unpleasantness about menstruation which needs to be either suppressed or exaggerated but always needs to be avoided.

Sex. Even more do we appear to need distance from sex and sexuality. The anatomy of sexuality is regarded as alarming enough, but in this society, the action and its accompanying impulses are so disconcerting, so illogical, so compelling, and yet so shaming that we forbid mentioning its name, just as many religions forbid uttering the name of the divinity. We may speak, carefully, of "sexual intercourse" or, boldly, of "having sex with" someone. We may perhaps name a few specialized varieties of the act, usually those we disapprove of, like "fornication," "adultery," or "cohabitation." But even these are specific enough to cause many people distress. Often, therefore, we simply refuse to name what we are talking about. We will say "doing it" or "it" or "getting it on" or "getting off," for example, or refer to "sleeping with," "going to bed with," "staying the night with," "making love to [or with]," or just "being with" someone else. Everybody recognizes the references for these signs, but the hopeful assumption appears to be that maybe if we don't say it out loud, we won't do it, either.

Much more common—not more polite or less taboo, but more common—are the derogatory terms, the half-joking, half-hostile dysphemisms for sexual contact. The grandparent of them all, and the most versatile, is "fuck," whose ultimate etymology the *O.E.D.*'s supplement has declared to be unknown. Its usage, however, is ancient (the *O.E.D.* records it in English first in 1503, but it is doubtless older than that); and the recorded values of "fuck" have stayed both consistent and impolite, if not always taboo. It is a noun, a verb, an adverb, an intensifier, a gerund, a participle (both past and present), an adjective, an expletive, and probably somewhere a conjunction and a preposition, too. It forms combinations with almost every conceivable affix, free base, and bound base. The word is as varied in its forms as is the act, and its connotations can range from the pleasant (rarely) or at least neutral to the much more commonly hostile or vengeful, as in "Fuck you!" or "fuck up."

Indeed, it is a curious characteristic of nearly all the taboo words for sexual intercourse that they convey connotations of distaste, mechanization, or blunt hostility, even when the word is male-oriented, as in "ball." (Is there any connection between these connotations and the usual social judgment that women should never hear, much less use, any of these words?) The ambivalence of attraction and repulsion shows up in such words as "rip off a piece," "plough," "prong," "lay" or "get laid," "get one's ashes hauled," "poke," "jump," "ram." These are not joyous actions, but hurtful, tiring, negative. Maybe we mean to convince ourselves that sex does not really have so much power over us after all, or at least that it is not very much fun.

Propaganda

In the course of a somewhat oversimplified look at political language, racist language, sexist language, and taboos and euphemisms, we have described several techniques that mark these kinds of language as propaganda. The Institute for Propaganda Analysis defined "propaganda" in a way that explicitly notes its linguistic-political, power-ploy function:

> . . . expression of opinion or action by individuals or groups deliberately designed to influence opinions or actions of other individuals or groups with reference to predetermined ends.[9]

Careful attention to the many ways language and language users work will show that detecting propaganda is not always so easy as this definition implies. It is clear that propaganda is different from pure research in science, where the answers are not shaped in advance; but how is propaganda different from persuasion generally? Persuasion, after all, is designed to influence opinion, is deliberate, and does have a predetermined end. Still, much speech behavior intended to be persuasive is not necessarily propagandistic. Without falling back on intuitional moralizing—that is, avoiding such two-valued, intensional statements as "Propaganda is dishonorable and immoral; persuasion is honorable and ethical"—we might offer the following three characteristics that often (not always, but often) distinguish propaganda from ordinary persuasion:

9. Clyde R. Miller, "How to Detect Propaganda," *Propaganda Analysis* (November 1937).

A consistent choice of loaded language over more value-free language. Where alternative words or constructions exist for conveying an idea (and English is rich and flexible enough that such alternatives are almost always available), the propagandist will consistently choose the loaded word: "rabble" instead of "crowd," "fat cats" instead of "rich people," "pushy" instead of "assertive," and so on. In particular, the propagandist favors the specialized kind of loading we have seen in this chapter, known by logicians as name calling: epithets, labels of primary potency, dysphemisms, and (for what he favors) euphemisms. Loaded words are obvious power words.

A heavy use of stock phrases. Again, where alternative words or constructions are available, the propagandist favors the known—we might even say the clichéd—over the new. Propaganda of all types is weighted down with stock phrases, ready-made terms, buzz words, fad words, baffle-gab, and fog. A dispute about integration of schools, for example, nearly always produces the collocation "legislated morality." Too many women always cry, "Chauvinist pig!" just as too many men always complain about "bitchy broads." Homosexuals are too often referred to as being either "in the closet" or "parading the streets," unless they are "molesting the children" in the schools. Democrats are "fuzzy-minded [or 'bleeding heart' or 'knee-jerk'] liberals," while Republicans are "toadying" to "vested-interest groups," and any level of government sooner or later is accused of "graft" or "bribery" or at least "wasteful spending."

The value of stock phrases in a language-power situation is twofold. First, nearly everyone knows the clichés, so they are easy and accessible, not requiring any explanations. Second, nearly everyone thinks he or she knows what the phrases mean, so they seem to have agreeably universal signification. Thus, the word-politician does not have to think very hard when he uses a cliché, for the stock signs carry with them a prepackaged signification, nor need the audience stretch their minds, either. Clichés are comfortable. And, because most stock phrases are also loaded one way or another, a clever word-politician can use the familiarity of clichés to sway his audience toward an unthinking acceptance of his argument, gliding past any troublesome points with yet another safe and pleasant bromide. But a reliance on stock phrases almost always leads to a reliance on standard ideas—at best, a sort of mental treading of water; at worst, stagnation or entropy.

A flavor of having the answers ready made. This characteristic is more difficult to define without lengthy analysis of speech or writing samples, but in general, the trait may be described as simplistic smugness. Even without obvious loading of language, and even without resorting to stock phrases, there are utterances that do not ask questions, but present answers; that do not search for truth, but imply truth is already known; and that do not allow for variation, alternatives, or gradations, but suggest that whatever the answer is (not "answers are"), whatever the truth is, the speaker has it, right here, in an easily digestible package that also does not cost very much. Just vote for (or against) Senator Phogbound or the Equal Rights Amendment or a reduction of taxes or wilderness areas or nuclear power plants or whatever, and all of our troubles will be over. This kind of language always smacks of an advertising campaign for a pill to solve your problems, not mentioning that the problems may not be so simple as is implied or that the pill itself may cause other problems.

Propaganda is, above all, persuasive language, but it is a back-door kind of persuasion, "hidden persuasion," manipulation of words so that emotions rather than reason become dominant in the listeners' minds. Propaganda is the antithesis of inquiry, the opposite of investigation. It reduces; it simplifies; it restructures a large and complex universe to something tiny and manageable; and it does so by diminishing liveliness of thought, variety of experience, and exploration of truth's multiple possibilities. Propaganda does all this, first, by evoking those connotations in words which are most likely to frighten or alarm us, making us more inclined to flee or fight than to think, and then by turning that fear into uncritical sentimentality or unthinking scorn. Like the other political uses of language which it epitomizes, perhaps the worst fault of propaganda is that it does not allow us to think for ourselves.

Review Questions

1. What is a political use of language? What are the aims of such a use?
2. Define "loaded words" and give some examples.
3. What three tactics do politicians employ in their manipulation of language?
4. What particular tactic does advertising language use?
5. What are participatory invitations? How do they work?
6. What constitutes racist language? How does it work?
7. What kinds of racist language qualify as euphemistic?
8. Define these terms: epithet, stereotype, label of primary potency, marking, propaganda.
9. What is sexist language? How does it work?
10. What are the major types of taboo in language? How does a taboo work in language?

Selected Reading

Allport, Gordon W. *The Nature of Prejudice.* Reading, Mass.: Addison-Wesley Publishing, 1954.

Arnold, Thurman W. *The Symbols of Government*. New Haven, Conn.: Yale University Press, 1935.

Barthes, Roland. *Mythologies*. New York: Hill and Wang, 1972.

Berne, Eric. *Games People Play: The Psychology of Human Relationships*. New York: Grove Press, 1964.

Grotjahn, Martin. *The Voice of the Symbol*. New York: Dell Publishing Co., 1971.

Hall, Edward T. *The Hidden Dimension*. New York: Doubleday & Co., 1959.

Harre, Tom. *Life Sentences: Aspects of the Social Role of Languages*. New York: John Wiley & Sons, 1976.

Hymes, Dell, ed. *Language in Culture and Society*. New York: Harper & Row, 1964.

Jameson, Frederick. *The Prison-House of Language*. Princeton, N.J.: Princeton University Press, 1972.

Lakoff, Robin. *Language and Woman's Place*. New York: Harper & Row, 1975.

Mayer, Martin. *Madison Avenue, U.S.A.* New York: Harper & Row, 1958.

McLuhan, Marshall. *Understanding Media*. New York: McGraw-Hill, 1964.

Meerloo, Joost A. M. *Unobtrusive Communication*. Assen, The Netherlands: Van Gorcum, 1964.

Miller, Casey, and Kate Swift. *Words and Women: Reality Askew in the English Language*. New York: Doubleday/Anchor Books, 1976.

Mueller, Claus. *The Politics of Communication*. New York: Oxford University Press, 1973.

Ogilvie, David. *Confessions of an Advertising Man*. New York: Atheneum Publishers, 1963.

Orwell, George. *Shooting an Elephant and Other Essays*. New York: Harcourt Brace Jovanovich, 1974 (1945).

Packard, Vance. *The Hidden Persuaders*. New York: David McKay Publishers, 1957.

Partridge, Eric. *A Dictionary of Clichés*, 4th ed. New York: The Macmillan Co., 1950.

Thorne, Barrie, and Nancy Henley, eds. *Language and Sex: Difference and Dominance*. Rowley, Mass.: Newbury House, 1975.

Wootton, A. J. *Dilemmas of Discourse: Controversies About the Sociological Interpretation of Language*. New York: Holmes and Meier Publishers, 1976.

Wright, Will. *Six-Guns and Society*. Berkeley: University of California Press, 1975.

Journals *Journal of Abnormal and Social Psychology; Journal of Popular Culture; Psychology Today*

11
The Writing of Language

The word "writing" generally has three related but distinct meanings: system or characters, such as alphabetic letters; penmanship, or handwriting; and composition, or creation of written documents, whether bills of lading, poems, plays, essays, resumés, or whatever. All three associative fields stem from the same source—the characters or letters—but each field also covers a separate area of meaning, unrelated to the others. Because of the word's variety of meaning, "writing" per se is difficult to discuss in a coherent but brief manner. Somewhat arbitrarily, therefore, we will restrict our focus in this chapter to the first and the third of those three common meanings, omit penmanship, and acknowledge that there is a big division between writing as system and writing as composition.

It must also be acknowledged, however, that the connection between system and composition is important: the particular form of language use, the written form. Writing, either as system or as composition, is not merely a pale form of speech but a distinct form of language, parallel with, and in some situations as important as, the spoken form. Writing has its own evolution, its own requirements, and its own value and signification. Sometimes the evolution, requirements, and value/signification are identical with or parallel to those of speech, but sometimes they are not.

Writing and Speech

The first universal principle of language (chapter 3) is that the spoken form is primary: it is acquired first, is used more often, and is *linguistically* more significant than the written form. Linguistically, speech is more important because it more accurately reflects the performance of language behaviors than does writing and is therefore a more reliable source of data about language competence. But it cannot be denied that in some respects, writing as a sociocultural instrument is much more important than speech. True, children learn to write relatively late in their language-acquiring and language-using careers; and true, many fewer people can write or read than can speak. Nevertheless, without writing, the civilizations of the world probably would not now exist in their present forms.

In its earliest stages, writing was primarily a technique for keeping records: how much corn was stored this year, how many people came to pay tribute, who went to war with whom. Eventually, however, writing turned into a communication technique that in some ways is quite different from the spoken form of language. The two forms are related, of course, for both have to do with language; but three differences between them are extremely important.

The first is that writing developed as a language form much later than speech did: perhaps half a million years ago for speech, but only ten thousand years—at the most—for writing. Second, we do not have to speculate so much about the origin of writing as about the origin of speech; we can trace the development of the written form almost from its beginnings. Indeed, the permanence of written forms is strong evidence for the inevitability of language change. Third, the permanence of writing, as contrasted with the ephemeral and fleeting nature of speech, means that written language is inherently more conservative than speech. Writing systems do change, as we shall see, and writing as an art form—composition—also changes; but neither changes so quickly as speech.

This permanence and conservatism of writing has both advantages and disadvantages. A principal advantage is that records, language forms, and written arts are preserved, as spoken materials could not be. Additionally, communication across time and space is possible through the written medium, but not ordinarily through the spoken: until the telegraph and then the telephone gave us control of distance, we were limited to writing letters. But a disadvantage inherent in the permanence of writing is that sooner or later, spoken forms become altered beyond the phonetic capacity of written mechanisms for recording language. No matter how closely a written form might originally have represented sound, eventually there will be a gap between speech sounds and written forms. That gap produces orthographic (spelling) problems in every language that uses writing. Furthermore, the greater the distinctions between the written and the spoken forms of a language, the more difficult it is for speakers to learn the writing system.

Writing Systems

People who are literate (can read and write) in English, or in most of the Indo-European languages, sometimes wrongly assume that the Latin or Roman characters are the only writing system. But many written languages not only do not use the Roman alphabet; they use no alphabet at all. So in addition to alphabets, we shall investigate three other kinds of writing systems: pictographs, logographs, and syllabaries. These three types were also predecessors of alphabets, so our investigation of writing systems will be

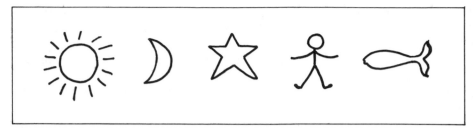

Figure 11.1   Pictographic Signs

both diachronic (historical) and synchronic (contemporary). There are no widely used pictographic writing systems functioning now, but logographic and syllabaric, as well as alphabetic, systems are in use today.

Pictographs. Pictographs are "picture writings," characters that are essentially pictorial rather than graphic. Some theorists suggest that pictography should not be classified as a writing system, for the characters do not involve words at all. Indeed, a distinct advantage of pictographs is that one need not necessarily know the language to interpret the characters, for many pictographic signs have virtually universal significance (figure 11.1).

It is clear, however, that as soon as the concept (what is signified) becomes nonliteral or nonreferential, a pictograph ceases to be universal. The sun is a thing, an object, as are the moon, a star, the human figure, and fish. We need not know any language to recognize what is represented by the pictographs. But many referents are culture- and language-based and have particular names derived from particular cultures and languages. I cannot use the sun-picture, for example, to stand for the concept *noon* (not the word "noon," but the idea) unless both I and my interpreters can make several presuppositions about the concept of time, the segmentation of time, times other than noon, and similar limitations and restrictions on the pictograph. Nonreferential ideas, such as time, are difficult to render pictographically.

That is why most pictographic systems are really more like rebuses than like true pictographs. Rebuses, you may recall, are puzzles whose solutions depend partly on recognizing pictures, partly on recognizing letters, and partly on recognizing sound, as in figure 11.2.

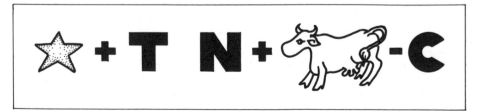

Figure 11.2   A Rebus

The drawing of the star gives the English sounds /star/, to which one adds the sound /t/; then the second letter gives the sound /n/; the second drawing gives the /kauw/, and finally, one subtracts the /k/ sound. The result: /start nauw/, "start now." Egyptian hieroglyphic characters are essentially rebuses, not pure pictographs, for most of the Egyptian characters represent pictures of objects as they are named in the Egyptian language. All of the hieroglyphs (the word means "sacred carvings") may originally have been true pictographs, like ◁◉▷ , which refers to an eye. But most of the hieroglyphs involve particularly Egyptian—no longer universal—ideas or sounds. For example, the glyph 𝟇 is the sign for "to rule." It is a stylized drawing of a flail, which became the Pharaoh's staff, which became the symbol of ruling.

Most pictographic writing systems really involve rebus writing, but are conventionally called pictographic anyway. Conventional pictographs still appear in alphabet-using cultures anywhere it is important that nonliterate or preliterate people, or people who use different languages, be able to understand something quickly. For instance, a few years ago, the European countries devised a system of pictographic traffic signs that could be interpreted internationally, regardless of the speaker's native language. Some examples are given in figure 11.3. Similarly, the National Park Service in America has adopted pictographic signs to use in its facilities (figure 11.4). In contrast with the rebus, which requires some knowledge of specific-language sounds and letters, one need not know a specific language, nor even be able to read, to understand what the traffic or the Park Service signs signify. But one does need to know that in America, as in most Western countries, women are usually symbolized as wearing dresses.

Logographs. The word "logograph" comes, etymologically, from two Greek words: *logos,* "word" (actually, more like "sign") and *graph,* "write." A logograph, then, is a single character that stands for a whole idea or for a complete morpheme. Sometimes the morpheme represented by the logograph will be a free base, a word, so occasionally logography is referred to as "word-writing," but "morpheme-writing" would be more accurate. Sometimes logographs are also referred to as ideographs, or "idea-writing." Whatever one calls this group, it is distinct from pictographs or rebuses, because logographs are tied to language forms rather than to the direct depiction of the object. Logographs are therefore truly linguistic signs.

No writing system in use today is completely logographic, although Chinese characters come closest. The graph 重 , for example, means "heavy"; it uses one character for one word, where English writing requires five separate characters. But even Chinese blends logography with

Figure 11.3   International Traffic-Symbol Pictographs

Figure 11.4   U. S. National Park Service Pictographs

pictography, so that some of the characters represent morphemes, some represent ideas (often with no need to know the word in order to make sense of the graph), and some are combinations of characters. The graph 凵屮 is not now pictographic, but it was derived from a pictograph: ⋀⋀⋀ (mountain). And the combination sign 重 力, meaning "to move," is composed of the character "heavy" plus the graph for "strength."

It must be apparent that a logographic writing system, like a pictographic one, is *non*arbitrary, in that there is very nearly a one-to-one correlation between signifier (character) and signified (object, attitude, or idea). This nonarbitrariness of signification means that both pictographic and logographic writing systems require an enormous number of characters, roughly one for each individual referent. Consequently, it is extremely difficult to learn to read a logographic system. To read a Chinese newspaper, for instance, one needs to know about five thousand characters, and a dictionary for written Chinese contains over forty thousand different characters.[1] As a

---

1. In mainland China, however, the differences among the various dialects (such as Mandarin, Cantonese, and Wu) are so great as to constitute essentially a difference between languages. But the writing system is the same throughout China. Thus, two literate Chinese may not be able to talk to one another, but they can still write to each other.

result, most writing systems that were originally logographic, such as the Sumerian (in Mesopotamia in the Middle East, about 3000 to 4000 B.C.), eventually became syllabaric or alphabetic.

Syllabaries. Speaking metaphorically, we may say that pictographs are related to writing as gesture is related to speech, both being visually oriented forerunners of the written or spoken form. Logographs might then be regarded as analogous to the holophrastic state in language acquisition, for both logography and holophrasis convey entire idea units with a single written or spoken sign. Similarly, the syllabaric writing system is related to an alphabetic one as the telegraphic phase (joining and connection) are related to the recursive phase in language acquisition. Syllabaries and telegraphy signal one of the most remarkable features of increasingly sophisticated language use, the segmentation of whole-unit forms into manipulable parts. Telegraphy's segmentation occurs with the introduction of inflections and function words in speech; a syllabary's segmentation occurs when the word or morpheme is recognized as containing syllables. When a writing system changes from the logographic to the syllabaric, the system begins to represent sounds rather than morphemes. As a consequence, a syllabaric system is more arbitrary and more economical than a pictographic or a logographic one.

For a hypothetical example of the different representations, look back at the rebus shown in figure 11.2. Suppose we took the first character to signify "*object* in the sky which becomes visible only at night and seems to twinkle." That usage would be pictographic. Next, let us say that the same character signifies the *word* "star"; now it is logographic. If we abstract the sounds in the word, /star/, and say that stands for those *sounds,* as it does in the rebus, then the character has become syllabaric. We would use any time the sounds /star/ might appear in the language: "star," "stars," "start," "upstart," "startling," "starling," and so on.[2]

Many ancient languages, such as Sumerian (± 3000 B.C.), Egyptian (± 3000 B.C.), Akkadian (± 2500 B.C.), and Phoenician (± 1500 B.C.), either were syllabaric or contained syllabaric elements mixed in with logographic characters. The cuneiform characters used by the Sumerians are the oldest nonpictographic writing forms known. Cuneiform writing is called that because of the wedgelike (Latin *cuneus,* wedge) shape of the characters, made as wooden styluses were pressed into clay tablets. This form of writing was adopted by the Babylonians, the Assyrians, the Akkadians, the Phoenicians,

---

2. In English, however, this list represents three different morphemes, not one. The {star} of "star" and "stars" is not the same as the {start} base, and neither is the same as the {starling} base. The coincidence of similar phonemes is merely quasi-homonymic accident.

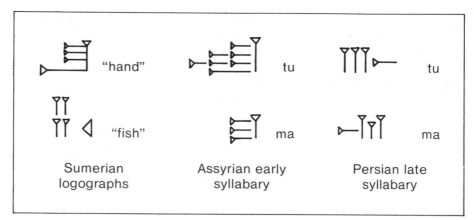

Figure 11.5 Western Semitic Cuneiform Characters

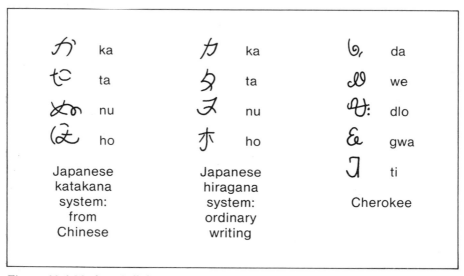

Figure 11.6 Modern Syllabaries: Japanese and Cherokee

and finally, around 500 B.C., the Persians, and had earlier been picked up by the Greeks by about 800 B.C. Examples of Sumerian, Assyrian, and Persian cuneiform syllabaric characters are given in figure 11.5. Note that the characters have become quite abstract; they no longer look anything like the sounds or original objects signified. The only major language in use today that is written as a syllabary is Japanese, although the Amerindian leader Sequoyah developed a Cherokee syllabary in the nineteenth century. Examples of the Japanese and the Cherokee syllabaries are given in figure 11.6.

Most of the ancient syllabaries were actually mixtures of older logographic signs together with syllabaric forms. The Semitic languages in Mesopotamia retained logographic symbols for thousands of years, but the gradual change to a syllabaric form greatly reduced the number of characters in the writing system. Between ± 4000 B.C. and ± 2000 B.C., it is estimated that the West Semitic syllabary in use throughout the Middle East had been reduced from about two thousand logographic characters to around one hundred syllabaric characters. Because of the morphophonemic structure of these languages, the characters all represented consonants. West Semitic languages used a consonant-vowel (CV) pattern of phonemes, consonantal sounds always bracketed by vocalic sounds in an alternating pattern of consonant-vowel-consonant-vowel (CVCV) sounds. Inflectional changes were internal, rather than following the affixative pattern common in English, so a single syllabaric character could represent both the consonant and the following vowel.

As long as the consonant-vowel sound alternation is regular, such a syllabary works quite well; vowels need not be separately identified. But if either consonant or vowel sounds begin to cluster together rather than to alternate with each other—as in English "scream," CCCVC /skrim/—then an immediate difficulty appears. If we try to use a West Semitic-type CV syllabary to write such a word as /skrim/, we will have great trouble indicating that the /s/ is not followed by a vowel, nor is the /k/. Only the /r/ is followed by a vowel sound. The same difficulty arises when two vowels not only cluster but must be kept phonemically distinct, not diphthongized, as in "miasma" /miæzmə/: CVVCCV. A CV-type syllabary is simply not adequate for cases such as those.

Alphabets. In response to such difficulties, there appeared first the Phoenician (± 1500 B.C.) and then (± 800 B.C.) the Greek alphabets. The Phoenicians indicated vowels when they needed to avoid ambiguity, but only sporadically; the Greeks' great contribution to writing systems was the systematic use of vowel characters. The Greeks needed vocalic characters, separate from consonantal characters and from each other, because Greek syllables often show a clustering of sounds rather than ordinary CV alternation. Greek phonology simply could not be accurately recorded with a CV system. By introducing vowel characters, the Greeks produced the first true alphabet.

The word "alphabet" is a shortened form of the names of the first two letters in the Greek system, *alpha* and *beta*. An alphabet system, unlike the others, is based on the sounds that comprise morphemes—not on the shapes of objects, nor on the morphemes, nor on the syllables, but on sounds that make up syllables and morphemes. (Some examples of contemporary alphabets are given in table 11.1.) Alphabets are the most arbitrary of the writing systems, and the development of alphabets is analogous to the development of recursiveness in language acquisition. With a very small

Greek		Latin		Cyrillic			Hebrew		
A α	alpha /a/	A a		А а	/a/		א	' aleph /'/	
B β	beta /b/	B b		Б б	/b/		ב	beth /bh/	
Γ γ	gamma /g(n)/	C c		В в	/v/		ג	gimel /gh/	
Δ δ	delta /d/	D d		Г г	/g/		ד	daleth /dh/	
E ε	epsilon /ε/	E e		Д д	/d/		ה	he /h/	
Z ζ	zeta /z/	F f		Е е	/jə/		ו	waw /w/	
H η	eta /i/	G g		Ё ё	/jo/		ז	zayin /z/	
Θ θ	theta /θ/	H h		Ж ж	/ž/		ח	heth /h'/	
I ι	iota /ι/	I i		З з	/zə/		ט	teth /t/	
K κ	kappa /k/	J j		И и	/i/		י	yodh /j/	
Λ λ	lambda /l/	K k		Й й	/ I /		ך כ	kaph /kh/	
M μ	mu /m/	L l		К к	/k/		ל	lamedh /l/	
N ν	nu /n/	M m		Л л	/l/		ם מ	mem /m/	
Ξ ξ	xi /ks/	N n		М м	/m/		ן נ	nun /n/	
O o	omicron /ɔ/	O o		Н н	/n/		ס	samekh /s/	
Π π	pi /p/	P p		О о	/o/		ע	ayin /'/	
P ρ	rho /rh/	Q q		П п	/p/		ף פ	pe /ph/	
Σ ς	sigma /s/	R r		Р р	/r/		ץ צ	sadhe /s'/	
T τ	tau /t/	S s		С с	/s/		ק	qoph /k/	
Y υ	upsilon /u/	T t		Т т	/t/		ר	resh /r/	
Φ φ	phi /f/	U u		У у	/u/		שׂ	sin /s/	
X χ	chi /kh/	V v		Ф ф	/f/		שׁ	shin /s/	
Ψ ψ	psi /ps/	W w		Х х	/kh/		ת	taw /th/	
Ω ω	omega /o/	X x		Ц ц	/ts/				
		Y y		Ч ч	/c/				
		Z z		Ш ш	/sa/				
				Щ щ	/tsca/				
				Э э	/jə/				
				Ю ю	/ju/				
				Я я	/ja/				

Table 11.1 Four Contemporary Alphabets. From left to right: Greek (24 characters);
Latin (26 characters); Cyrillic (30 characters); Hebrew (23 characters).

number of basic tools (characters), a writer can manipulate all of the segmental phonemes—around thirty-three in English—and, more impressive still, all of the morphemes and words in his language. The number of significant sounds in a language is smaller than the number of significant morphemes. Since English has in current usage upwards of 500,000 words, the economy of an alphabet over any of the other forms is obvious.

But no alphabet in ordinary use is truly phonetic. Rather, alphabets are phonemic, but only to a certain extent: no ordinary alphabet exactly transcribes the significant sounds that speakers utter. As we saw in chapter 4, only the IPA can come close to accurate phonetic transcription. Ordinary alphabets need to be flexible enough to allow for both synchronic and diachronic variation, for pronunciation varies from one dialect to another and from one historical period to another. If alphabets were not flexible in this manner, much of the conservative, preservative function of writing would be lost. As it is, we can still read documents hundreds, even thousands of years old, and even if I say /pɛn/ and you say /pɪn/, we can recognize the written form <pen> as the common referent.

Modern Alphabetic Orthography

Nevertheless, there is no denying that even alphabets, economic and efficient as they are, cause many a writer many pains. As we have already noted, the chief source of distress, especially in English, is orthography. How is it that the same combinations of letters are pronounced so many different ways (e.g., "he*a*rd" /hɛrd/, "be*a*rd" /bɪərd/, "de*a*d" /dɛd/, "me*a*t" /mit/)? And how is it that the same sound, say /f/, can be spelled so many different ways: "cou*gh*," "blu*ff*," "*f*rom," "*ph*ysical"? Very generally, we may suggest two reasons: the language "reform" that took place in England in the seventeenth and eighteenth centuries, and the enormous number of imported words in English.

Language reform. When the grammarians attempted to make English grammar regular and respectable (in relationship to Latin, that is), they also attempted to standardize the spelling. Until the period of reform, spelling was almost a matter of individual whim (Shakespeare spelled his own name five or six different ways), but in the 1600s and 1700s the great "freezing" effect on orthography took place. The grammarians of that time tried to represent sounds accurately where they could, but pronunciation has changed considerably over the span of 250 years and the width of the Atlantic. The Great Vowel Shift (see p. 111) was not entirely completed until after the language "reformation," so we still have the <ea> spelling, which in the Renaissance was pronounced /æ/, for modern pronunciations ranging from /i/ to /ei/. Some of our current spellings reflect even older pronunciations: <knight> used to be /knɪxt/ and <thought> used to be /θɔxt/ in the Old English, velar period.

Importations. Beginning in the 1500s and especially in the 1600s, the English language imported a great many words from Classical (Greek and Roman-Latin) sources. Almost always, the imported word retained its original spelling and pronunciation. Thus, for example, we have many Latin words which contain <tio> or <tion>, but which are pronounced /šo/ or /šɔn/, because that was how the Romans pronounced them. Similarly, the <ph> spelling in Greek-derived words is pronounced /f/, as the Greeks would have said in a word like the English "philosophy."

Many of the imported words contained sounds, and letters signaling sounds, that were phonemic in the original language but gradually became redundant (nondistinctive) in English. Particularly is the leveling of phonemic significance true in the many Classical words spelled with a mediate (in the middle of the word) <i>, <e>, or <a>. The pronunciations of those sounds in their original language, usually Latin, would have been more clearly differentiated than they are now, for Modern English has tended to reduce or level all of these mediate vowels to *schwa*, /ə/. Consequently, many people today have trouble remembering whether the /ə/ sound is spelled with an <e>, an <a>, an <i>, or an <o>: "compl*i*ment" versus "compl*e*ment"; "compar*i*son" versus "compar*a*tive"; {or} inflections versus {er} inflections ("advis*o*r," "survey*o*r," "operat*o*r," but "writ*e*r," "help*e*r," "transcrib*e*r").[3] The *schwa* letters, it seems likely, will simply have to be memorized, although the variant spellings may eventually become leveled, as the sounds have been. Similarly, it is possible that regular past-tense inflections, such as /t/ and /d/ (usually written as <ed>), may disappear in writing as they are currently disappearing in speech. The words "released," "used," and "supposed," for example, are frequently spelled without the <d> because the <d> is not pronounced, especially before "to" or other plosives: /ri'lis/, /jus/, /sə'poz/.

Orthography also has some influence on pronunciation, although perhaps not so strong as the influence of sounds on writing. It is not at all uncommon, for example, for a speaker who has never heard a word but has seen it written to try a kind of improvised phonetic pronunciation, as in /ɔftɛn/ "often" or /'æntəgon/ "Antigone." Spelling pronunciation like this has already influenced American English speech in such words as the now-common /soljɛr/ "soldier," which used to be pronounced /sojɛr/. Many observers believe that the /w/–/hw/ distinction noted on page 138 is becoming a matter of spelling pronunciation only. The marks of punctuation used in writing, however—commas, apostrophes, and the like—to distinguish one syntactic or morphemic unit from another rarely have an effect on pronunciation.

Later spelling reforms. No alphabetic writing system is completely free of problems in spelling, because no alphabetic writing (with the exception of the IPA) is completely phonetic. Why do we not shift to a more accurate

---

3. The common substitution, in writing, of "could of" for "could have" or "could've" is another example of *schwa* leveling, since in many dialects of English, it is impossible to distinguish the /əv/ of <'ve> from the /əv/ of <of>.

system than the cumbersome spellings that so plague us today? Why not spell words by ear, as they sound? Basically, there are three reasons, besides the obvious one that doing so would mean learning a whole new system of writing.

1. Diachronically, we would lose touch with older written materials; the great literature and the historical documents of the past would no longer be accessible to us.
2. Synchronically, we would have great difficulty reading other dialects than our own.
3. Consequently, writing would no longer be a communally shared system for representing *la langue,* but an idiolectic form that would have to be constantly modified for dialect and constantly updated. As a result, the virtues of arbitrariness and conventionality would be altogether lost from writing.

To many observers, however, these virtues do not outweigh the confusion inherent in English (or any other alphabetic) writing. Many people have therefore proposed either partial reforms or a complete discarding of the spelling system in favor of an artificially created orthography. The hope is that the artificial system would be more phonetic without sacrificing arbitrariness and conventionality. As early as the seventeenth century, English reformers were trying to match letters to sounds. In the nineteenth century, Noah Webster's influential dictionary of American English (1828) was almost single-handedly responsible for Americans' dropping the <u> from words like "colour" and "honour" (as they are still spelled by the British). In the later nineteenth and early twentieth centuries, many well-known figures, such as Charles Darwin, Lord Tennyson, George Bernard Shaw, and President Theodore Roosevelt, advocated spelling reform.[4] But the reform movements usually did not produce much effect except exasperation (Congress called President Roosevelt's attempts "tampering with our language"), and their momentum soon was buried by inertia.

Engineered languages. But the problems that inspired the spelling-reform attempts did not go away, nor are they likely to. All written languages that started out as speech confront much the same problems English does, but other languages have had more success in enforcing reforms. Engineered languages are deliberately modified through some extralinguistic means. For example, when Israel became a political entity, Hebrew was revitalized as a

---

4. It was Shaw, for example, who pointed out that English letters and sounds are so inconsistent that we could conceivably spell "fish" as *ghoti:* <gh> as in "enou*gh*"; <o> as in "*wo*men"; and <ti> as in "-*ti*on."

spoken language after it had existed for many thousands of years principally in a written, devotional form.

A more extreme form of language engineering occurs with a made-up language, like Esperanto. (The name means "hope" in that language.) Recognizing that Latin was no longer a common language, or *lingua franca,* among the populations of Europe in the late nineteenth century, the Russian physician L. L. Zamenhof created a new language that he hoped would serve the same interlinguistic function Latin had, allowing French-speakers to converse with Dutch-speakers, Norwegians with English, Germans with Flemish, and so on. There are at present upwards of six million speakers of Esperanto, and supporters claim the language is easy to learn,[5] is orthographically much more phonetic than most Indo-European languages, and so far seems to be comparatively stable diachronically. The major drawback of Esperanto, and of its interlanguage successors like Idiom Neutral and Interlingua, is that they are Indo-European in origin and in function. These interlanguages are therefore as difficult for speakers of Chinese or Turkish or Hebrew to learn as are the Indo-European languages themselves.

Composition

Earlier in this chapter, we mentioned that the word "writing" had several meanings, the two principal ones being characters (writing as system) and composition (writing as art). Obviously, the second meaning could not exist without the first, for the creation of essays, stories, plays, poems, letters, lists, or books depends on there being something to create with—graphs: handwritten, typed, or printed; alphabetic, syllabic, or logographic. Oral story telling and the creation of poetry existed long before graphs did, but when writing systems and creativity converged in the Western world roughly in the eighth century B.C., history was born. (The term *prehistoric,* in fact, usually means "preliterate.") When writing permitted creative or business or legal materials to be written down, then ideas and records were no longer ephemeral, no longer dependent on memory alone, and no longer limited by physical proximity.

Composition is by nature a more frozen medium (see chapter 8) than is speech. The weight of precedent and the resistance to change that surround written signifiers seem also to accompany what is signified in writing. Consequently, as we have already indicated, written language forms change much more slowly and conservatively than do the forms of speech. People are more careful about their writing than about their speech, and more

5. Try this sentence, for example: *La inteligenta persono lernas Esperanton, la lingvo universala, rapide.*

apprehensive about it as well, perhaps because unlike speaking, which for most of us almost comes naturally, writing is a skill that must be learned painfully. It also must be learned in two distinct stages: first, printing and handwriting in the primary grades; then, composition. The learning and refining of compositional skills never seems to stop, either; one's skill as a writer is always subject to criticism by somebody.

Rhetoric. For many centuries, until the Western nations began their push in the nineteenth century for universal literacy, writing was a skill possessed by only a few people, the wealthy or the clergy.[6] But the kinds of issues and impulses with which writers are concerned belong to everyone, literate or not, and were discussed by many people besides those who could write. Many modern notions about composition were shaped by earlier thinkers who could not write but who spoke particularly effectively, as public orators, and whose skills were noted down by their literate contemporaries. A good deal of what is commonly taught in many composition classes today is ultimately derived from Greek and Roman notes on rhetoric, also called oratory, the art of effective speaking.

For example, the consciousness of one's audience, which we mentioned in connection with registers in chapter 8, is a rhetorical concern. So is the customary division of an essay into three major parts: introduction, body, and conclusion. Formal attention to the use of figurative language (chapter 9) was first drawn by rhetoricians and later adapted by writers. Style generally was much discussed by rhetoricians: choice of words, pacing and phrasing of sentences, length and ordering of sentences, the presence of a distinctive and consistent "voice," or persona, throughout the oration or composition. A recognition of context as well as of audience stems from rhetoric's principle that persuasion or argument are essentially different from narration and require different skills. Above all, the principle that compositions have an extrinsic purpose—are not just exercises in self-expression—is a rhetorical axiom.

Of course, it would be inaccurate to say that the guidelines for effective writing were solidified by Plato, Aristotle, Cicero, and Quintilian, remaining unaltered or unchallenged for more than two thousand years. Peter Ramus in the sixteenth century turned rhetoric into little more than elocution, or elegantly proper speaking, only minimally concerned with ideas and logic. Kenneth Burke, in the twentieth century, has had much influence on both oratory and composition with his insistence that identification rather than persuasion is the heart of human discourse. Burke and his followers believe that a speaker's or writer's task is not so much to sway audiences this way or

---

6. That is why the earliest documents in English, on which are based our knowledge of the history of the language (chapter 7), come from the pens of clerical copyists

that, but to establish consubstantiality—a common ground, a base for agreement and thus for social cohesion—between speaker/writer and audience.

Generally, too, the fluorescence of electronic technology in the twentieth century has altered our perception of what is effective in compositions. Marshall McLuhan suggested that "the medium is the message," that is, television's format—short, entertaining shows constantly interrupted by advertisements—has prejudiced us against anything very lengthy or difficult to understand. Consequently, it has been proposed, we no longer value elegance and structure in writing; we want short, snappy, not overly complicated memos, preferably with a quick solution. Journalistic writing provides a good example of our changing tastes. If you look at a newspaper story of only fifty years ago, you will see something more like what we would now call an essay, quite different from the brisk, easily digestible pyramid opening ("5 W's + H": who, what, where, why, when, how) that we are used to today in news articles.

Process versus product. The art of writing, whether creative or factual, was for many centuries taught as a mimetic or imitative art. A child would hone his skills as a writer by practicing different forms, modeling his essays, poems, plays, or arguments on what other writers before him had produced. Good writing was thought to be perhaps one-tenth inherent talent, nine-tenths craft acquired from contact, through imitation, with the masters. Writing was judged as good, bad, or indifferent on the basis largely of the result, the product, the written document, whatever it might be: treaty, prayer, play script, sermon. To a considerable degree, that is still how each of us learns to write. We imitate the teacher's letters on the blackboard; we make up stories like the ones in the primer; we progress to more complicated and more specialized models: Tolstoy, Faulkner, Chaucer, Joyce, Hemingway, Twain, the *New York Times* or the Associated Press, the Chicago or the MLA style sheets. We learn through experience that this supervisor wants this kind of format in a business letter, a resumé, or report, but that instructor prefers that kind of format. We still imitate the required models.

But there is no longer anything like the consensus that seemed to hold, until perhaps the eighteenth century, about what good writing is or should be. As a result, there is no longer any consensus that imitation is the best way to learn to write. Many people believe that mimesis stifles creativity and that teaching the product (the composition) is less important than teaching the actual process of writing. As linguistics has contributed much in recent years to our understanding of language and language processes, and as it has become more and more apparent that speech—not writing—is the primary form of human communication, many observers have concluded that we should pay more attention to discovering what internal activities go on in a writer's mind as he gets ready to write and as he moves through successive drafts and refinements of his composition. In other words, what psycholinguistic information can we show a writer to help him write more effectively? In particular, how can the processes involved in effective writing be directed toward immediately useful ends?[7] Process-oriented writing courses tend to go in one of two general directions: toward oral composition or toward practical composition (as contrasted with creative, self-expressive writing). Often these trends are combined in the same class, but we will look at them separately here.

Oral composition. Here, the idea is that students should practice out loud, with each other, all the preliminary steps involved in the writing process before they actually sit down to write. Then, when they have finished their compositions, they should trade papers with one another and analyze them, using peer evaluation, before turning the papers in for grades. The central premise underlying the concept of oral composition, sometimes called ''talk/write,'' is that many students do not know the techniques a writer can use to prepare himself before he begins to write, nor the techniques to use in revising his rough drafts. It is therefore supposed that talking with other students, using oral rather than written composition skills, will help the student learn these techniques.

The techniques themselves are no different from those used by a writer trained in the older, mimetic, solitary tradition. What is different here is that instead of working all alone, with his head and a scratch pad and perhaps some resource texts, the writer now works with other writers as well. The techniques are familiar to all writers and essentially are problem-solving strategies.

The preliminary (prewriting) phase goes through three, often simultaneous stages: identification, organization, and focusing. That is, the writer should first identify the task, topic, or issue in question; gather information about it, recollect experiences, or observe behavior or appearance and take stock of his own basic beliefs and assumptions as they bear on the subject or task at hand. Next, the writer begins restricting the topic to something manageable, outlining a general approach or theme, a general organization for the supportive evidence, and a functional and effective conclusion. Third, the writer should focus the topic, the development, and the outline in terms of the particular audience and occasion or other special demands of this writing task, such as predetermined length, necessity for using (or not using) library sources, and so forth.

Once he has a written draft, the writer begins the polishing, or rewriting, phase. There may actually be several revisions, but essentially the same

---

7. Behind this question lies the—not necessarily legitimate—presupposition that most general composition courses have not had practical application as a goal; in other words, that composition usually is taught as a ''creative'' (therefore, in two-valued terms, a useless) art.

techniques will be applied for each revision. These, too, will frequently overlap with one another. A writer should read the composition aloud to see how a passage sounds or to see how an idea fits in this or that context. He should also check to see that the organization has worked, that nothing has been repeated, omitted, or misplaced, and that enough support of the right kind has been located in the right places. In addition, the writer must make sure that the word choice is appropriate, the sentences not too long or too short, the paragraphs complete and fully developed. Above all, a writer must keep testing everything in the composition against the task or topic: Did he say what he meant to say? Is it clear to someone else? Does what he says here have some connection with what was said in another section? What sort of difference will the composition make in a reader's life when he has finished it?

A writer working by himself will do all of these prewriting and rewriting tasks on paper, trying to be both creative and critical as he moves through each stage of the paper's development. If he is lucky, he may find someone willing to read and comment on his successive drafts. Oral composition improves the writer's chances of being lucky, because he is provided with listeners right from the start, people on whom to test his ideas and assumptions, who will help him think his way through, and who can help him polish the final drafts. The actual writing is still up to the author, of course, but in oral composition, he has assistance in working through the processes involved in writing. This process-oriented technique in writing, then, is analogous to our bringing individual competence in language use up to the surface of consciousness and translating it into actual performance.

Practical composition. Just as all effective writers use the techniques noted above, whether they are working by themselves or with other people, so do all writers sooner or later face practical-writing situations. Eventually, nearly all writing develops a specific and immediate purpose beyond the creative and shaping impulses in composition itself. Courses that emphasize the practicality of writing merely bring those aims up to the forefront of students' attention, as courses emphasizing oral composition stress the acts involved in writing and revising. Most general writing classes make at least some practical assignments along with creative/expressive assignments, just as most writing courses involve the students in process-oriented skills.

See table 11.2 for examples of "expressive" and "practical" assignments. Note the considerable blending between the modes, as well as the distinctions between them.

A course devoted entirely to practical matters may direct students' energies more toward the older mimetic approach than toward expressiveness or process orientation. Business writing, technical writing, journalism, advertising, script writing, and so on, all require imitation and mastery of standard

Expressive Topics	*Practical Topics*
1. I hate people who ———.	1. Persuade an income-tax adjuster that your deductions are legitimate.
2. My first ———.	2. Prepare a job resumé and a letter that explains the value of your work experience.
3. What I am most afraid of.	3. Complain about a product so you will get it fixed or get a refund.
4. Getting in trouble at school.	4. Praise a policeman for helping you under arduous circumstances.
5. Caught in a bar with a fake ID.	5. Write a letter to a good friend who owes you money, phrased so you get to keep the money and the friend.
6. A fight with somebdy about something he/she didn't want to hear.	6. Sell a product to a hostile audience.
7. Embarrassing incident.	7. Develop a position paper for a company's management to show why the company should market a certain product.
8. Somebody should do something about ———.	8. Explain why you are going to spend your money on X instead of Y.
9. A crucial decision.	9. Decline a marriage proposal in an honest but affectionate way.
10. How to become a nonconformist.	10. Prepare a concise and forthright description of a territory for someone thinking of setting up a business there.
11. What time of day is best.	11. Tell someone off constructively.
12. Who really reads *Playboy?*	12. Honestly analyze the behavior of someone you find peculiar.
13. Games people play.	13. Evaluate the advantages/disadvantages of a career.
14. Who I would choose to be if I could be someone else.	14. Get an offensive advertisement taken off television.

Table 11.2   Examples of Composition Assignments

forms, jargon, or approaches: where the salutation goes in a business letter, how to write an abstract of a technical report, what to lead off with in a feature story or in an advertisement, how to cue the cameramen or soundmen to dolly in, fade, dissolve, or pan from an establishing shot. The expectation of a practical-compositon writing class is that students who successfully imitate and manipulate the standard terms and forms will get the results they want—at least partly because of their mimetic abilities.

Good practical writing depends, much more than does good expressive writing, on adhering to models and formats, on using correct (prestigious) patterns of spelling, punctuation, and so forth, and on staying within the fairly conservative limits of tolerance for individual idiolect. That does not mean, however, that good practical writing is purely formulaic, any more than good expressive writing is purely a matter of the writer's whim. Practical and expressive writing are not antonymous behaviors; there is a gradable scale between those two poles and, consequently, a good deal of common ground. One common area we have already mentioned: the process of composing and the stages in the process. Another area in common is the quality of the product. A good business letter (practical) has many of the features of a good short story (expressive), even though their purposes, their audiences, and their theses may be quite different. When we ask what those features are, we move into the realm of style.

Style

Like the word "meaning," the word "style" is extremely difficult to pin down referentially. The *O.E.D.* gives almost eight full columns to defining the word's various usages as noun and verb. The etymology of "style" (Latin *stilus*, a pointed writing instrument) explicitly links it to writing, and one of the principal definitions in the *O.E.D.* is: "a writer's mode of expression considered in regard to clearness, effectiveness, beauty, and the like" (1971, p. 1206). Like the two-way pull in language between the general *(la langue)* and the particular *(la parole),* style shows a tug between general principles and particular expression. On one side, clarity, effectiveness, beauty, and the like are seen as very nearly universal requirements of good style; on the other side is the requirement that the individual writer's own personality or "voice" show through his words. Most critics of style would agree that the best stylists meet both of these apparently contradictory demands, as well as the demands of audience, occasion, purpose, supportive detail, and organization. In a very general sense, "style" can be applied to any kind of writing or speaking (or dressing, walking, lovemaking, or anything else that human beings do). When we ask more specifically what constitutes good writing style, however, we may run into some conflicts.

One immediate problem is historical-diachronic, for the definition of "good" style has changed radically over the centuries. In Shakespeare's time, for instance, an elaborate use of imagery was one of the requirements of good writing, whether poetry or prose, whether practical or expressive. Milton's *Areopagitica* (extract 7.3) is a good example of that kind of "high" style. Beginning in the early eighteenth century, however, the "plain" style began to be more favored, especially for public writing, and the division between expression and practicality, which we still follow today, appeared.

The second problem arises from that division. It is a contextual-synchronic issue: what is good style in an advertisement may be wildly inappropriate in a report on pipeline technology, and neither mode may work well in a love poem. In a very general sense, good business letters and good short stories do share some qualities, but because of our current inclination to separate writing into kinds or types, depending on purpose and audience, we have also tended to draw up different requirements for each type. A real and pressing concern of a writer must be that division, and he must understand which requirements need to be applied in which contexts.

But what about that most general sense, in which style is good (or bad) regardless of the type of writing mode used? Recognizing the inherent risk in making generalizations, what qualities can we say make good writing good, at least in our times? A writer usually is thought to follow three processes when he generates a product that other people admire: mechanics, organization, and word choice.

Mechanics. The jargon word "mechanics" has a specialized meaning when applied to compositions and style. It refers to spelling, punctuation, usage (current prescriptive attitudes about grammar and word choice), format, and simple legibility.

All of these mechanical aspects cause writers trouble. Many writers, in fact, believe that mechanics are the most vexing aspects of composition, and, conversely, that once the mechanics are taken care of, the writing will automatically be good. Unfortunately, that is not so. Good spelling does not mean good writing, nor does bad spelling mean bad writing. Despite the emphasis given them in many classrooms, mechanics have very little to do with style. True, illegible papers are irritating, and capricious punctuation can be a positive drawback to understanding. A great deal of social pressure is put on writers to learn and use prestigious patterns in mechanics. The pressure is very real, and every writer must come to grips with it, to accommodate or to resist it in some way, but one thing a writer must not do is mistake that pressure for a stylistic one. In truth, all of the aspects of mechanics can—and, many think, should—be handled after the composing process is complete. Correcting spelling and punctuation is an editorial or proofreading activity, not a compositional one.

Ideas and organization. With ideas and organization, we move into true stylistic concerns. The question at this point is not so much what the ideas are but how they are handled. Are the main points clear and dealt with at greater length than the less important, subordinate issues? Is there enough particular detail, support, and illustration to bring out the significance of each major point? Does the whole composition have a discernible plan, a sense of controlled and directed motion from point A to B to X, Y, and Z? Is that overall plan the most appropriate one for the ideas involved, or would another organization make the ideas clearer? For example, would arranging the major items sequentially or chronologically make more sense than discussing them in a comparison-contrast structure?

Word choice. This last aspect, sometimes called diction, is probably what most people have in mind when they refer to written style. Whether the product be a memo or a love letter, good writers care passionately about words. Good writers recognize that words are signs, not merely signifiers, but they also recognize that words are functional, creative tools as well, even in the most practical of writing situations. To put the point negatively, poor writers tend to use the same words everyone else does: stock phrases, clichés, collocations, truisms, buzz and fad words, anything already tested and worn out by other writers. Or they go to the opposite extreme and disregard the signification altogether, forcing words into peculiar or pompous patterns. Poor writing is dull, like a committee report, with no sense of experiment, exploration, discovery. Good writing shows dash, flair, personality.

All well and good, but how? How does a writer develop whatever "dash," "flair," and "personality" mean? The answer to those questions will not be very satisfactory here, because this is a book about language and not about composition. Recognizing that limitation, four tactics can be suggested for developing a feel for vivid diction:

1. Read everything you can, about anything, and ask "Why?" a lot. Why did this writer choose that word, why this kind of sentence, why that phrasing?
2. Practice using (not just memorizing) new and striking words so that you have a large repertory at your command. But stay away from inflated fog and outrageous or silly diction.
3. Develop a feel for synonymy and antonymy of all types and for the problems that arise with each type.
4. Use imagery as well as denotative language, but do not strain yourself or your reader by stretching a simile or metaphor too far.

Probably the most useful technique, however, is to find a good critic, someone who cares about language and about you. A good critic will listen to your words and interrupt you when they are not clear. He will serve as a kind of skeptical antagonist who helps you shape your writing into its best possible form. He will challenge your muddy thinking and your shallow generalizing, will point out that you skipped three issues you should have examined, will catch you short when your connotations outrun your intentions. Eventually, whether the critic is someone else or yourself, you will discover that good criticism works with you by working against you. It is invaluable in helping you continue the lifelong process of learning how to write.

Review Questions

1. What are the three different meanings of "writing"?
2. Describe the major differences between writing and speech.
3. Give an example of a pictograph, a logograph, a rebus.
4. Discuss the advantages of a syllabary over pictographs and logographs.
5. What Middle Eastern peoples are ordinarily given credit for the invention or discovery of the alphabet? What particular contributions did the Greeks make?
6. What makes an alphabet different from the earlier writing systems?
7. Discuss the advantages and disadvantages of reforming the Latin alphabet toward a more phonetic system of orthography.
8. Define these terms: *schwa*-leveling, *lingua franca,* literate, mimetic.
9. Compare oral composition with practical composition, and both with traditionally rhetorical composition.
10. What are the major components of style in language use?

Selected Reading

Abercrombie, David. *Studies in Phonetics and Linguistics.* New York: Oxford University Press, 1965.

Arena, Louis A. *Linguistics and Composition.* Washington, D.C.: Georgetown University Press, 1975.

Burns, Shannon, et al., eds. *An Annotated Bibliography of Texts on Writing Skills.* New York: Garland Publishing, Inc., 1976.

Chatman, Seymour, and Samuel R. Levin, eds. *Essays on the Language of Literature.* Boston: Houghton Mifflin Co., 1967.

Darbyshire, A. E. *A Grammar of Style.* London: Andre Deutsch, Ltd., 1971.

Diederich, Paul B. *Measuring Growth in English.* Urbana, Ill.: National Council of Teachers of English, 1974.

Diringer, D. *The Alphabet.* New York: Philosophical Library, 1948.

Elgin, Suzette Hadin. *Pouring Down Words.* Englewood Cliffs, N.J.: Prentice-Hall, Inc., 1975.

Empson, William. *Seven Types of Ambiguity,* 3rd ed. London: Chatto and Windus, 1933.

Gelb, Ignace J. *A Study of Writing,* rev. ed. Chicago: University of Chicago Press, 1963.

Godshalk, Fred I., Frances Swinford, and William E. Coffman. *The Measurement of Writing Ability.* New York: College Entrance Examination Board, 1966.

Graham, Sheila Y. *Sentencecraft.* Englewood Cliffs, N.J.: Prentice-Hall, Inc., 1976.

Hart, Kathleen, and Alice Helm. *Sentences, Paragraphs, and Essays*. Boston: Little, Brown & Co., 1979.

Heatherington, Madelon E. *Outside-In*. Glenview, Ill.: Scott, Foresman and Co., 1971.

Hiatt, Mary P. *Artful Balance: The Parallel Structures of Style*. New York: Columbia Teachers College Press, 1975.

Jacobs, Roderick A., and Peter S. Rosenbaum. *Transformations, Style, and Meaning*. Waltham, Mass.: Xerox College Publishing, 1971.

Lawrence, Mary S. *Writing as a Thinking Process*. Ann Arbor: University of Michigan Press, 1972.

Sebeok, Thomas A., ed. *Style in Language*. Cambridge, Mass.: M.I.T. Press, 1960.

Spitzer, Leo. *Linguistics and Literary History*. Princeton, N.J.: Princeton University Press, 1948.

Tate, Gary, ed. *Teaching Composition: 10 Bibliographical Essays*. Fort Worth: Texas Christian University Press, 1976.

Vachek, Josef. *Written Language: General Problems and Problems of English*. The Hague: Mouton Publishing Co., 1973.

Journals *Anthropological Linguistics; College Composition and Communication; College English; English Journal;* NCTE *publications*

12
The Teaching of Language

Teaching does not occur only in a classroom, nor does learning occur only between recess periods. Children probably begin learning language almost as soon as they are born; their most impressive language learning, as we saw in chapter 2, has already been accomplished by the time they start school. Every speaker around a young child is his teacher, whether consciously or not. It has been a central premise of this book that all of us need to bring our competence up to a conscious level and thereby become more alert to our performance. The premise can now be applied to the unconscious, day-by-day, informal teaching we do as parents, peers, older brothers or sisters, babysitters, roommates, spouses, or friends. We need to become aware of what we are teaching, why we are teaching it, and how we are teaching it. Because the instructor in the classroom, from kindergarten on, has to work with the language foundation we have informally helped our children build, let us become aware of what that foundation is.

Prescription and Description

Perhaps the most important point to remember about language awareness is the difference between prescription and description. They are two quite different behaviors, with two quite different purposes, and it is crucial in our teaching that we not confuse the two. Prescription is the social "should" list of prestigious/nonprestigious linguistic shibboleths,[1] heavily weighted in favor of *don't:* Don't start a sentence with "and" or end it with a preposition; don't use "ain't," double negatives, or swear words; don't say "myself" when you mean "I" or "me," and so on. Prescriptions about usage are the equivalent of Emily Post's or Amy Vanderbilt's instructions on the etiquette of what to wear to a semiformal wedding at four o'clock. They depend on what a certain segment of society values as manners or decorum, and like all other fashions, they change. What is prescriptively sound today

---

1. "Shibboleth," from a Hebrew word used in *Judges* 12:4–6, refers to any custom, especially of language use, that reliably distinguishes one group from another. Interestingly, "shibboleth" was used as a password originally, in a military situation, to separate enemies from allies. Those who could not pronounce the initial /š/ in the word were killed because of their dialect.

may be out of style tomorrow, as the reflexive pronoun form (''myself'') is coming to substitute for both the subjective (''I'') and the objective forms (''me''), no matter how firm the prescription against the practice.

Nevertheless, most such prescriptions are uttered with the illocutionary force of permanent, unchanging, graven-in-stone, undeniable, and perpetual truths: thou shalt not drop thy <g>'s nor say, ''Robert and myself saw a movie last night.'' Most people who make metalinguistic statements about language or its usage do so in prescriptive terms with the belief (and this point is important) that they are conveying accurate descriptions. But description is concerned with what people actually do; prescription with what someone thinks people should do. The two actions are not identical, but they are often made to seem so by people who believe that there is one single, unalterably, eternally correct way of speaking or writing, and that their statements about double negatives or {ed} inflections are a factual description of that single unchanging, eternal truth.

We have seen, however, that linguistically—objectively, descriptively— there is no such thing as *the* correct way to use language. Indeed, in linguistic terms, there is not even such a thing as ''correct'' speech. ''Correct'' is a heavily loaded prescriptive term, implying all sorts of unspoken moral values. A child who uses correct language is presumably neat, polite, well groomed, and a paragon of virtue, whereas a child who uses incorrect language probably falls asleep in church, plays hooky from school, dissects cats, and takes dope.

The exaggeration in the preceding sentence was intentional, to point out in hyperbolic terms the inescapable fact that language, as a sociocultural function, catches the fallout from other sociocultural functions. We make social judgments about people on the basis of their language use, whether we intend to make such judgments or not. As a result, few adults feel comfortable about their use of language, for they have been exposed for many years to the social indictments handed down about their ''incorrect'' language. Nearly all such indictments, unfortunately, imply that a person who does not speak properly is somehow a bad person.

It would be absurd to argue that parents should stop trying to teach their children linguistic manners (prescriptions), for parents will no more give up trying to civilize their children (in language use or in other ways) than children will stop resisting such training. Rather, the point is merely that we should be clear about what we are doing. We should recognize that training in linguistic etiquette is simply that—education in manners—and need not be imposed as a statement about the child's entire soul or psyche. To put this extremely important distinction briefly: descriptively, all language behaviors are equal; prescriptively, some language behaviors carry more social prestige than others in certain contexts. Phrased that way, as social rather than moral injunctions, instructions about language use are more effective and less psychically damaging in modifying a child's linguistic behavior than are hard-line prescriptions.

Standard and Nonstandard Dialects

The objective is to teach the children the prestige dialect not because it is "correct," but because it is socially useful to them. The key is to phrase the prescriptions, or judgments about etiquette (in terms of the prestige dialect), so that they are clearly social rather than moral cues. In working toward that objective, it may be useful to avoid the word "correct" altogether and use instead the more accurate and objective word "standard." "Standard" is not a euphemism for "correct," because no judgment is made about the moral value of language practices when we describe them as standard. "Standard" is a descriptive term only, referring to quantity, not quality or prestige: standard language practices are those used either by a majority of speakers within a language or by a significant number of prestige-dialect users. Thus, standard practices are neither correct nor incorrect; they are simply those in current use among X number of Y-type speakers on occasion Z.

Competence and performance. We are saying, then, that the parent or teacher must treat language and its use in an objective manner and must help his or her students to do the same. It is quite possible to help even very young children understand the nature of usage and dialects without relying on any linguistic jargon whatever. (Indeed, one *should not* use the jargon at all in teaching young children.) One way to begin is by asking the children themselves to identify examples of variant pronunciations, lexical items, collocations, and syntax—that is, to draw on their own competence and experience. How do the children themselves say this or that word? Can they understand each other? Can they understand the teacher if his or her pronunciation, lexicon, and so forth are radically different from theirs? How do people say the word on television? How do the neighbors say it? Can the children understand all of those pronunciations? What changes in language use might they have observed? Use the children's competence in order to encourage them to see for themselves that "different" need not equal "bad." This is descriptive behavior, eliciting descriptive responses.

But since all human beings live in a stratified society, description alone will not help the children whose dialects are so different, so nonstandard, that social punishment will hinder their social progress. The teacher is therefore obliged to help the speakers of non-S.E. dialects acquire the standard one, just as he or she is obliged to help them acquire arithmetic, penmanship, reading, and whatever other social and intellectual skills the community values. Some children's competence may need redirecting into different kinds of performance, and again, the most appropriate starting point is their own experience. What have they heard and observed from their parents, their neighborhoods, their radio and television sets that could be collated into an improvised dictionary of standard language practices? How do most people pronounce this or that word, produce this or that inflection, generate this or that transformation? Collect samples from the children's observations and let them discover for themselves the differences between their dialects and the prestige one. Then practice the prestige sounds and forms, but never to the point of tedium.

Receptive and productive competence. Always keep in mind the stages of language acquisition. Remember that children can understand and recognize much linguistic variety before they can produce anything like the range they hear. This difference has been phrased as receptive competence versus productive competence. Especially in kindergarten and the early grades, it is important that the teacher not confuse incomplete productive competence with speech pathology or with dialect variance, for many young children may lack the muscular coordination required to deal with phonemic distinctions such as /r/-/w/ or /l/-/r/ or /s/-/θ/. But as young children's receptive competence is relatively high even in primary grades, the teacher can begin quite early to help those who show dialect variance to recognize the variation and, ultimately, to practice identifying and using standard practices.

Another key is always to justify and support in linguistic terms any nonstandard practice before you point out the relatively low social value of the practice. If, for example, a child consistently uses double negatives ("I do*n't* have *no* sisters"), remark that double negatives were quite common even in prestigious English speech until not so very long ago. Point out that it is very common in many languages even now to use that construction. Note that the construction is perfectly understandable to any English speaker who hears it. Only then go on to observe that in English, there is another way of constructing a negative, the standard, more socially valued—but no more "correct"—technique of single-word negation: "*not* . . . any."

Bidialectalism. Not so long ago, pedagogical thinking held that nonstandard dialects should be eradicated. Chicano students and black students and any other non-WASP students were (at worst) punished for using their dialects, (at best) gently instructed in the standard WASP dialect and told to drop their own. Such eradication seems unnecessary if one views dialect, any dialect, as metaphorically a miniature equivalent of a language. We do not ask English-speaking students in a foreign-language class to unlearn their native language altogether, so why should we ask students in an S.E. class to unlearn their native dialects? Similarly, if we look at nonstandard practices as microcosmic dialects instead of as horrible sins, then why can we not apply the same principle? If a child's idiolect calls for constructions like "Me and him was going," there is no need to try forcing him to stop using that construction altogether. He won't do it anyway. It would be much more realistic and just as useful to him if the teacher merely pointed out that in thus and such a social context, "Me and him was going" is effective, but in another context, "He and I were going" may be more effective. Bidialectalism, or the promotion of two (or more) dialects, is a tactic that lets us have it both ways—description and observation, together with nonthreatening prescription. And bidialectalism as a teaching technique is both more humane and more effective than is attempted eradication in promoting the appropriate use of Standard English.

Refinements on the Theme for Older Children

As children grow older, they can profit from increased familiarity with metalinguistic concepts, although they do not need to have the term "competence" in their lexicon to be competent, nor need they know the word "performance" to perform language acts. Generally speaking, the less formal terminology of grammar, the better, especially with young children. No correlation at all has been demonstrated between a student's ability to parse a sentence—in Traditional, Structural, or Transformational terms—and his ability to speak, read, interpret, spell, or compose. It is not appropriate to teach children that they are studying "syntax" and that the name of the study of syntax is "grammar"; what they do need to learn is how English syntax works. More accurately, we should say that children already know how it works (are competent), but they need some help in seeing what they know. Thus, again, one should begin with their competence, not with the S.E. prescriptions.

Sentence combining and usage. First-graders and second-graders can handle very simple test frames and trees; older children, in middle school or junior high, can deal with more complicated patterns, building on the competence they have identified earlier. Along with the trees, it can be useful to start introducing basic notions of transformations and sentence combining, which uses principles of coordination, subordination, and modification to specify or qualify the main clause, as in the exercise in table 12.1. Note that no one of the combinations is "correct"; all of them are. The emphasis in sentence combining is on what can be done, not on what cannot.

Always stressing the concepts of bidialectalism, prescription/description, and language change, but without overloading the children with jargon, the teacher can also begin introducing primary-grade children to conventions of

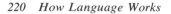

Trees		*Transformations*

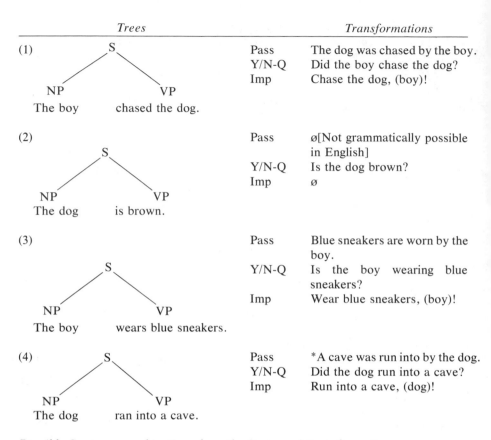

(1) S
   NP   VP
   The boy   chased the dog.

Pass   The dog was chased by the boy.
Y/N-Q   Did the boy chase the dog?
Imp   Chase the dog, (boy)!

(2) S
   NP   VP
   The dog   is brown.

Pass   ø[Not grammatically possible in English]
Y/N-Q   Is the dog brown?
Imp   ø

(3) S
   NP   VP
   The boy   wears blue sneakers.

Pass   Blue sneakers are worn by the boy.
Y/N-Q   Is the boy wearing blue sneakers?
Imp   Wear blue sneakers, (boy)!

(4) S
   NP   VP
   The dog   ran into a cave.

Pass   *A cave was run into by the dog.
Y/N-Q   Did the dog run into a cave?
Imp   Run into a cave, (dog)!

Possible Sentence-combinations from the Trees and Transformations:

The boy chased the brown dog.
The boy was wearing blue sneakers and he chased the brown dog.
The boy wearing blue sneakers chased the brown dog.
The boy who was wearing blue sneakers chased the brown dog.
The blue-sneakered boy chased the brown dog.
Chasing the brown dog was the boy in blue sneakers.
The boy wearing blue sneakers chased the brown dog, but the dog ran into a cave.
The brown dog, which was being chased by the boy wearing blue sneakers, ran into a cave.
Into a cave ran the brown dog, chased by the boy wearing blue sneakers.
Wearing blue sneakers, the boy chased the brown dog, which ran into a cave.

Other combinations are possible.

Unlikely construction in English.

Table 12.1   Simple Trees, Transformations, and Sentence Combinations

standard usage in spelling, punctuation, and penmanship when they begin to learn to write. For example, capital letters, periods, and basic comma rules naturally accompany writing. But in the lower grades, it is often best not to concentrate so much on these mechanics that the children see writing as nothing but correct punctuation. A primary-grade teacher would be wise *not* to correct every error of mechanics, lest the children learn to avoid such errors by writing unnecessarily simple sentences far below their level of spoken competence. Excessive correction by the teacher will not help the children learn how to use commas; it will merely teach them to avoid any constructions that might require commas.

Using drills. In either spoken or written form, drills probably should be used with care, for it is an old pedagogical axiom that one never undertakes a drill until the need for it is clear. Be sure that the children really are deficient in some aspect of productive competence before you prepare a drill. For example, first identify whether the class needs an exercise in /əd/-inflections; ask the children, randomly and rapidly—speed of reply is essential here—to manipulate a sentence such as "Today we wash the laundry," using variant openings: "Yesterday we . . . "; "Every day we . . . "; "On Sundays we . . . "; "Last week we . . . ." Only if a significant number of children do not make the S.E. /əd/ distinction for past tense should the teacher drill on it, and then only briefly, for exercises provide controlled practice in a skill but do not teach the skill itself. The skill comes, if at all, from ordinary usage in nonformal situations. In exercises and practice sessions at all levels, it is important to stress the practical advantages of knowing and being able to use a wide variety of registers, styles, and dialects in various written or spoken contexts, inside and outside the classroom.

Using the media. Since all children now have been influenced by television and other electronic media, a teacher would surely want to use these, along with books and other print media, as sources for teaching language. Most children remember television shows better than they remember books, for they have been watching television and believing it from infancy. Television is a good source for phonology and dialectology, as we have noted, but it is also a useful repository of other linguistic evidence from which older children can learn: the loading of language in advertisements or in electioneering; racial/ethnic and sex-role stereotyping in programs and advertisements; pragmatics behaviors in various contexts; collocations of all sorts, from imagery to cliches. Television and newspapers or magazines provide excellent material for discussing and practicing both written and oral composition. Have the class refute an advertiser, plead a case against a tax inspector, provide alternative plot conclusions, flesh out a minor character in a script, turn a stereotype upside down, sell an impossible product or person to a skeptical audience, parody a popular show's style.

Handbooks, Manuals, and Dictionaries

The general strategy in children's earlier years is a two-stage one. First, focus their natural curiosity about everything specifically onto language, drawing heavily on their own experiential competence. Then, direct that competence and curiosity into performances specifically modified in terms of bidialectalism and practical adaptability. Sooner or later, however, these descriptive techniques are going to bump into the harshly prescriptive universe outside. Somebody will say, flatly, "That's dumb!" or somebody else will say, "Yes, but can he spell?" (A remarkable number of people honestly believe that teaching language means teaching spelling.) Sooner or later, in short, a teacher has to account for his time, list his objectives and defend his methods of reaching them, and produce evidence that he is working on them. This kind of accountability is nearly always measured, not in terms of a child's understanding of registers or dialects, but in terms of his grasp of such mechanical matters as the comma.

Limitations.   Until a majority of the world's language users understand that skill in S.E. usage is a function of response to social pressure, not a measure of intelligence or ethics, the majority of the world's language teachers will rely on handbooks, manuals, and dictionaries. Handbooks, however, do not teach language, do not teach writing, and do not solve any but the most specific problems about language use. If a student already knows the right questions to ask, handbooks are invaluable. If he does not, they are worthless. Recognizing their limitations is the first step a teacher must take in using these resource books.

The second step is to understand that the vast majority of handbooks, manuals, and dictionaries are prescriptively biased. The function of a handbook is to lay down rules of "correct" and "incorrect" usage: "Do not use slang or archaic words or capitalized mass nouns. Avoid dangling modifiers. Do not use comma splices and fused sentences." The prescriptions are so numerous, so capricious, and so internally contradictory that no human being alive could reconcile or even remember them all. Therefore, it is wise to use handbooks selectively, with a cautious and skeptical eye on their biases, and to test them constantly against the standards of usage in current practice.

Uses.   Having acknowledged them as limited, however, the teacher's third step is to teach the students their uses, which are immediate and practical.

Even the most heavy-handed or old-fashioned handbook is a valuable tool in the acquisition of S.E. dialect. Especially for written language, the standard forms, standard constructions, and standard fashions change comparatively slowly.[2] Consequently, once children are comfortable with the notion that they can acquire S.E.—that S.E. is accessible as another dialect, not remote or punitive—then handbooks, manuals, and dictionaries become tools like calculators, hammers, or scissors. They are the psycholinguistic equivalents of the levers and pulleys that let us extend our control over the physical universe.

So a teacher should begin early, in primary school, suggesting that children check a dictionary for S.E. pronunciation, for etymology, for syntax, and let them test those prescriptions for themselves against their own competence. A little later, a teacher might start the children on using a handbook written for their level of comprehension. They can look up what it prescribes about S.E. usage on such matters as capital letters, pronoun references, or adjective modification. Later still, it might be useful to compile a handbook or a manual of S.E. usage from the students' own modified competence, letting them discover again that they know more than they think they know. They will usually see that their acquired prescriptions about S.E. are not so different from what the commercial handbooks prescribe. And in the process of producing such a handbook, they will frequently come to learn more about their own usage and its variation from what they believe S.E. expectations to be than they might have learned through the drills or exercises a teacher could offer them.

Linguistics and Language Teaching

It has often been observed that linguistics is not at present a pedagogical discipline, for it does not now offer any method for teaching the many subjects with which its branches are concerned. An accurate description of language patterns and practices—of phonology, morphology, syntax, signs, and dialects—does not yet readily translate into a set of instructions for teaching these concepts to someone else.

So of what value, we might reasonably ask, is learning about linguistics, if most of its information is essentially theoretical? Put another way, how can we informally transfer the skills and concepts of theoretical linguistics into applied practice, actual teaching situations, day-by-day work at home or in a classroom? The usual responses to such practical questions are that any

2. Note the qualifying word "comparatively": *some* forms, constructions, and fashions change quite rapidly. Rapid change is particularly characteristic at the lexical level. All aspects of language change eventually, of course, and language change is one of the features a teacher must be familiar with and must convey to students.

knowledge is valuable for its own sake and that not knowing is often more harmful than knowing, whatever the subject under discussion. Those are sound and humane responses, but not very helpful to a harried teacher.

Attitudes and models. Possibly more helpful is the suggestion that a language teacher should know something about linguistics, whether or not that knowledge can immediately be translated into classroom practice, for two principle reasons. First, studying linguistics can bring about a profound change in the teacher's own attitude toward language and its practices, an attitude change that has a direct bearing on the response of the students with whom that teacher will be dealing. Second, linguistics provides its students with facts in some cases, rather than prejudgmental assumptions or wishes, and in other cases provides students with a model or theory that indicates where other facts are still needed.

When we examine the matter of attitude in more detail, we invite a review of this entire book. *How Language Works* has been, from the start, an implicit plea that we *not* take language for granted, *not* assume we already know what it is and how it works, and, above all, *not* continue to pass on to our children the biases, prescriptions, and suppositions that were passed on to us. Studying linguistics is first and foremost an inquiry into, and therefore an experiential/referential testing of, a complicated area many of us have never examined before. In few other areas of our lives do we function so much on untested assumptions, unexamined premises, and uncritical judgments as we do in our use and teaching of language. But in few other areas are our assumptions, premises, and judgments as important as they are in teaching and using language, for language permeates everything else that we do. If nothing else, the study of linguistics should help us take a closer look at our language practices and the assumptions we have about them.

In particular, linguistics provides us with a good deal of objective information about language practices: about levels of language production from sound to form to word to sentence, about language acquisition by children, about language development historically and comparatively, about variations in space as well as in time, and about the nature of linguistic signs in theory and in practice. Where data are missing or inadequate, the theories developed from linguistic study can prompt researchers to ask the right kinds of questions to fill in the gaps.

We do not now know, for example, the details of how the brain works in its generation of language, but we know enough to recognize that more detailed studies need to be done in neurophysiology. We do not yet know why some children are successful bilinguals or bidialectals and why others are less successful, but we know that more research is needed there. At present, we do not know whether syntactic or lexical features are dominant in the production of grammatical sentences, nor how much of language use is specifically human and how much is shared with other primates, nor why some aphasiacs lose recall of noun patterns generally and some of particular nouns only. We have, in sum, enough data now, which we did not have twenty-five or fifty years ago, to tell us what else we still need to investigate. As in all other cognitive disciplines, what we know we *don't* know can be as useful as what we *do* know, for recognition of ignorance is perhaps the most critical step toward enlightenment.

What should a language teacher teach? Let us suppose that whether a language teacher is functioning formally in a classroom or nonformally at home, he or she has achieved enlightenment and does understand the linguistic topics we have addressed in this book. What aspects of that enlightenment should a teacher have in mind to pass on to the children? What can we summarize as being most important from the preceding sections in this chapter and the preceding chapters in the book?

First of all, let us consider what need *not* be taught, at least not to young children (infancy through first or second grade). Terminology *qua* terminology, for its own sake, we can usefully skip: children need to know syntax, but not the formal nomenclature of lexicon, grammar, or syntax. By all means, introduce them to test frames and simple trees, but do not burden them with the jargon. Also, spelling and punctuation can be introduced comparatively early, but in very simplified forms and as an accompaniment to reading and writing—not as ends in themselves, but as part of the written-language package. Finally, very young children need only minimal formal instruction in patterns of standard spoken usage; they will be picking up a good deal of informal instruction, anyway. Remember that many children are still overgeneralizing and still formulating their own competence in recursiveness. Save the details of comma splices, prenominal modification, and absolute constructions until later, in the upper primary or middle-school grades.[3]

Rather than drills and exercises on unrelated details, what should be emphasized with young children are concepts and practice in the application of those concepts in their own speech. Four concepts in particular need attention, not through naming them, but through using them:

---

3. A filler from *The New Yorker* (June 26, 1978, p. 89) contains this quoted paragraph from *Newsweek,* with *The New Yorker's* wry comment added:

> Try to parse this sentence: "When *anyone* crosses the street, *they* take the chance of being run over." Or: "In this land of the free, *everybody* is entitled to *their* rights." Here we have two examples of a plural pronoun referring to a singular substantive, which, as any third-grader can tell you, is a grammatical solecism of the first magnitude.
> —Philip Dunne in *Newsweek*
> As soon as he takes the lollipop out of his mouth.

1. Competence versus performance, or instilling in the children the understanding that "grammar" (i.e., syntax) is not something one learns, but something one has.
2. Language change, or the recognition that what is prescribed today may be denied later, as social fashions in language catch up with actual practice.
3. Bidialectalism, or the recognition that all dialects work equally well in practical terms, but some dialects have more social value than others.
4. The standard dialect, its phonemes, morphemes, and syntax, its lexicon and semantics, and above all, its sociolinguistic function in the real, lively, filled-with-conflict universe that the children inhabit.

To teach them the details of that S.E. dialect will of course require ongoing attention for many years and is usually regarded as the province more of the classroom instructor than of the parents.

What should a language teacher know? To answer this question, we first ask another: What kind of language teacher is meant? If we mean a specialist in ESD (English as a Second Dialect), in ESL (English as a Second Language), or in TESOL (Teaching English to Speakers of Other Languages), then clearly that person will need a great deal of training beyond what a second-grade teacher in a largely upper-middle-class school would need. For purposes of general discussion here, let us therefore hypothesize a theoretically "average" elementary-school teacher, whose classes contain roughly a 50–50 mixture of S.E. and non-S.E. speakers, none of whom is bilingual and none of whom has any speech or cognitive pathologies. That is, all of the children are healthy and "normally" bright, and there is "normal" dialectic variation among the speakers. Most of the regions are represented, many of the ethnic dialects, both of the genders.

What, then, should this hypothetical language teacher know about linguistics, in addition to the practical (applied) and pedagogical (instructional) techniques that we informally derived from theoretical linguistics? The bare minimum requirements should probably be five:

Another language besides English. There are two reasons for this requirement. One is that knowledge of a foreign language increases the likelihood that the teacher can regard English as *a* language rather than as *the* language and thus will be able to demonstrate more objectivity about English and its workings. Second, if a teacher works in an area of the country where another language is commonly used—Spanish in the Southwest or French in parts of the Southeast, the Northeast, and the northern Middle West—then his teaching will be vastly enhanced by his fluency in the language used by the students. Besides, it is only courtesy to learn that second language in an area where, for many people, it is the only language spoken.

Phonetics. Being able to use phonetics means knowing the IPA chart well enough not to have to refer to it in order to transcribe sounds. It means knowing what an allophone is and how to recognize one when it is spoken. (How many allophones are there in English of /l/, for example? Of /r/? Of /s/?) The teacher should be familiar enough with articulatory phonetics that he can recognize what all labiodental sounds, all fricatives, and so on have in common, so he can distinguish redundant from distinctive features. He should have a good sense of the speech organs, of the difference between vowel production and consonant production, and of the approximate position of vowel phones in the oral cavity, especially as these positions often change from dialect to dialect.

Morphology. Here, a general idea of the historical development of English is appropriate, together with a general idea of how morphemes function (base, affix; free, bound). It would also be appropriate to have an understanding of the various processes and directions of synchronic and diachronic change in English morphology. In particular, the teacher should know that English is a word-order (analytic) language, in contrast with many Indo-European languages, and should know what effect that analytic structure has on the linearity of English syntax.

Syntax. A good grasp of English syntax means a practical comprehension of such concerns as tense construction and the Auxiliary rewrite rule, inflectional morphemes, the parts of speech, basic phrase structure and basic transformation rules, test frames, IC analysis, sentence formulas, and surface structure versus deep structure. It would not hurt, also, to know what a feature matrix is and its relationship to deep structure and surface structure. Special care should be given to the differences between standard and nonstandard syntaxes, particularly to those nonstandard features that are remnants of earlier periods in the history of the language (e.g., double negatives).

Dialects. Finally, a teacher should have a practical grasp of the dialects used in the region where he is teaching. Actually, this requirement carries another one, piggyback: the teacher should be thoroughly versed in the standard dialect (S.E.); but we will assume that most teachers are. In any event, the teacher should become aware of what dialects are spoken where he is teaching, in order that he not mistake dialectic differences for incompetence. A teacher whose own dialect is Bostonian but who is teaching in Atlanta, for example, must make an effort not to impose the Boston dialect on his students as if that were the only correct way of speaking. In the South, the Boston dialect is not necessarily correct. The teacher himself must understand what the regional, ethnic, and social norms are, in addition to helping the children understand the same point. If he wishes to teach S.E., then both he and the children will have to recognize that neither Boston nor Atlanta has a monopoly on it.

In addition to these five minimal requirements, a language teacher at any level could profit from having some sense of the differences between speech and writing, an awareness of different approaches to compositional theory, and a grasp of the basic aspects of "meaning": field analysis (homonyms, antonyms, synonyms); semiotics (sign, signifier, signified); pragmatics (illocutionary force, conversational principles, presuppositions); and semantics (two-valued logic, extensional versus intensional meaning, indexing). Any teacher working a good deal with students who use nonstandard dialects, whose primary language is not English, or who have physiological or cognitive trouble with speech acquisition will of course need to undertake more specialized study in the pertinent fields: ESD, ESL/TESOL, speech pathology, and so on.

Now let us return for a moment to the beginning of this chapter and reconsider what a nonformal teacher needs to know, a parent, an older sibling, a babysitter, or anyone who wants to become informed about language. What is most important for the layman concerned about language? Three main points we derived from the chapter on universals of language will serve us best here:

1. The spoken language is primary, and significantly different from the written forms.
2. All languages change in various ways, synchronically (via dialects, contexts, processes, and directions) as well as diachronically over time.
3. All languages are symbolic in various ways: lexically, syntactically, culturally.

If you know the details behind the meaning of these three principles, then you have a good basic understanding of how language works.

Review Questions

1. What is the difference between prescription and description? How are both related to the teaching of language?
2. What is the prestige dialect? How is it related to the concept of bidialectalism?
3. Distinguish between receptive and productive competence.
4. What techniques from Structural and Transformational grammars would be suitable for use in teaching young children syntax?
5. Of what should a teacher beware when using handbooks, manuals, and dictionaries in teaching language? Of what use are these tools?
6. What should a language teacher know about linguistics? What five concepts and skills in particular are useful? What three other skills probably would be useful?

7. Distinguish among "usage," "grammar," and "syntax."
8. What should a language teacher *not* teach to young children? Why not?
9. What *should* a language teacher teach? Why?
10. What should anyone (language teacher or not) know about language?

Selected Reading

Abrahams, Roger D., and Rudolph C. Troike, eds. *Language and Cultural Diversity in American Education.* Englewood Cliffs, N.J.: Prentice-Hall, Inc., 1972.

Alatis, James E., ed. *Linguistics and the Teaching of Standard English to Speakers of Other Languages or Dialects.* Washington, D.C.: Georgetown University Press, 1969.

Allen, Harold B., ed. *Readings in Applied English Linguistics,* 2nd ed. New York: Appleton-Century-Crofts, 1964.

Eisenhardt, Catheryn T. *Applying Linguistics in the Teaching of Reading and the Language Arts.* Columbus, Ohio: Charles E. Merrill Publishing Co., 1972.

Evans, Bergen, and Cornelia Evans. *A Dictionary of Contemporary American Usage.* New York: Random House, 1957.

Fries, Charles C. *The Teaching of English.* Ann Arbor, Mich.: George Wahr Publishing Co., 1949.

Guth, Hans P. *Teaching English Today.* New York: McGraw-Hill Book Co., 1970.

Imhoof, Maurice I., ed. *Social and Educational Insights Into Teaching Standard English to Speakers of Other Dialects.* Bloomington: Indiana University School of Education, 1971.

Kehoe, Monika, ed. *Applied Linguistics: A Survey for Language Teachers.* New York: The Macmillan Co., 1968.

Laird, Charlton. *And Gladly Teche: Notes on Instructing the Natives in Their Native Tongue.* Englewood Cliffs, N.J.: Prentice-Hall, Inc., 1970.

Pooley, R. C. *Teaching English Usage,* 2nd ed. Urbana, Ill.: National Council of Teachers of English, 1974.

Savage, John F., ed. *Linguistics for Teachers: Selected Readings.* Chicago: Science Research Associates, Inc., 1973.

Shugrue, Michael F. *English in a Decade of Change.* New York: Western Publishing Company/Pegasus, 1968.

Shuman, R. Baird, ed. *Questions English Teachers Ask.* Rochelle Park, N.J.: Hayden Book Co., 1977.

Spolsky, Bernard. *Educational Linguistics.* Rowley, Mass.: Newbury House, 1977.

Strunk, William, Jr.; rev. E. B. White. *The Elements of Style,* 2nd ed. New York: The Macmillian Co., 1972.

Williams, Frederick, ed. *Explorations of the Linguistic Attitudes of Teachers.* Rowley, Mass.: Newbury House, 1976.

Journals   *The CEA Critic; Change; College English; Elementary English; English Education; English Journal;* ERIC resources; *Journal of Education Research; Journal of Speech and Hearing Disorders; Journal of Verbal Learning and Verbal Behavior; Language; Learning;* NCTE publications; *Research in the Teaching of English; Today's Education*

General Bibliography

Allen, Harold B. *Linguistics and English Linguistics.* (Goldentree Bibliographies in Language and Literature.) New York: Appleton-Century-Crofts, 1966.

Anderson, Wallace L., and Norman C. Stageberg, eds. *Introductory Readings on Language,* 4th ed. New York: Holt, Rinehart and Winston, Inc., 1975.

Barber, Charles L. *The Story of Speech and Language.* New York: Thomas Y. Crowell Company, 1964.

Bolinger, Dwight. *Aspects of Language,* 2nd ed. New York: Harcourt Brace Jovanovich, Inc., 1975.

Brown, Roger. *Words and Things.* New York: The Free Press/Macmillan, 1958 (reptd. 1971).

Clark, Virginia P., Paul A. Eschholz, and Alfred E. Rosa, eds. *Language: Introductory Readings,* 2nd ed. New York: St. Martin's Press, 1977.

Crystal, David. *Linguistics.* Baltimore: Penguin Books, 1971.

Dean, Leonard F., and Kenneth G. Wilson, eds. *Essays on Language and Usage,* 2nd ed. New York: Oxford University Press, 1963.

Dineen, Francis P. *An Introduction to General Linguistics.* New York: Holt, Rinehart and Winston, 1967.

Ducrot, Oswald, and Tzvetan Todorov. *Encyclopedic Dictionary of the Sciences of Language.* Baltimore: Johns Hopkins University Press, 1979.

Falk, Julia S. *Linguistics and Language,* 2nd ed. New York: John Wiley & Sons, 1978.

Farb, Peter. *Word Play.* New York: Alfred A. Knopf/Bantam, 1975.

Fromkin, Victoria, and Robert Rodman. *An Introduction to Language,* 2nd ed. New York: Holt, Rinehart and Winston, 1978.

Goshgarian, Gary, ed. *Exploring Language.* Boston: Little, Brown & Co., 1977.

Greenberg, Joseph H. *A New Invitation to Linguistics.* New York: Doubleday/Anchor, 1977.

Hall, Robert A., Jr. *Linguistics and Your Language.* New York: Doubleday/Anchor, 1960.

Hockett, Charles F. *A Course in Modern Linguistics.* New York: The Macmillan Co., 1958.

Hungerford, Harold, Jay Robinson, and James Sledd, eds. *English Linguistics: An Introductory Reader.* Glenview, Ill.: Scott, Foresman & Co., 1970.

Laird, Charlton. *The Miracle of Language*. New York: World Publishing Co., 1953.

Langacker, Ronald W. *Language and Its Structure,* 2nd ed. New York: Harcourt Brace Jovanovich, 1973.

Lenneberg, Eric H., ed. *New Directions in the Study of Language*. Cambridge, Mass.: M.I.T. Press, 1966.

Marckwardt, Albert H., ed. *Studies in Language and Linguistics*. Ann Arbor: The English Language Institute of the University of Michigan, 1964.

Minnis, Noel, ed. *Linguistics at Large*. New York: The Viking Press, 1971.

Ornstein, Jacob, and William W. Gage. *The ABC's of Language and Linguistics*. Silver Spring, Md.: SR Publishers, 1964 (reptd. 1978).

Past, Ray. *Language as a Lively Art*. Dubuque, Iowa: William C. Brown Co., 1970.

Pei, Mario. *The Story of Language*. New York: New American Library, 1960.

Roberts, Paul. *Understanding English*. New York: Harper & Row, 1958.

Sebeok, Thomas A., ed. *Current Trends in Linguistics*. The Hague: Mouton Press, 1973.

Somer, John, and James F. Hoy, eds. *The Language Experience*. New York: Dell Publishing Co., Inc., 1974.

Wardhaugh, Ronald. *Introduction to Linguistics,* 2nd ed. New York: McGraw-Hill, 1977.

Waterman, John T. *Perspectives in Linguistics*. Chicago: University of Chicago Press/Phoenix, 1963.

West, Fred. *The Way of Language*. New York: Harcourt Brace Jovanovich, 1975.

Journals

Columbia University Working Papers in Linguistics; Daedalus; Journal of English Linguistics; Journal of Linguistics; Language; Linguistics; Modern Language Journal; Word

Index